**IDEA MAGAZINE FOR TEACHERS®**

# The MAILBOX®

## 2013–2014 YEARBOOK

The Education Center, LLC
Greensboro, North Carolina

*The Mailbox® 2013–2014 Grades 2–3 Yearbook*

**Managing Editor, *The Mailbox* Magazine:** Jennifer Bragg

**Editorial Team:** Becky S. Andrews, Diane Badden, Kimberley Bruck, Karen A. Brudnak, Catherine Caudill, Pam Crane, Chris Curry, David Drews, Tazmen Fisher Hansen, Marsha Heim, Lori Z. Henry, Troy Lawrence, Gary Phillips (COVER ARTIST), Mark Rainey, Greg D. Rieves, Rebecca Saunders, Donna K. Teal, Sharon M. Tresino, Zane Williard

ISBN13 978-1-61276-531-0
ISSN 1930-3580

©2014 The Education Center, LLC, PO Box 9753, Greensboro, NC 27429-0753

Printed in the United States of America.

*The Mailbox*® Yearbook
PO Box 6189
Harlan, IA 51593-1689

HPS 256264

# Contents

**TheMailbox.com**

# Common Core Skills

# LANGUAGE ARTS

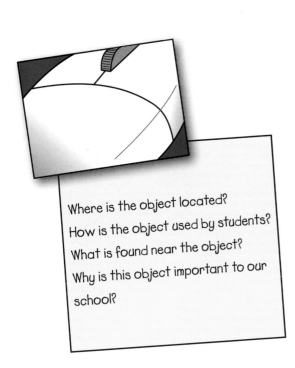

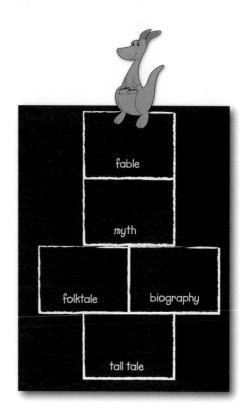

Where is the object located?
How is the object used by students?
What is found near the object?
Why is this object important to our school?

## Focus on the Big Picture

### *Asking questions (RL.2.1; RI.2.1; RL.3.1; RI.3.1)*

Set students on course to asking text questions with this small-group activity. In advance, take close-up pictures of objects around your school, such as part of a railing, a portion of a playground structure, or a computer mouse. Print the pictures and give one to each small group. Instruct students to write four questions they might ask to help them figure out what the object in the picture is. Provide time for each group to share its questions; then lead a discussion of which questions would lead to more detailed responses and which would provide short answers. Then, if time allows, take students on a quick walk to show them the objects photographed.

Judith Lesnansky, Kirkmere Elementary, Youngstown, OH

## Hop to It!

### *Genres*

Learning about and tracking different types of literature is what this idea is all about. First, use a white crayon to draw a hopscotch grid on a large sheet of black paper. Label each section with a different genre of literature your students will read during the year. If desired, add descriptions of each genre in the corresponding spaces. Then copy the kangaroo pattern on page 17 and cut it out. Place the cutout on the first genre students will read. Later, as each new genre is introduced or as a genre regains focus in the classroom, move the cutout to the matching section.

adapted from an idea by April Parker, St. Pius X School, Greensboro, NC

 If you have a class mascot, post an enlarged picture of that animal on your display instead.

# READING

## tips & tools

# READING
### tips & tools

## A Game Plan

### Word analysis (RF.2.3; RF.3.3)

Play your cards right and students will have a blast decoding words! To prepare, type sight words or words with a desired decoding concept onto a supply of self-adhesive removable labels. Place a label on each card from a deck of War, Crazy Eights, or other card game your students enjoy. Follow the game's standard rules, but lead students to read the word on the card in play aloud before playing it. Whether you play with students or have them play on their own, they're sure to benefit from the extra reading practice.

Susan Farmer, Lincoln Elementary, Rexburg, ID

## Slow and Steady

### Key ideas and details (RL.2.1–3; RL.3.1–3)

Train your students to be reading winners! Copy a bookmark from page 18 for each child and allow him to color it. If desired, laminate the bookmarks for durability. When students read a story, have them refer to the bookmark and answer the questions. To extend the activity, assign a question for students to write a written response to in their reading journals.

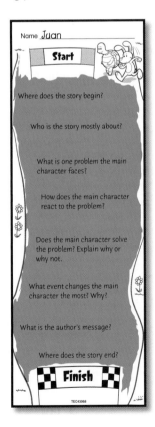

Name Juan

**Start**

Where does the story begin?

Who is the story mostly about?

What is one problem the main character faces?

How does the main character react to the problem?

Does the main character solve the problem? Explain why or why not.

What event changes the main character the most? Why?

What is the author's message?

Where does the story end?

**Finish**

TEC43068

## Better and Better

### Fluency (RF.2.4b; RF.3.4b)

To help students see their reading growth, enlist the help of your parent volunteers. At the beginning of the week, have each student read aloud a predetermined reading passage to a volunteer. Have the volunteer determine the number of words correctly read by the child in a minute's time. Then, at the end of the week, have a parent volunteer collect the same data on the same passage. Provide each student with a chart to track her progress during the week and as the year progresses.

Kim Ruefle, Walkersville Elementary Walkersville, MD

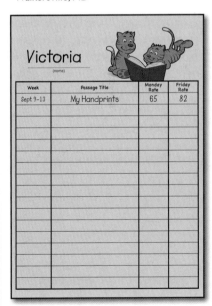

Victoria
(name)

| Week | Passage Title | Monday Rate | Friday Rate |
|---|---|---|---|
| Sept 9–13 | My Handprints | 65 | 82 |
|  |  |  |  |
|  |  |  |  |
|  |  |  |  |
|  |  |  |  |
|  |  |  |  |
|  |  |  |  |
|  |  |  |  |
|  |  |  |  |
|  |  |  |  |
|  |  |  |  |
|  |  |  |  |
|  |  |  |  |
|  |  |  |  |

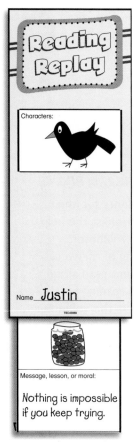

## Reading Replay

### Recount stories (RL.2.2; RL.3.2)

Guide students to identify a story's key ideas and details with this handy reference. To begin, give each student a card stock copy of the left side of page 19. Instruct him to cut it out and make two slits where indicated. Next, give the child a paper copy of the right side of page 19. Direct him to draw or write details about the story to complete each section of the strip. Then have him cut out the strip and write the title on the back. The child pulls the strip through the slits and folds each end back. To recount a story, the child pulls the strip and refers to each section to jump-start the information he shares aloud. Later, when he's ready to discuss a new story, have him remove the paper strip and insert a new one.

**To vary the activity,** go online for a programmable strip. Program the strip with story details you want students to focus on. Or make copies of the blank form; then have students order the main events of the story in each section and label the writing lines with brief descriptions of the events.

Josephine Flammer, Adirondack, NY

## On the Air

### Read irregularly spelled words (RF.2.3f; RF.3.3d)

Not only will students enjoy this top-notch center, but it also allows you to keep a record of students' reading progress! First, make a copy of the activity card on page 20 and put it in a plastic page protector for durability. Place the activity card and a titled list of irregularly spelled words near a recording device (tablet, webcam, voice recorder, etc.). Demonstrate how to use the recording device. Then invite students to visit the center and follow the directions on the card.

**To meet the needs of all your learners,** prepare several different word lists and write a different title on each list. Place the lists with the materials at a center. Each time a child visits the center, direct him to read a specific list.

# READING
## tips & tools

## Crazy Eight
### Vowel teams (RF.2.3b)

To help students identify spelling-sound correspondences for the long *a* sound, direct each student to draw and label a large eight on her paper. Challenge the child to use a current reading to write words with as many different long *a* spellings as she can. Provide time for students to share their findings, recording words on a large class chart set up in the same manner, with vowel spellings serving as headings for lists of words. **To vary the activity,** direct the child to cut from magazines pictures that represent words with long *a* spellings. Have her glue the pictures to her paper and then label each picture.

Bonnie Gaynor, Franklin, NJ

## Daily Dose of Meaning
### Literal and nonliteral language (L.3.5a)

Expose students to figurative language on a daily basis using materials you already have! First, write a different example of figurative language on the back sides of a supply of small sticky notes. Then place a sticky note on each section of your monthly classroom calendar. Each day, invite a student to flip the sticky note up and read the example aloud. Take a few minutes to compare its literal meaning to its nonliteral meaning. As students become more familiar with the task, challenge them to contribute examples to an upcoming calendar. With this daily exposure, students will be better prepared to tackle figurative language in their reading.

Heather Aulisio, Tobyhanna Elementary Center, Pocono Pines, PA

## Merging Two Into One
### Compound words (L.2.4d)

Lead students to say each part of the following sentence and complete the corresponding hand gesture every time you provide practice with compound words. "A compound word is two words (*hold up each index finger*) put together (*interlock index fingers*) to make one word (*hold up index finger from one hand*)." With repeated practice, students will have no trouble identifying a compound word.

Jamie Catalina, W. Z. "Doc" Burke Elementary, San Antonio, TX

## Front-Page News
### *Main idea (RI.3.2)*

Whether your students are subjected to snow days or not, this hands-on weather-related activity helps them piece together related text. Start by telling students they have been asked to organize the front page of a newspaper, matching headlines (titles), articles (text), and graphic features. To do this, each student reads his copies of pages 21 and 22 and then cuts out each headline, article, and graphic feature. Next, the child sorts the pieces by main idea and then glues them to a sheet of 11" x 17" paper. Finally, he glues the newspaper name across the top of his paper. (Tell students headline and article placements may vary.) **To extend the activity**, the student labels each text feature shown on his completed newspaper page (RI.2.5).

Susan B. Smith, Fairview Elementary
Monroe, NC

 Before gluing the pieces to the paper, have the child color-code those that go together.

## Red Rover...
### *Suffixes (RF.2.3d; RF.3.3b)*

To prepare this whole-class game, make a set of base word and suffix cards so there is one card for each child. Take students to a large space, such as a multipurpose room, and divide the class into two teams. Give each child in one line a suffix card and each child in the other line a base word card; then have each team stand in a line facing the other team displaying the word parts on their cards. To play, one team (the calling team) chooses one of its words. Then team members decide who from the opposing team they want to call over and say, "Red Rover, Red Rover, send [*-ful*] right over to make [*helpful*]." That child runs, skips, or hops to the line and, if you agree that the two word parts make a real word, she joins the team. If they do not, she gets to take a player back to her team. Then the other team takes a turn. Play continues until no more words can be made. **To make the game more challenging**, have the calling team give a meaning of the words they make (L.3.4b).

Shelly Tamburro, Putnam Elementary School of Science, Fort Collins, CO

## Race Game
### *Dictionary skills (L.2.4e; L.3.4.d)*

This fast-paced activity leads students to navigate the dictionary more quickly as they increase their alphabetical order skills. In advance, write four to six words on separate index cards. Invite students to hold the cards while another student plays the contestant. Set a timer for one minute and guide the contestant to arrange the cards so the words are in alphabetical order. When she is satisfied with her order, have her ring a bell. If the words are ordered correctly, her turn ends. If the words are not ordered correctly and there is still time left, tell her how many words are in the correct location and direct her to keep going.

Brenda Wilke
Davidson Elementary
Detroit, MI

# READING
## tips & tools

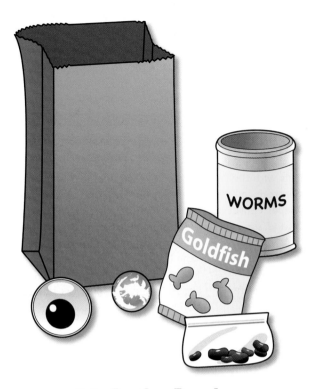

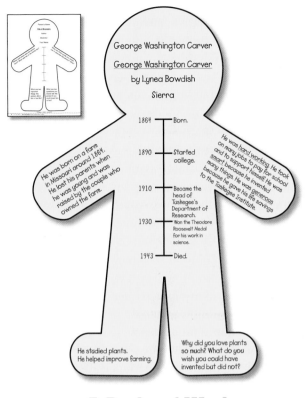

## It's In the Bag!

### *Literal and nonliteral language (L.3.5a)*

To expose students to idioms, place in a paper bag a can labeled "worms" (*open a can of worms*), a bouncy ball (*have a ball*), a wiggle eye (*I've got my eye on you*), some fish-shaped crackers (*something's fishy in here*), and some dry beans (*spill the beans*). Start by discussing with students the sentence "Don't let the cat out of the bag." Explain to students that the expression "let the cat out of the bag" has a nonliteral meaning—one that doesn't mean exactly what it says. Then pull each item out of the bag, name the related idiom, and have students tell the nonliteral meaning. **As a follow-up activity,** assign each child two or more different idioms and have him prepare a bag to share with the class in a similar manner. Learning idioms will be a piece of cake!

Jessica Womack, Finley-Oates Elementary, Bonham, TX

## A Body of Work

### *Answering questions (RI.2.1; RI.3.1)*

Make no bones about it—this activity guides students to provide answers about an informational text. After reading a biography of her choice, a child cuts a simple body outline from a sheet of poster board. She refers to a copy of page 23 to write details about the person and his life on her cutout. Then, in the center of her project, she draws a simple timeline showing five important life events and, if desired, adds decorative details to the back.

**Oral presentation extension (SL.2.2; SL.3.2)** Have the child introduce her classmates to the person she studied by holding her project and sharing the details she recorded on it.

Jessica Mayes, Fairhill Elementary, Fairfax, VA

# READING
## tips & tools

# READING

## tips & tools

### On the Job

**Literature discussion groups**

Students will sit up and take notice of these comfy classroom additions. To prepare, use a permanent marker to label each of six inexpensive seat cushions with a different literature circle job, such as those shown. Honor one group of readers each day with the privilege of using the cushions as they discuss a book, directing each child to sit on his assigned cushion. When they're not in use, keep the cushions near your class library and invite students to sit on them while reading independently.

adapted from an idea by April Parker
St. Pius X School, Greensboro, NC

Summarizer
Questioner
Researcher
Illustrator
Word Wizard
Connector

### Gary the Gulper

**Main ideas and details (RI.3.2)**

Help students separate the big ideas from a text's shrimpy details with this two-part activity. To start, introduce your readers to a toy or paper cutout of an animal that gulps its food, such as a pelican or dolphin. Tell students his name is Gary and that he searches for the big fish when he reads—or the big ideas that tell what a reading is mostly about. Also, tell students the smaller fish (the details) make his meal (the story) more interesting. Then, when students read, have them use a copy of the fish pattern on page 24 to identify the main idea. **To extend the activity,** give students a copy of the organizer from the bottom of page 24. Direct the child to complete it after reading an informational text.

Barclay Marcell, Roosevelt Elementary
Park Ridge, IL

### Read and Respond

**Answering questions; characters; setting and plot (RL. 2.1, 3, 7)**

Good things come in small packages, and this booklet is no exception! Copy pages 25 and 26 back to back; then fold them in half to make a booklet. If desired, laminate it for durability. Set the booklet out as a free-time activity or at a reading center. A child reads the passage and then answers the questions on a sheet of paper.

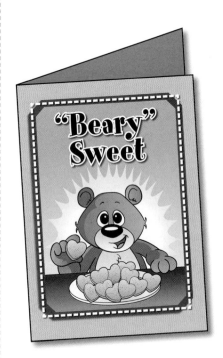

T = title

H = headings

I = illustrations and photographs

V = vocabulary (bold, italics)

E = extra information (graphs, charts, timelines, diagrams, sidebars, etc.)

R = reading passage

**Bravest Character**
awarded to

## Matilda

for helping her teacher and saving the school from Miss Trunchbull's evil ways.

Adaly

May 23, 2014

## Rhymes With Giver

### Nonfiction text features (RI.2.5; RI.3.5)

Guide students to use this mnemonic device for previewing and reading informational text. Display the acronym shown and explain that each letter stands for a part of informational text that a student should look for and read to aid understanding. As you identify each letter, guide students to locate the matching text feature in an informational reading. **For independent practice,** give each child a copy of a reading. As he reads, direct him to highlight the text for each feature listed and then label the highlighted text with the matching letter.

Melissa Renae Ashbaugh, Almont Community School, Almont, MI

## Award Worthy

### Characters (RL.2.3; RL.3.3)

Roll out the red carpet and give students a chance to recognize their favorite story characters! First, challenge students to name favorite characters from the year's whole-group readings and read-alouds. List the results on the board. Next, direct each child to choose a character and create an appropriate award, such as Bravest Character, Funniest Character, or Worst Villain. Direct the student to include reasons to support her award. Then lay a red paper walkway (red carpet) along the front of your room and have each child walk on it before she presents her award in front of the class.

Heather Aulisio, Tobyhanna Elementary Center, Pocono Pines, PA

# READING

## tips & tools

# READING

## Words in Bloom

### *Decoding words with suffixes*
### *(RF.2.3d; RF.3.3b)*

To prepare this small-group game, label each of a supply of cards with a different word that contains a suffix. Stack the cards facedown. Then draw and label a flower, as shown, for each team. To play, show the top card to a player from Team 1 and have him read the word aloud. If he does so correctly, give him the card. If he is unable to read the word correctly, put it at the bottom of the stack. Then move to Team 2 and continue in this manner until a team has collected three cards. When that happens, the students return their cards to the bottom of the stack and a child colors one section of his team's flower. The first team to completely color its flower wins.

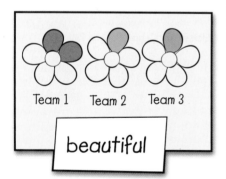

Team 1    Team 2    Team 3

beautiful

## Flip for It

### *Cause-and-effect relationships*
### *(RI.3.3)*

Help students see the relationship between a series of events, ideas, or steps. To begin, have each child read an informational text and write its title on a copy of page 27. Also project the page onto the board. Invite a child to flip a coin. If it lands on heads, write a detail from the reading that causes another event or result; then have each child copy the cause and write its related effect. If the coin lands on tails, list an effect. Have each student copy it and then list its cause. Repeat with two more coin tosses and follow up with a discussion of students' responses.

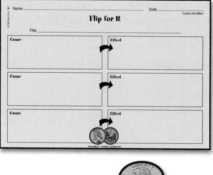

## There's More to This Story

### *Reading literature (RL.2.1–5)*

These post-reading activities not only get students thinking about a recently read story, they also give students choices. In advance, make a copy of page 28, program the page with the number of activities you want students to complete, and then make students copies of the programmed sheet. Direct students to write the story title on their papers and refer to the story as they complete the programmed number of activities on another sheet (or sheets) of paper. After a child completes an activity, she colors its number.

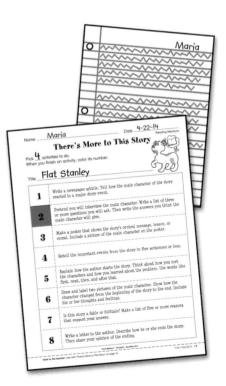

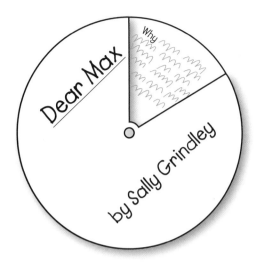

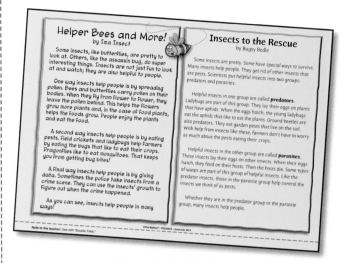

## Go for a Spin

### Ask and answer questions about text *(RL.2.1; RL.3.1)*

Send comprehension skills into overdrive with this reader response wheel. To prepare, make two copies of the reading wheel on page 29 for each student. Instruct each child to cut out both patterns. Next, have him cut a section out of one cutout, turn it over, and write the title and author of a current reading. Then guide him to place the title cutout atop the other and secure them with a brad to make a wheel. Finally, choose one option below; then lead the student to complete the task.

**During reading:** Post on the board six story-specific questions. Then have students number the sections of the wheel from 1 to 6. He writes the answer in the corresponding section as he reads the text.

**Post reading:** Guide the student to write a different question about the text on each section of the wheel. If desired, post on the board a list of question starters for students to use. Then have the child write the answers.

## Double Take

### Compare and contrast texts on the same topic *(RI.2.9; RI.3.9)*

Project the passages from page 30 onto the board. Guide students to read both passages; then use the questions provided to lead students in a discussion of the texts' similarities and differences.

- What are both passages about? *(Insects can be helpful.)*

- Which facts or details do the passages have in common? *(Ladybugs help farmers by eating pests that threaten their crops.)*

- How are the passages different? *("Helper Bees and More!") gives examples of different ways insects help. It names insects that help in each way. "Insects to the Rescue" puts helpful insects into two groups: predators and parasites.)*

- If the authors are writing about the same topic, why did they use different details? *(Even though each author is telling how insects can be helpful, each author has different key points. Therefore, there are different details.)*

# READING

## tips & tools

 **Alternatives to Book Reports**

## Literary Yard Sale

An imaginary yard sale is the setting for this book report alternative. To start, tell students they will be participating in a yard sale where only books are sold, and to sell a recently read book, they must create a price tag. Give each child an index card with a hole punched in one corner and a length of yarn. Instruct each student to write on his card the title and author's name for the book he will write a report about and then have him write a brief but descriptive summary of the plot. If desired, instruct the child to affix a round adhesive sticker to the card and write a price under one dollar on the sticker. After he feeds his yarn through the hole, help him tie it around the book so the book cannot be opened. Provide time for students to browse the summaries and, if desired, have each child use play money to "purchase" one of the books for free-time reading.

April Parker, St. Pius X School, Greensboro, NC

## Reading Fair

Instead of displaying projects for a science fair, use trifold display boards for a reading fair. Here's how. First, guide each student to decorate the left section of a display board with the narrative elements of the story they read. Then instruct the child to decorate the middle section with the story's title, author's name, illustrator's name (if applicable), and a picture that depicts a main event from the story. Finally, lead the student to complete an author study and list her findings on the right panel of the board. Have each child set up her display board and place a copy of the book in front of it. Then have students visit the different displays and learn about the great books! **To extend the activity**, assign each display a number. Prepare for each student a numbered list with the matching book titles. As the child reviews each display, have her check off which books she would like to read over the summer.

Heather Aulisio, Tobyhanna Elementary Center, Pocono Pines, PA

Find **reading practice sheets** on pages 31–41.

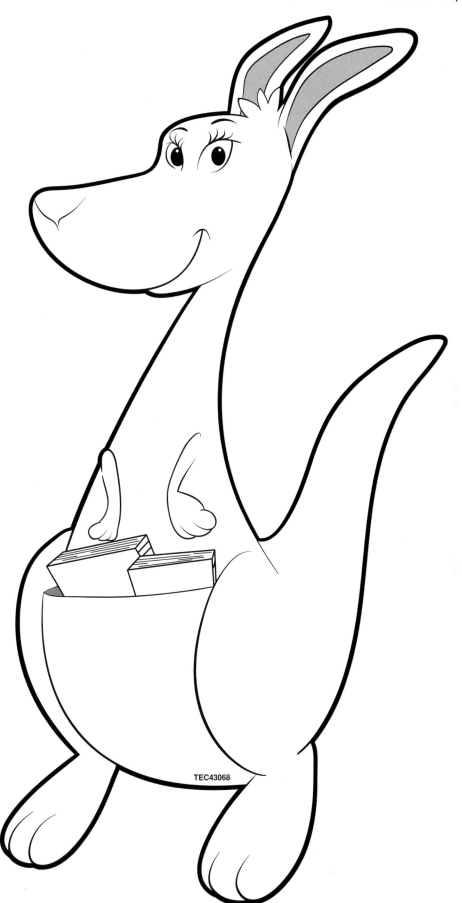

TEC43068

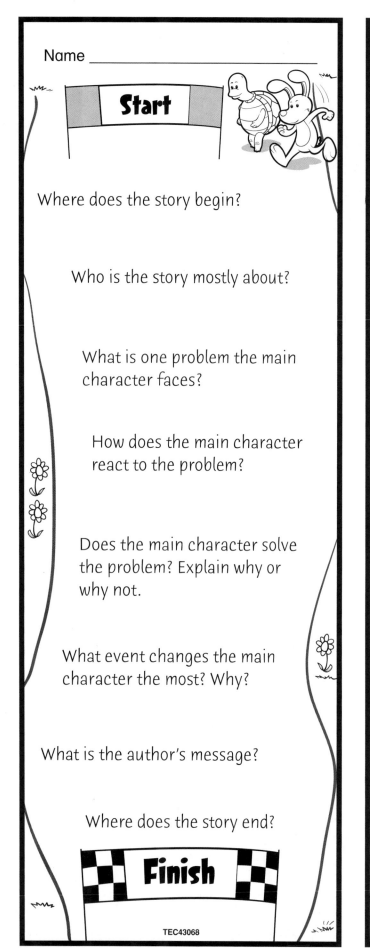

Name _____

Start

Where does the story begin?

Who is the story mostly about?

What is one problem the main character faces?

How does the main character react to the problem?

Does the main character solve the problem? Explain why or why not.

What event changes the main character the most? Why?

What is the author's message?

Where does the story end?

Finish

TEC43068

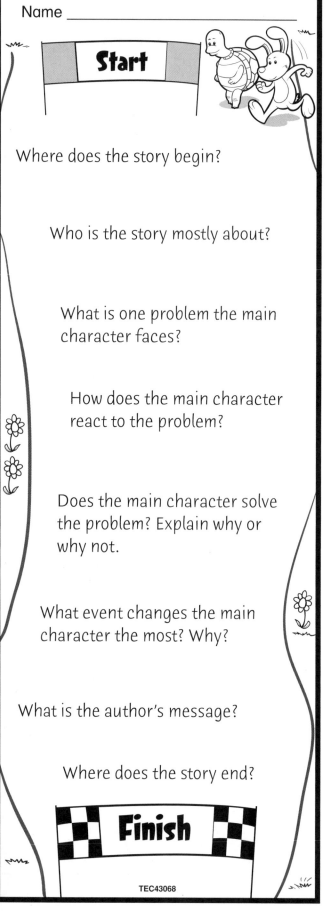

Name _____

Start

Where does the story begin?

Who is the story mostly about?

What is one problem the main character faces?

How does the main character react to the problem?

Does the main character solve the problem? Explain why or why not.

What event changes the main character the most? Why?

What is the author's message?

Where does the story end?

Finish

TEC43068

**Note to the teacher:** Use with "Slow and Steady" on page 7.

# Booklet Cover and Story Strip

Use with "Reading Replay" on page 8.

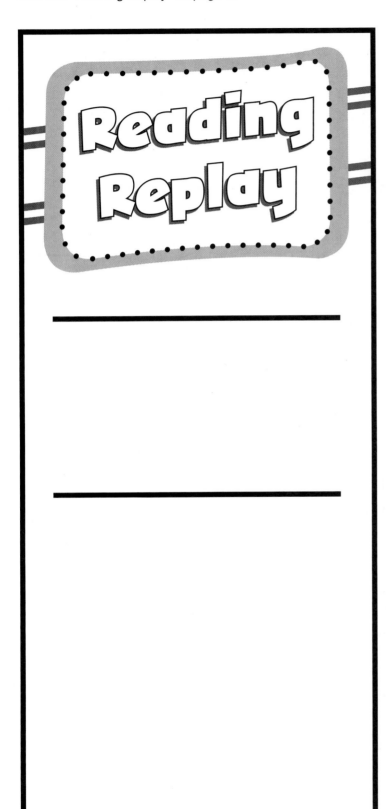

Reading Replay

Name_____

TEC43069

| Fold. |
|---|
| Characters: |
| Setting: |
| Problem: |
| Solution: |
| Message, lesson, or moral: |
| Fold. |

# On the Air

**What You Need**

- recording device
- word list

**①** Read the list of words to yourself three times.

List A

**②** Turn on the recording device.

on

**③** Say your name, the date, and the title of the list.

D. J.,
October 1, 2013,
List A.

List A

**④** Read each word aloud. Take your time and speak clearly!

List A

**⑤** Replay your reading.

- If you like how it sounds, go to Step 6.

- If you think you can do better, repeat Steps 3 and 4. Then go to Step 6.

**⑥** Turn off the recording device.

©The Mailbox® • TEC43069 • Oct./Nov. 2013 • (RF.2.3f; RF.3.3d)

**Note to the teacher:** Use with "On the Air" on page 8.

## Fun in the Snow

## More Snow Ahead

## Snowstorm Strikes City!

By Sam Jones

Hillville—A winter storm system dumped as much as two feet of snow in our area Tuesday night. Road crews worked around the clock to keep the streets clear. The power company worked quickly to restore power to homes and neighborhoods. Many schools and businesses were closed on Wednesday.

Rosalie Sanchez, speaking for the local school system, said, "We chose to cancel classes to keep our students safe."

Sanchez added that the makeup day for this snow event will be March 11.

By Devon Davis

Hillville—Instead of doing reading, writing, and 'rithmetic Wednesday, hundreds of excited school children got a break and played in the snow. All around town, snowy hills became sledding paths. Snowmen sprang up in yards, and snowballs flew through the air.

Marvin Cross, a second grader at Long Pond School, said, "I love snow! I wish it would snow every day!"

With reports of another front coming this way, Marvin may get his wish.

By Cary Charles

Hillville—Weather reports show another big storm to our west. Meteorologists expect this storm to arrive late Friday. It could add as much as a foot of snow to the snow already on the ground. Areas south of the city may only see five to six inches.

# The Hillville Daily News

**Thursday, January 16, 2014**

csp13391650

Road crews made several passes at city streets to keep them clear for residents.

*"Today was the perfect day! We had a snowball war, sledded down every hill in my neighborhood, and warmed up with giant mugs of hot cocoa. Plus I didn't have to take my spelling test!"*

—Sarah McSilver

## Predicted Snowfall (inches)

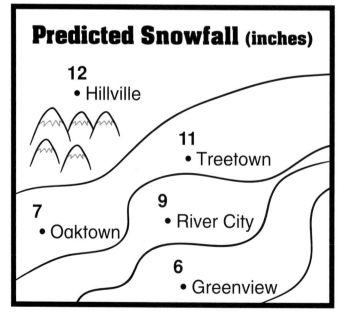

12
• Hillville

11
• Treetown

7
• Oaktown

9
• River City

6
• Greenview

**Note to the teacher:** Use with "Front-Page News" on page 10 and headlines and articles on page 21.

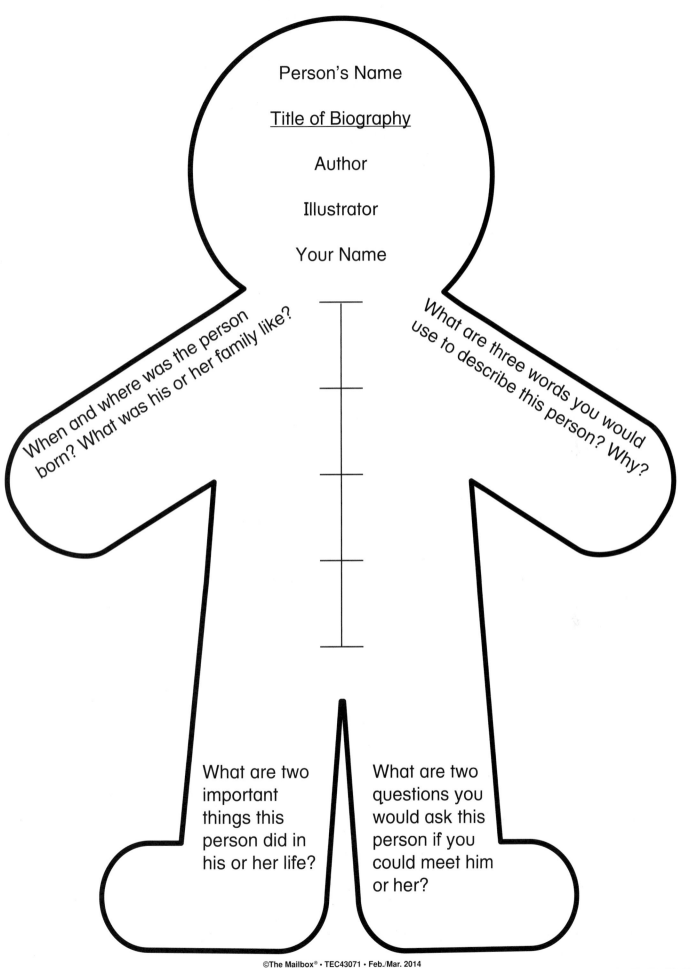

Person's Name

Title of Biography

Author

Illustrator

Your Name

When and where was the person born? What was his or her family like?

What are three words you would use to describe this person? Why?

What are two important things this person did in his or her life?

What are two questions you would ask this person if you could meet him or her?

©The Mailbox® • TEC43071 • Feb./Mar. 2014

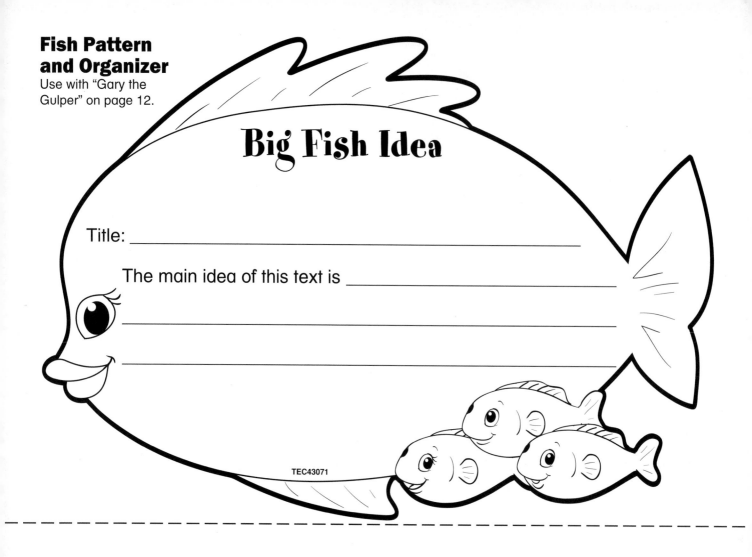

# Big Fish Idea

Title: _____

The main idea of this text is _____

_____

_____

TEC43071

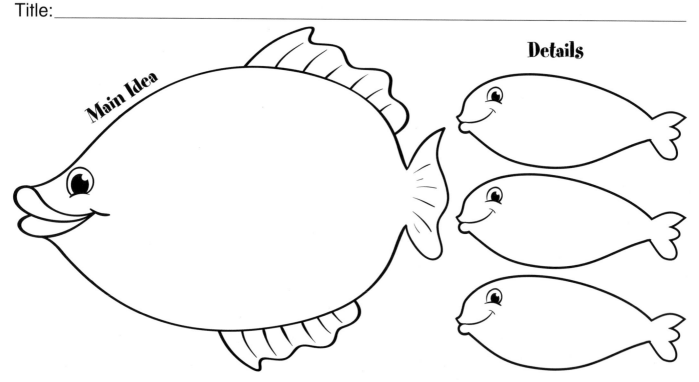

Name _____     Date _____

Main idea and details

Title: _____

Main Idea

Details

## "Beary" Sweet

### Your Opinion Counts!

Who was the nicer character in this story? Tell why you think so.

**Note to the teacher:** Use with "Read and Respond" on page 12.

Bud E. Bear liked to help. One Saturday, he told his mom he would go shopping for her. The store was not far from his home, so his mom agreed. She handed Bud a list of eight items, gave him a peck on the cheek, and sent him on his way.

It didn't take long for Bud to walk to the store. He took out the list and got a cart. The cart had a wobbly wheel and was hard to steer! Bud took a basket instead and started to shop. First, he got the butter. Next, he picked up some eggs and a carton of milk. Then he grabbed some flour, baking soda, baking powder, and sugar. Finally, he found the vanilla. He was almost ready to go.

Bud paid the bill. He walked outside with a bag in each hand. Then rain began to fall. Bud did not want the groceries to get wet. He hurried home.

Soon, Bud was back home. His mom took one look at him and said, "My grizzly bear has become a drizzly bear!" Bud started to say he was sorry for getting himself wet, but his mom sent him off to change his clothes.

When Bud came back to the kitchen, a surprise was waiting for him. His mom had used the groceries to make sugar cookies. They were piled high on a plate set next to a glass of milk. She said to Bud, "You were so sweet to help me shop. I wanted to do something nice for you. Now dig in!"

Bud took a cookie from the pile. He gave it to his mom. Then he ate one himself. It was the best cookie he ever ate!

---

# Write your answers on another sheet of paper.

1. Who are the main characters?

2. What is the setting at the beginning of the story?

   What is the setting in the middle of the story?

   What is the setting at the end of the story?

3. What does Bud do to show he is *helpful?*

4. What problem does Bud face after he finishes shopping? What does he do?

5. Do Bud's actions solve his problem? How do you know?

6. How does Bud's mom surprise him?

Name _____  Date _____

Cause and effect

# Flip for It

Title _____

| Cause | | Effect |
|---|---|---|
| | → | |

| Cause | | Effect |
|---|---|---|
| | → | |

| Cause | | Effect |
|---|---|---|
| | → | |

©The Mailbox® • TEC43072 • April/May 2014

**Note to the teacher:** Use with "Flip for It" on page 14.

Reading literature

# There's More to This Story

Pick ___ activities to do.
When you finish an activity, color its number.

Title _____

| | |
|---|---|
| **1** | Write a newspaper article. Tell how the main character of the story reacted to a major story event. |
| **2** | Pretend you will interview the main character. Write a list of three or more questions you will ask. Then write the answers you think the main character will give. |
| **3** | Make a poster that shows the story's central message, lesson, or moral. Include a picture of the main character on the poster. |
| **4** | Retell the important events from the story in five sentences or less. |
| **5** | Explain how the author starts the story. Think about how you met the characters and how you learned about the problem. Use words like *first*, *next*, *then*, and *after that*. |
| **6** | Draw and label two pictures of the main character. Show how the character changed from the beginning of the story to the end. Include his or her thoughts and feelings. |
| **7** | Is this story a fable or folktale? Make a list of five or more reasons that support your answer. |
| **8** | Write a letter to the author. Describe how he or she ends the story. Then share your opinion of the ending. |

©The Mailbox® • TEC43072 • April/May 2014

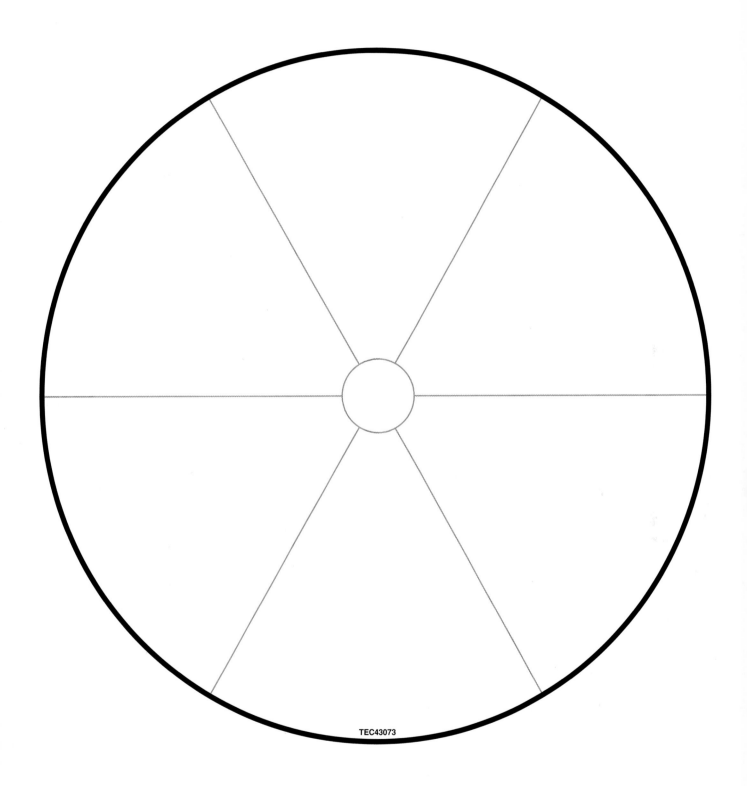

TEC43073

# Helper Bees and More!

by Ima Insect

Some insects, like butterflies, are pretty to look at. Others, like the assassin bug, do super interesting things. Insects are not just fun to look at and watch; they are also helpful to people.

One way insects help people is by spreading pollen. Bees and butterflies carry pollen on their bodies. When they fly from flower to flower, they leave the pollen behind. This helps the flowers grow more plants and, in the case of food plants, helps the foods grow. People enjoy the plants and eat the food.

A second way insects help people is by eating pests. Field crickets and ladybugs help farmers by eating the bugs that like to eat their crops. Dragonflies like to eat mosquitoes. That keeps you from getting bug bites!

A final way insects help people is by giving data. Sometimes the police take insects from a crime scene. They can use the insects' growth to figure out when the crime happened.

As you can see, insects help people in many ways!

# Insects to the Rescue

by Bugsy Bedle

Some insects are pretty. Some have special ways to survive. Many insects help people. They get rid of other insects that are pests. Scientists put helpful insects into two groups: predators and parasites.

Helpful insects in one group are called **predators**. Ladybugs are part of this group. They lay their eggs on plants that have aphids. When the eggs hatch, the young ladybugs eat the aphids that like to eat the plants. Ground beetles are also predators. They eat garden pests that live on the soil. With help from insects like these, farmers don't have to worry as much about the pests eating their crops.

Helpful insects in the other group are called **parasites**. These insects lay their eggs on other insects. When their eggs hatch, they feed on their hosts. Then the hosts die. Some types of wasps are part of this group of helpful insects. Like the predator insects, those in the parasite group help control the insects we think of as pests.

Whether they are in the predator group or the parasite group, many insects help people.

©The Mailbox® • TEC43073 • June/July 2014

Note to the teacher: Use with "Double Take" on page 15.

How reasons support text

# To the Point

**Title:** _____

What main points are made by the author?

What reasons does the author use to support the points?

because

because

because

*Based on the key details and the reasons the author used to support them, why did the author write this text?*

☐ to describe something ☐ to tell what happened in a real event

☐ to give information about a person, event, or thing ☐ to tell how something is alike or different from something else

**How to Use**   After reading an informational text, have each child complete a copy of this organizer. Or program a copy of this page with key details from the text, make student copies, and have students write the reasons the author gives.

# How Does Your Understanding Stack Up?

**Thin questions** start with words like *Did, How many, What, Where,* and *Who.* They have short answers and the answers can be found right in the text.

**Thick questions** start with words like *How did, What if, What might,* and *Why do you think*. They have more detailed answers that come from thinking about the text.

Title

Write and answer three thin questions about the reading.

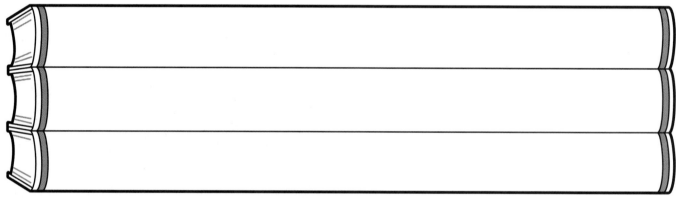

Write and answer three **thick questions** about the reading. (If needed, continue your answers on the back or on another sheet of paper.)

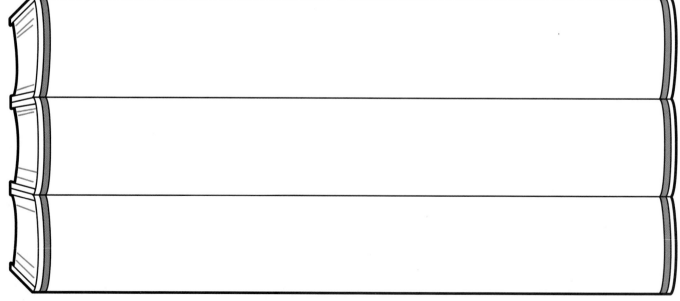

©The Mailbox® • TEC43070 • Dec./Jan. 2013–14 • (RI.3.1)

**Note to the teacher:** Have each child complete a copy of this page as a post-reading activity. If desired, have students write on the left side of each book the paragraphs in the text or the page numbers where the answers can be found.

# Penny's Pail

Miss Penny found a quarter
As she traveled down the path.
Then she happened on a nickel
And quickly did some math.

Thirty cents in her bucket,
Miss Penny bounced down the trail.
She came upon seven dimes
And dropped them in her pail.

Before long, Penny was home.
Then everyone heard her holler.
Inside her pail, there was a hole—
She had lost her dollar.

Read the poem.
Answer the questions.

1. What did Penny do with the money she found on the path? _____

_____

2. How did Penny feel about finding 30 cents? How do you know? _____

_____

_____

3. How did Penny feel when she arrived back home? How do you know? _____

_____

_____

4. What happened to the money Penny found? _____

_____

**Bonus:** Draw a picture to show how Penny might have looked when she hollered.

# That's a Mammal?

Pretend you are asked to draw a picture of a mammal. What do you draw? Do you make a furry critter, like a dog or a bear? Maybe you show a hairy bat or even a dolphin. They are all mammals. What about this guy? Can a mammal wear a shell of bony plates? You bet!

The armadillo is a mammal. It is the only living mammal that wears a shell. This shell of bony plates covers its back, head, legs, and tail. But like other mammals, it also has hair. Wiry hair is found on its sides and belly. Still, its name comes from a Spanish word meaning "little armored one."

Only one type of armadillo hides in its shell for protection. When in danger, it rolls itself into a tight ball. This leaves only its shell exposed. Predators, like foxes or wolves, cannot get a grip on the armadillo. Some armadillos run away to stay safe, while others dig new tunnels to get away.

This mammal is built for digging. Its snout may be pointy or shaped like a shovel. It has strong front feet and curved claws. It uses these tools to dig up meals of ants, beetles, and other insects. (A long, sticky tongue helps it pull termites from tight spaces too.) The armadillo also digs burrows underground. Here it sleeps and raises its young.

Armadillos give birth to live young, just like other mammals. Their young are called *pups*. Most types of armadillos have just one or two pups at a time. One type of armadillo has a litter of four pups. At first, a pup's shell is soft and feels like leather. It takes a few days to harden.

## Read.
## Write your answers on another sheet of paper.

1. What kind of animal is an armadillo?

2. What might an armadillo do if it is in danger?

3. How is an armadillo pup different than its parents?

4. Why are armadillos great diggers?

5. Name two ways an armadillo is like other mammals. Use examples from the text.

6. Name two ways an armadillo gets its food.

7. Describe the animal in the photo. Use the text to help you.

8. Based on the photo, title, and the text, what is the main idea of this reading?

**Bonus:** How does this photo help you better understand the reading?

# Game-Day Decisions

As usual, Crash is running late. He grabs his cleats, dashes out of his room, and plows down the hall. Just before he reaches the stairs, Crash slams into his little brother, Flip. The brothers sit on the floor for just a moment before Crash offers Flip his hand. "Sorry, bro. Are you okay?" Crash asks. "That was nothing," Flip says as he stands up. Crash steps back and lets Flip go down the stairs first.

Finally, Crash makes it out of his house. He sprints down the street toward the soccer park. When he gets to the intersection, he has to stop and wait for the "walk" signal to flash. Crash taps his foot and checks his watch. Five minutes to game time. Then Crash sees Mrs. Dinky moseying toward the corner. He knows she will need help getting across the street. When the "walk" signal flashes, he takes Mrs. Dinky's arm and guides her safely to the other side. Then Crash takes off for the park.

Crash is huffing and puffing when he reaches the soccer park. Coach Gruff looks at him and shakes his head. "You're late," he barks. Rather than explain his story, Crash nods his head and then looks down at his feet. Coach points to the bench and says, "Have a seat. You may be my best player, but everyone needs to follow the rules and that includes being on time." Crash sits down and cheers on his team. A few minutes later, Coach sends Crash in to play. Crash is so excited to get on the field, he nearly knocks over his coach! They don't call him "Crash" for nothing!

① Why does Crash dash out of his room?

② How does Crash feel about Flip? How do you know?

③ How does Crash feel when he gets to the intersection? How do you know?

④ Based on how he treats Mrs. Dinky, which character trait best describes Crash? Why?

bossy   thoughtful   loyal

⑤ Name three decisions Crash makes that could change how the story ends.

©The Mailbox® • TEC43069 • Oct./Nov. 2013 • Key p. 307 • (RL.3.3)

**How to Use**  Project this page onto your whiteboard. Use the questions to lead a class discussion. Or make copies of this page and have each student write the answers on another sheet of paper.

## Bus Ride

Here it comes, the yellow bus,
And we know what that means for us.
Without complaint, without a fuss,
It's time to go to school.

We happily walk down the aisle.
Our noisy friends all wave and smile.
The trusty bus rolls on for miles
Before we get to school.

When we arrive, the bus will park.
And then it's time to disembark.
Our faithful bus has found its mark
And brought us all to school.

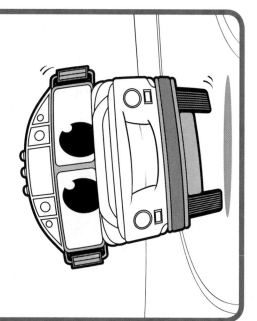

1. Underline the five words in the poem that have either a prefix or suffix. Circle the prefix or suffix in each word.

2. Read each meaning. Write one of the circled suffixes next to each one.

   having: _____

   in some manner or state: _____

   full of: _____

3. Write the letter of the matching meaning.

   happily _____        A. having noise

   noisy _____          B. full of faith

   faithful _____       C. in a happy manner or state

4. If *embark* means to board a vehicle for transportation, what does *disembark* mean?

5. Think about the events of each stanza. If each stanza had a subtitle based on its events, what would you call each stanza?

   First stanza: _____

   Second stanza: _____

   Third stanza: _____

Name _____

# Not So Nice Ice

① **Hail** is a type of precipitation. It falls to the earth as lumps of ice. These lumps are called **hailstones.**

② Hailstones are hard. They can be round or bumpy. They can break windows and dent cars when they fall to the earth. They can also hurt crops. Some hailstones are small. They are smaller than a pea. Other hailstones are large. The biggest hailstones on record were eight inches across. That is about the size of the short side of this paper!

③ Why are some hailstones big while others are small? To answer that, you first need to know where and when they form. Hailstones form in the clouds during a thunderstorm. Some of the air in the thunderstorm cloud flows up. It is warm. Some of the air flows down. It is cold.

④ Each hailstone starts as frozen rain or snow. It is called a **hail embryo** \em-brē-ō\. First, the hail embryo falls toward the earth. Then warm air pushes it back into the clouds. The hail embryo freezes in the cold clouds. It falls toward the earth again. Sometimes the warm air knocks the embryo back up into the cold air. This cycle of falling down and going back up may happen many times. The hail embryo gets bigger each time it goes back into the cold air. Finally, the hail embryo gets too heavy for the air. It falls to the earth as a hailstone.

## How Hail Forms

cloud

hail embryo

cold air

warm air

hailstones

©The Mailbox® • TEC43070 • Dec./Jan. 2013–14 • Key p. 307 • (RI.2.7)

Read.
Write your answers on another sheet of paper.

1. What does the diagram show?

2. How does the diagram help the reader understand key ideas in the text?

3. Which paragraphs explain the key ideas shown on the diagram?

4. What does the reading tell you about hail that the diagram does not?

5. If the diagram was not included, do you think the reading would have been harder to understand or about the same? Explain.

**Bonus:** Why do you think the author chose to include this diagram, instead of a photo of a hailstone or table of facts?

# A Bargain?

Jan got an advertisement
From a newly opened store.
The shop was having a massive sale,
So Jan went through its door.

Inside the store were items
That surprised, then baffled, Jan.
She saw half a coat and half a bed
And half a frying pan!

There were half a pair of pants
And half a shovel and a pail.
Jan was confused but soon remembered—
The ad read "Half-Off Sale!"

Use the poem to answer the questions.

1. A memory is something from the past that you still think about. Draw a box around the word with the same root.

2. Circle the two words that have nearly the same meaning.

    surprised     baffled     confused

    Think of a word that means nearly the same as the uncircled word. Write the word. _____

3. Underline the reason Jan went to the store.

4. What is the setting for most of the poem? _____

    How do you know? _____

5. Why do you think the author uses a question mark in the title? _____

_____

**Bonus:** If you were shopping in this store on the same day as Jan, do you think you could buy one earring? Why or why not? Use the poem to support your answer.

Name _____  Date _____

Context clues

# After Dark

Write the word that means almost the same as each **bold word**.
Use the word bank.
Underline the clues that lead you to the meaning.

_____ **1** Jack's tooth falls out. Then he **misplaces** it. He cannot find it anywhere.

_____ **2** Jack scrunches up his face. He turns to his mom and says in a shaky voice, "I am **concerned**. Do you think the tooth fairy will come?"

_____ **3** "The tooth fairy can **locate** any lost tooth. I am sure she will find it!" Mom says.

_____ **4** Jack sighs. Slowly, he gets ready for bed. He **reluctantly** gets under the covers.

_____ **5** A few hours pass. The tooth fairy arrives. She plans to **nab** Jack's tooth from him and leave without being seen.

_____ **6** She **hovers** in the air above Jack's bed as she looks for his tooth.

_____ **7** The tooth is **concealed** in the carpet. The tall fibers cover the tooth, but the tooth fairy spots it right away.

_____ **8** Suddenly, the flying tooth fairy **swoops** down to grab the tooth.

_____ **9** The tooth fairy knows what she will put in the tooth's place. She **deposits** a shiny gold coin under Jack's pillow.

_____ **10** The tooth fairy is **exhausted**. She is ready to go home and rest after her busy night.

## Word Bank

| | | | | |
|---|---|---|---|---|
| dives | hidden | take | find | worried |
| tired | floats | loses | leaves | not willingly |

**Bonus:** Which sentence gives more clues to the meaning of the bold word? Explain.
A. When the tooth fairy got home, she found her puppy curled up with a pillow and **snoozing** on her bed.
B. The tooth fairy's puppy was **snoozing**.

©The Mailbox® • TEC43072 • April/May 2014 • Key p. 307 • (L.2.4a)

THE MAILBOX **39**

# More Than a Weed

## Dandelions

Some people think of dandelions as weeds. They try to remove them from their lawns. The settlers who came to the New World many years ago did not think this plant was a pest. They grew these plants in their gardens and used many of their parts. Did you know the leaves from young dandelion plants can be tossed in salads or cooked like spinach? The liquid that is found in its stem can be used to treat bee stings. The roots can be roasted or used as tea.

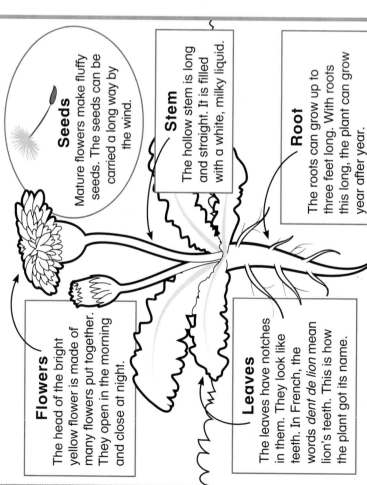

**Seeds**

Mature flowers make fluffy seeds. The seeds can be carried a long way by the wind.

**Stem**

The hollow stem is long and straight. It is filled with a white, milky liquid.

**Root**

The roots can grow up to three feet long. With roots this long, the plant can grow year after year.

**Flowers**

The head of the bright yellow flower is made of many flowers put together. They open in the morning and close at night.

**Leaves**

The leaves have notches in them. They look like teeth. In French, the words *dent de lion* mean lion's teeth. This is how the plant got its name.

Use the paragraph and the diagram to answer the questions.

1. What does a dandelion's flower look like? Color it to match. _____

2. How did the dandelion get its name? _____
_____

3. What is found inside a dandelion's stem? How is it useful? _____
_____

4. What parts of a dandelion can be eaten? How might they be prepared? _____
_____

5. What part of the dandelion can be up to three feet long? _____
_____

**Bonus:** How did the dandelion diagram help you understand the facts in the paragraph?

©The Mailbox® • TEC43072 • April/May 2014 • Key p. 307 • (RI.3.7)

# Kids Will Be Kids

Today the orthodontist
Told Gregory the news.
His teeth have become crooked
From the objects that he chews.

He snacks on things like boxes,
Old sneakers and shoelaces,
Garden tools, and tin cans.
So now he will need braces.

Gregory is sorry and
Regrets the things he did.
But he really couldn't help it.
After all, he's just a kid!

Use the poem and the illustration to answer the questions.

1. What news did Gregory get today?
_____
_____

2. The author calls Gregory a kid. Use the illustration to write a definition for how *kid* is used in the poem.
_____
_____

3. Circle two words in the poem that show how Gregory feels about his choices to chew on things.

4. Underline the five things Gregory chewed that caused his problem.

5. Based on the illustration, do you think Gregory learned his lesson? Why or why not?
_____
_____

**Bonus:** What part of the poem might help a reader understand what an orthodontist does? Draw a star next to it. Then color the part of the illustration that gives clues.

©The Mailbox® • TEC43073 • June/July 2014 • Key p. 307 • (RL.2.7)

**Note to the teacher:** To engage students in an interesting text discussion, display the poem by itself first. Then reveal the illustration. Have students explain how the illustration clarifies the poem.

# Ready to Retell!

We know your students are reading and responding to a variety of fiction texts. These quick-to-prepare ideas help them build on basic story element knowledge to specifically recount fables, folktales, and myths. (RL.2.2; RL.3.2)

## Just the Basics

This student-friendly reference tool helps you introduce the key differences among each type of reading while leading students to better retellings. First, make student copies of page 43. (Second-grade teachers can cover the myth column before copying for a grade-specific form.) Have each child staple the organizer into his reading folder or response journal. To identify a reading as a fable, folktale, or myth, instruct each student to use the descriptions at the top of the chart. Then have him include the information at the bottom of the chart when he retells one of the featured types of texts.

## Read Around the World

As students read about faraway places, keep a log of each trip they "take." To do this, label a sheet of chart paper for each inhabited continent and program the left side of each paper as shown. Post the charts near a large world map. Each time students read a different fable, folktale, or myth, help them identify its origin. Then, for each story, have students retell the story's title and author (if known); the story elements; and the moral, message, or theme. Write each answer on a separate like-colored sticky note; then place the sticky notes in a column on the corresponding chart. Use the sticky notes to compare and contrast stories from the same continent or across continents, or to find similarities within different versions of the same tale.

## Lessons Learned

To set up this simple center, set out a collection of picture books that include morals or lessons. After reading a book, a child writes its title on a sheet of paper and creates a mini poster that reveals the moral or message. Add each completed mini poster to a class book titled "Learning From Literature" and keep it at the center for students to reference. **To make this center easier,** provide audio recordings for students to listen to as they read and a list of morals or messages from which to choose.

**The Empty Pot by Demi**

It pays to be honest.

### North America

| | The Rough-Face Girl by Rafe Martin | Smoky Mountain Rose: An Appalachian Cinderella by Alan Schroeder | Domitila: A Cinderella Tale From the Mexican Tradition by Jewell Reinhart Coburn |
|---|---|---|---|
| Title and author | | | |
| Origin | | | |
| Characters | | | |
| Setting | | | |
| Problem | | | |
| Solution | | | |
| Lesson, moral, or theme | | | |

# Fable

- short story
- only one to three characters
- characters are objects or animals
- written to entertain
- teaches a lesson, which is shared at the end

**When you retell a fable, include**

- ☐ whether the characters are objects or animals
- ☐ the one or two events that lead to the solution
- ☐ the lesson learned from the characters' actions

# Folktale

- story has been told for a long time, passed down by storytelling
- shows the values of the place the story started from
- problem tests the main character
- main character changes at end

*Fairy tales, tall tales, and legends are all types of folktales.*

**When you retell a folktale, include**

- ☐ the place where the story came from
- ☐ how the problem tests the main character
- ☐ details about how the main character changes from the beginning of the story to the end

# Myth

- characters might be gods or goddesses or elements of nature with human traits
- characters have amazing powers
- story gives reasons for events
- some explain natural events; some tell why people do things
- story provides lessons about good and bad behavior

**When you retell a myth, include**

- ☐ details about the characters' strengths and powers
- ☐ how the main character's actions explain what causes a natural event or why people do certain things
- ☐ the lesson learned or shared

©The Mailbox® • TEC43069 • Oct./Nov. 2013

**Note to the teacher:** Use with "Just the Basics" on page 42.

# Conquering Content Area Words

(RI.2.4; RI.3.4)

## Hungry for Words

Create an appetite for new words with this class vocabulary monster. To prepare, color and cut out a copy of the monster pattern on page 45. Glue the pattern to the lid of a shoebox; then cut an opening in the monster's mouth and through the lid. Also cut out a supply of the word strip from page 45 and place the strips near the monster. Introduce students to the monster and tell them that for him to stay a happy, friendly fellow, he needs to eat new words every day. Encourage students to use new vocabulary words in their daily conversations or writing. When a child uses a word or knows of a classmate using a word, he writes the word on a word strip, explains the context in which it was used, and "feeds" it to the monster by sliding it through the opening. Periodically, remove the word strips from the monster and share with students. Encourage them to continue their progress or improve their efforts, as indicated by the number of strips in the box. *Melissa R. Ashbaugh, Orchard Primary, Almont, MI*

## Roll for Words

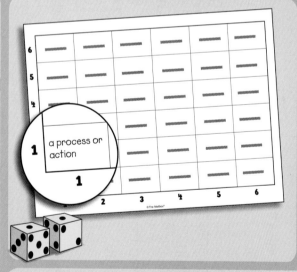

Students will have so much fun playing this game they'll forget that they're actually increasing their vocabulary knowledge! In advance, label a 6 x 6 grid with clues (definitions, synonyms, and cloze sentences) based on recent vocabulary words. Project the grid onto your board. To play, each team chooses a color. Then a student from Team 1 rolls two dice. She uses the numbers rolled as coordinates to find a clue on the grid. She reads the clue aloud; then she confers with her team to determine the matching word. If her answer is correct, she colors the grid space with her team's color. If her answer is incorrect, she leaves the space uncolored. If a roll results in a grid space already colored, the team's turn ends. Teams take turns in this manner. The first team to color four spaces vertically, horizontally, or diagonally wins. *Mary Miller, East Butler at Prague, Prague, NE*

## Stick With It

Help students make new words stick with this simple strategy. Identify two or three key words from your informational text. Prior to reading, give each student one sticky note for each word. Share definitions for the words; then direct each student to write each word and its meaning on a separate note. As the child reads the text, have him move the sticky notes from page to page. As he encounters a featured word, he writes the page number on the sticky note. Later, he moves the sticky notes to a journal, study sheet, or personal dictionary to use as a reference. *Cheryl Rayl, Mayville Elementary, Mayville, MI*

precipitation

moisture from the sky, like rain, snow, hail, sleet

page 48

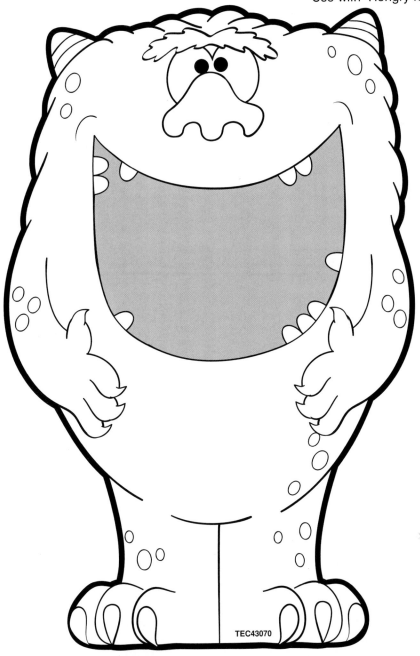

TEC43070

*word*

name

date

TEC43070

# NOW SHOWING
# Prefixes and Suffixes

Don't miss these blockbuster tips and activities! They're sure to be a megahit in your classroom! (RF.2.3d; RF.3.3a; L.3.4b)

## "Train-ing" Session

Use this engaging analogy to get students on track with reading new words. In advance, attach mailing labels to a three-part train (or train patterns), marking the engine car "prefix," the boxcar "root," and the caboose "suffix." Tell students that many words hook parts together to make one word, just as train cars are hooked together to make one train. Explain that prefixes are always found at the beginning of a base word, while suffixes appear at the end. Also tell students that when these different parts are added to root words, they can change how a word is used or what it means. To follow up the comparison, write words with affixes on the board and direct students to identify the word parts.

Cheryl Rayl, Mayville Elementary, Mayville, MI

## The Right Direction

Lead students to a better understanding of prefixes and suffixes with this simple tip. First, make student copies of the lists from page 47. Attach the prefix list to the upper left side of a child's desk; then attach the suffix list to the upper right side. The location of the lists helps students remember that prefixes come at the beginning of a root word while suffixes come at the end. The lists also help students determine word meaning when reading independently.

Cheryl Rayl

## Dig In!

For a simple center, copy the prefix, suffix, and root word cards from page 47; cut them out; and place them in an envelope. Set out the envelope with a compartmentalized paper plate labeled as shown. A student sorts the cards onto the corresponding sections. If desired, have him make a three-column chart that lists his results.

Heather Aulisio
Tobyhanna Elementary Center
Pocono Pines, PA

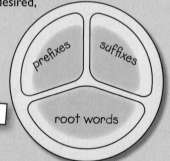

## Pop and Place

This whole-class game is sure to go over with a bang! To set up, write a list of eight to ten words that have prefixes. Write each of the different prefixes on a separate paper strip. Next, roll up the strips, place them in separate balloons, and blow up the balloons. Then write the root words from the list on two pieces of chart paper and hang the papers on opposite walls. Put Sticky-Tac or tape near the chart papers; then clear a path between the walls.

To play, divide the class into two teams. One player from each team meets halfway between the two walls (starting line). Give each child a balloon to pop. Then each player takes the paper strip from his balloon to his team's wall and attaches the prefix next to a root word to make a real word. He returns to his team, and then another player goes to the starting line. Play continues, but now, instead of popping a balloon, a player can move a prefix if he believes it is misplaced. The first team to correctly place all its prefix strips wins. **To vary the game,** label paper strips with suffixes.

Heather Aulisio

| | |
|---|---|
| un | real |
| pre | heat |
| | wind |
| re | write |
| | hook |
| | order |
| | draw |
| | school |

*tip* Be sure to warn your neighbors before playing this game or invite them to join you and play class against class!

A **prefix** is a word part that comes at the beginning of a root word.

- pre can mean *before or in front of*
- re can mean *again or back*
- un can mean *not or opposite of*
- dis can mean *not or opposite of*
- in can mean *not or opposite of*
- mis can mean *badly, opposite of, or not*

TEC43071

A **suffix** is a word part that comes at the end of a root word.

- ful can mean *full of or having the qualities of*
- less can mean *not having or unable to be acted on*
- ly can mean *having the characteristics of or every*
- able can mean *tending to, fit for, or worthy of*
- ation can mean *action or process*
- ible can mean *tending to, fit for, or worthy of*

TEC43071

## Prefix, Suffix, and Root Word Cards

Use with "Dig In!" on page 46.

| pre | help | ful |
|-----|------|-----|
| re | fuel | less |
| un | kind | ly |
| dis | honest | able |
| in | relax | ation |
| mis | teach | ible |

# Brain Boosters

**1** Rewrite each sentence to tell more.

I looked under my bed.

I opened my door.

**2** List five or more words that mean almost the same as *smart*.

**3** Describe things that are *pointy*.

**4** Circle the hidden number in each sentence. I will vote now.

A. It will amaze rodeo fans.
B. My teacher put a pen in each desk.
C. We walked on eggshells around her.
D. We will get extra recess if our class is good.
E. Is the number of students in our class even or odd?

**5** Write one word for each pair of meanings.

A. a young goat or to make fun of ____ ____
B. a storage building or to give off from a body ____ ____
C. a person who rules or a tool for measuring ____ ____
D. to guard from danger or a metal netting in a window or door ____ ____

**6** Which sentences would you use in a story to show that someone is angry? Which sentences would you use in a story to show that someone is excited? Explain your choices.

A. I can't believe you did that!
B. He stormed out of the room.
C. She was watching the clock, counting down the minutes until 3:00.

**7** Write as many regular verbs as you can to complete the chart. Start each verb with the letter *a*.

| Before | Now | Later |
|--------|-----|-------|
| acted | act | will act |

**8** Draw an *apostrophe*. Name two different places one can be found.

©The Mailbox® • TEC43068 • Aug./Sept. 2013 • Key p. 307

**How to Use** Give each student a copy of this page to work on during free time. Or, to use it as morning work or a warm-up activity, project a copy of the page and color the number of each task you want students to complete on their own papers.

# LANGUAGE ARTS

## Brain Boosters

**1** The answer is *haystack*. Write three or more questions that would have this answer.

**2** Complete each rhyming pair by writing a plural noun.

nice    *mice*

neat    _____

ten     _____

keep    _____

hear    _____

steeple _____

**3** Fall leaves can be *crunchy*. What else can be *crunchy*? Make a list of five or more items.

**4** Rewrite the letters to make a sentence. Add capital letters and punctuation.

iwillspendthanksgivingdayatbigbearlakeincalifornia

**5** What is the smartest month? "Know-vember," of course! Make a list of real words that start with *know*.

knows

**6** For each picture, write a past-tense irregular verb. Then use each verb in a sentence.

A.

B.

**7** Grandpa spends his autumn years traveling, fishing, and reading—all the things he didn't have time to do when he was working full time. What do you think *autumn years* means?

**8** What is the function of the bold word in each sentence?

A. The **crow** was perched on the fence, waiting for the farmer to leave his field.

B. I don't want to hear Sally **crow** about her trophy anymore.

**How to Use** Give each student a copy of this page to work on during free time. Or, to use as morning work or a warm-up activity, project a copy of the page and color the number of each task you want students to complete on their own papers.

# Brain Boosters

**1** Use the letters shown to write seven rhyming words. (Hint: There are two two-letter words, two three-letter words, and three four-letter words.)

b  g  k  l

n  o  w

**2** Study the equations. Write the word each symbol is replacing.

□ + ▷ = isn't

◇ + ○ = she'll

○ + ▷ = won't

□ = _____

▷ = _____

◇ = _____

○ = _____

**3** Write ten words that are related to winter.

**4** Write a different sentence for each word.

their

there

they're

**5** **Where do polar bears vote? The North "Poll"!**
Write four words from this riddle that sound like other words but are spelled differently. Then make a list of five more homophone pairs.

**6** Remove one letter from each word to form a new word. Tell what the set of new words has in common.

the   ⟶ _____

bit   ⟶ _____

web   ⟶ _____

shed  ⟶ _____

**7** When rolled, these dice made the word *click*. List five other words that could be rolled.

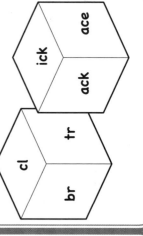

cl | ick | ace
br | tr | ack

**8** Read the cause. Write three effects.
Snow blanketed the roads.

©The Mailbox® • TEC43070 • Dec./Jan. 2013–14 • Key p. 307

**How to Use** Give each student a copy of this page to work on during free time. Or, to use as morning work or a warm-up activity, project a copy of the page and color the number of each task you want students to complete on their own papers.

# LANGUAGE ARTS

# Brain Boosters

**1** Make a list of geographic places, each beginning with a different letter of the alphabet.

### Australia, Brazil, Chicago...

**2** Write a sentence using the contraction *we'll*.

Write another sentence using the word *well*.

**3** Write one letter in each space to form four 3-letter words going down and one 5-letter name going across.

| I | F | A | D | A |
|---|---|---|---|---|
|   |   | P |   |   |
| E | N | E | G | D |

**4** Copy the riddle and punch line. Replace each ☘ with the missing letter or punctuation mark.

Wh☘ do mo☘t fr☘gs like ☘t. P☘tri☘k's Day☘

Bec☘☘se fr☘gs ☘lways w☘ar gr☘☘n

**5** List 5 things that could cause a person to shiver.

**6** These words can be used as nouns or verbs.

### bank   boot   burn   play

Write one word in each row so that another word is spelled in the circles.

Hint: The new word can also be used as a noun or verb.

**7** Use each word in a different sentence.

**fast**

**faster**

**fastest**

**8** Tell how catching a ball is different from catching a cold.

©The Mailbox® • TEC43071 • Feb./Mar. 2014 • Key p. 307

**How to Use** Give each student a copy of this page to work on during free time. Or, to use as morning work or a warm-up activity, project a copy of the page and color the number of each task you want students to complete on their own papers.

# Brain Boosters

**1** How are these pronouns alike? How are they different?

myself   himself

itself   ourselves

themselves

**4** The month of April has two birth flowers. To name them, use three different long-vowel teams to fill in the blanks.

d _____ sy and sw _____ t p _____

**5** The answer is *relaxation*. Write three questions that could have this answer.

**6** List five or more irregular verbs that start with *w*.

wrote

**2** Write ten classmates' names. For each classmate, write a product that starts with the same letter as his or her name.

Jen's jelly beans
Tom's taco sauce

**3** Which words have the prefix *pre* in them? Explain how you know.

spree

precut

pressed

prep

prefilled

**7** Gus wrote this quotation on his paper. Did he write it correctly? Why or why not?

The calculator was talking to the pencil. It said, "You can count on me"!

**8** Write three sentences. Use one of the words below as a noun in the first sentence. Use one of the remaining words as a verb in the second sentence. Use the final word as a proper noun in the third sentence.

plant   rose

sprout

©The Mailbox® • TEC43072 • April/May 2014 • Key p. 307

**How to Use** Give each student a copy of this page to work on during free time. Or, to use as morning work or a warm-up activity, project a copy of the page and color the number of each task you want students to complete on their own papers.

# LANGUAGE ARTS
## Brain Boosters

**1** The answer is *summer*. What are three or more questions that have this answer?

**2** *Rose* can mean the past tense of *rise* or a flower. List five or more words that each have more than one meaning and begin with *r*.

**3** Find a pair of rhyming words to match each clue.

The happy father is a *glad dad*.

A. a superheated place
B. a slender smile
C. a smart award
D. an aged sickness

**4** There are 30 days in June. Write 30 words that start with *j*. (List as many as you can before using a dictionary.)

**5** Write a sentence for each pattern.

A. noun + verb
B. adjective + noun + verb
C. adjective + noun + verb + adverb
D. pronoun + verb + adverb
E. pronoun + verb + noun

**6** What seven-letter word contains the word *heat*, names a place to see a show, and has three syllables?

**7** Would you rather be described as a gentle giant, as cute as a bug's ear, or as quiet as a mouse? Explain.

**8** Change one letter in each word to complete a phrase a parent might say.

A. Do so bet.
B. Cat sour bunch.
C. Lone lou!
D. He well sea.

**How to Use** Give each student a copy of this page to work on during free time. Or, to use it as morning work or a math warm-up activity, project a copy of the page and color the number of each task you want students to complete.

# Writing Tips & Tools

## Instant Inspiration
**Narrative writing (W.2.3; W.3.3)**

You're sure to make a mark with this prewriting idea! On a sunny day, give each student a piece of chalk; then take the class outside. Have each child draw a simple scene on a section of sidewalk or blacktop. When his picture is created, direct each student to raise his hand so you can take a picture of his scene. Print the photos and, at another time, direct each student to create a short story based on his picture. What a unique way to set the tone for a fun year of writing!

adapted from an idea by Heather Aulisio, Tobyhanna Elementary Center, Pocono Pines, PA

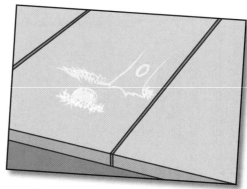

**tip** → Have parent volunteers available to help take pictures.

## Monthly Memories
**Informative writing (W.2.2; W.3.2)**

To start this year-long reflection journal, direct each child to fold a large sheet of construction paper in half (folder). Have her write a title, like the one shown; her name; and the school year. Next, direct the child to open the folder, trace her hand on the left side, and write the date inside the outline. Then have her complete a copy of page 63 (divider page) as shown and place it inside the folder. On a separate sheet of paper, direct her to describe her summer and her hopes for the school year. Then have her put that paper behind the divider page. Collect students' folders and redistribute them at the end of each month. At that time, provide each student with another divider page to complete and have her write about the events that occurred during the month. At the end of the year, bind each student's folder and pages into a book. Invite each child to trace her handprint on the right side of the inside cover and date it. Not only will students have a reminder of the events of the school year, they will see how they've grown as writers and as children.

Jennifer Fulfaro, Lehigh Elementary, Walnutport, PA

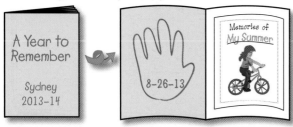

## Let Your Feelings Show
**Revising (W.2.3; W.3.3)**

Help students write to show details instead of telling the details. First, write the simple sentence shown on the board. Explain that the sentence tells how Lisa feels, but you want it revised to show that Lisa is happy. Have the class name ways people show they are happy, as well as events that might make people happy, as you list them on the board. Model how to rewrite the original sentence to show Lisa's feelings. **To extend the activity**, give each pair of students a simple telling sentence and have each duo rewrite its sentence to show instead of tell. Then remind students to apply this approach to their independent writing assignments.

Cheryl Rayl, Mayville Elementary, Mayville, MI

> Lisa was happy.
>
> | smiled | winning a prize |
> | laughed | opening a gift |
> | cheered | seeing a loved one |
>
> Lisa cheered loudly when she realized she had won a new car.

# Just Curious...

**Recalling information from experiences (W.2.8; W.3.8)**

With your students' help, you'll have a ready supply of journal prompts everyone will be eager to respond to. Give each child a sticky note and instruct her to write a question she would like her classmates to answer. Have students place their sticky notes on the board. Each day, select a different child to choose a sticky note. Then write the question on the board as the daily journal prompt. For added fun and inspiration, use seasonal or themed sticky notes.

Heather Aulisio, Tobyhanna Elementary Center, Pocono Pines, PA

What was the best thing you did over the summer?

How did you feel on the first day of school?

How did you celebrate your last birthday?

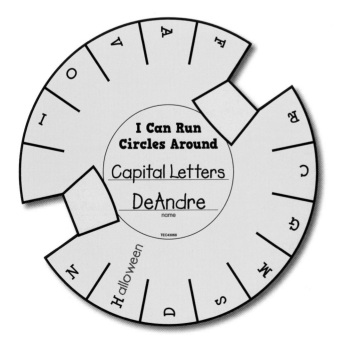

# Knowing Their Way Around

**Capitalization (L.2.2a)**

This handy organizer provides plenty of opportunities for practicing new capitalization rules. In advance, make a tagboard copy of page 64 for each child. Direct each student to complete the title as shown, cut out the circle, and snip the lines between the letters. Then challenge him to write a holiday, product name, or geographic place for each letter on the circle. After he writes the word with the matching capital letter, he folds the flap over. After students have had time to complete their circles, provide time for each child to share an example from his organizer. **To vary the activity**, challenge students to use the letters on the circle to compile lists of irregular verbs (L.2.1d; L.3.1d) or adjectives (L.2.1e).

adapted from an idea by Heather Aulisio

# Writing Tips & Tools

## Writers in Training
### Linking words (W.2.1, 3; W.3.1c; W.3.2c)

Get all your writers on board with using transition words! Make enlarged copies of the train patterns on page 65, cut them out, and write a different transition word on each cutout. Post the train near your writing area or in an easy-to-see location. As you come across examples of the transition words in text, make a copy of the page, highlight the transition word, and post it under the corresponding cutout. Lead students to refer to the display every time they write, and before long, your writers will be well-trained to use transitions!

**To vary the activity,** post temporal words (W.2.3; W.3.3c) on the train instead.

Tomika Altman-Lewis, Burton Elementary, Durham, NC

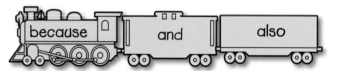

## Getting Thoughts on Paper
### Planning (W.3.5)

Sharing ideas with a partner is a great way to help your youngsters plan their writing, but only if they follow up by actually writing! To help students transition from the sharing stage to the writing stage, say, "Now your thoughts need to go from your brain *(point to your head)* to your pencil *(move your finger from your head down your arm)* to your paper *(point to an imaginary paper near your hand)*—not from your brain *(point to head)* to your mouth *(point to your mouth)* and to your neighbor *(move your thumb over to an imaginary person)*."

Sarah Newton
Logan Elementary
Topeka, KS

## Save the Day!
### Contractions (L.2.2c)

Dut, da, da, dah! This quick activity is perfect for your aspiring superheroes! First, post the helping verbs shown. Next, give each child a copy of page 66. Instruct him to write a sentence in each row of the left column, describing life as a superhero and using a different helping verb in each one. Then, in the right column, have the child rewrite each sentence, replacing the helping verb with a related contraction. Direct the student to trace each apostrophe with a crayon.

Terry Healy, Marlatt Elementary, Manhattan, KS

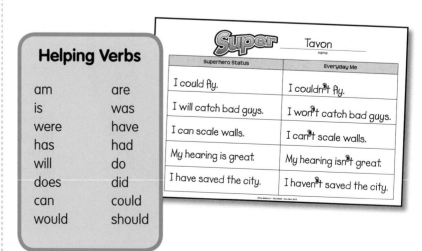

**Helping Verbs**

| | |
|---|---|
| am | are |
| is | was |
| were | have |
| has | had |
| will | do |
| does | did |
| can | could |
| would | should |

**Super** — Tavon
name

| Superhero Status | Everyday Me |
|---|---|
| I could fly. | I couldn't fly. |
| I will catch bad guys. | I won't catch bad guys. |
| I can scale walls. | I can't scale walls. |
| My hearing is great. | My hearing isn't great. |
| I have saved the city. | I haven't saved the city. |

# A Cut Above
**Writing**

With a little help from sales circulars, these activities lead students to practice different types of writing! To start any of the activities below, have each child select a familiar product from a sales circular, cut it out, and glue it to the top of a sheet of writing paper. Then have her complete one of the following tasks.

**Opinion-writing practice (W.2.1; W.3.1):** The student writes a sentence telling whether she thinks the product is popular with buyers. Then she writes three sentences to support her opinion.

**Informative-writing practice (W.2.2; W.3.2):** The child introduces the product to the reader. Then she gives the steps that explain how to use or prepare the product.

**Narrative-writing practice (W.2.3; W.3.3):** The student writes a real or imagined story where the product plays a key role in the plot.

Michelle Bayless, Croughton, England

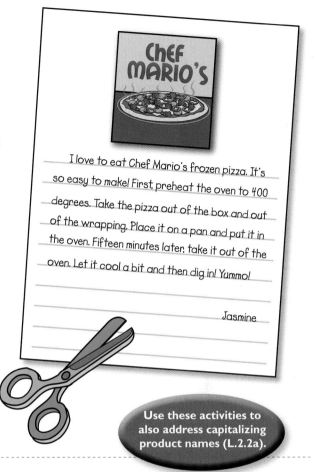

CHEF MARIO'S

I love to eat Chef Mario's frozen pizza. It's so easy to make! First, preheat the oven to 400 degrees. Take the pizza out of the box and out of the wrapping. Place it on a pan and put it in the oven. Fifteen minutes later, take it out of the oven. Let it cool a bit and then dig in! Yummo!

Jasmine

GLUE

Use these activities to also address capitalizing product names (L.2.2a).

# Poppin' Good
**Pronouns (L.2.1c; L.3.1a)**

Looking for anchor-chart inspiration? Check out these attention grabbers! In advance, draw a popcorn container on a sheet of chart paper. Use student input as you record important information about pronouns (reflexive or the function of) along the sides of the paper and below the popcorn container. Add examples of pronouns above the container, drawing a popcorn shape around each word or pair of words. Post the chart as a ready reference for students.

Staci Balmer, Silver Creek Elementary, Sellersburg, IN

# Writing Tips & Tools

## Check the Lineup
### Narrative writing (W.2.3; W.3.3)

Students plan and use unique story characters with this clever idea. To start, a child chooses a character outline from a copy of the character planner on page 67 and adds details to make a main character of his liking. Then he writes "1" on the character's shirt and drafts a story with this main character. The child keeps the planner in a writing folder. When he's ready to start another story, he chooses a different outline, adds details, and writes "2" on the shirt. He continues in this manner as characters are needed for his stories.

Heather Aulisio, Tobyhanna Elementary Center, Pocono Pines, PA

## Sounds Good!
### Revising (W.2.5; W.3.5)

To help your young authors correct or improve their writing, prepare a simple chart like the one shown. Post it where students can easily see it. When students read their drafts aloud, direct their classmates to refer to the poster to provide compliments or offer suggestions for improving how the writing sounds. **As an alternative**, prepare a chart titled "Stories That Look Good" to help students edit for conventions as they review their writing or their peers' writing.

April LoTempio, Ben Franklin Elementary, Kenmore, NY

> **Stories that sound good:**
> Can you follow the story from one event to another?
> Do you hear transition words like **first**, **next**, **later**, and **after that**?
> Can you see in your mind exactly what is happening in the story?
> Does the author use **specific nouns** and **verbs** instead of pronouns?
> Do you feel like you are part of the story?
> Do you hear sensory details? Do the words in the story help you know what the characters are **seeing**, **feeling**, **tasting**, **smelling**, and **hearing**?

## Extra Oomph
### Using onomatopoeia

This idea is sure to create a buzz as you lead students to more descriptive writing. To start, challenge small groups of students to list their favorite sound words and, if desired, have them include characters or objects that might make each sound on their posters. Display the posters around the room. When a student writes, instruct her to include at least three examples of onomatopoeia in her story without using examples from her own group's poster.

Heather Aulisio

# Writing Tips & Tools

## Silly Stories
**Writing motivation**

Here's a fun way to get students to write and get some of their wiggles out! First, set up student chairs around the room as you would for musical chairs. Next, give each child a clipboard stocked with a few sheets of paper and direct her to sit on a chair. When everyone is settled, instruct each student to write her name on the top paper and start writing a story. After a few minutes, direct students to stand and put their clipboards on their chairs. Play music and, when you stop it, have each student sit in the nearest empty chair and continue the story left there. Continue to play and stop music every few minutes. Then, after 15 to 20 minutes, guide students to return to their original chairs and read the resulting stories.

Heather Aulisio, Tobyhanna Elementary Center, Pocono Pines, PA

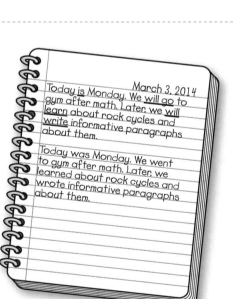

March 3, 2014

Today is Monday. We will go to gym after math. Later we will learn about rock cycles and write informative paragraphs about them.

Today was Monday. We went to gym after math. Later, we learned about rock cycles and wrote informative paragraphs about them.

## Quick Change
**Past tense verbs (L.3.1d, e)**

Squeeze a little grammar practice into the beginning and end of your day. In the morning, post a few sentences about the day's events on the board (morning message). Direct students to copy the morning message and underline the verbs. Then, at the end of the day, have students rewrite the sentences to show the past tense of the underlined verbs. Quick and easy, but great practice!

Nellie Franco, PS 376, Brooklyn, NY

## The End
**Writing conclusions (W.2.3; W.3.3d)**

Wrapping up a story can be a challenge for young authors. To make the task a little easier, reference stories your students already know! Here's how. Make a chart that lists different genres your students have read. Guide students to think about stories they're read or heard in each genre and tell how their endings are similar. Write the similarities on the chart. Then choose a story from one of the genres and read the story aloud, stopping before the story ends. Refer to the chart and have each student write the ending based on how stories in the genre typically end. Repeat the activity at different times, reading stories from the same genre and then stories from different genres to help students gain confidence and experience with their story conclusions.

April Parker, St. Pius X School, Greensboro, NC

| fairy tales | have a happy ending |
|---|---|
| fables | end with a moral or lesson |
| mysteries | end with the case being solved |

# On-Screen Planning

**Using technology to produce writing (W.2.6; W.3.6)**

To guide students to shape their writing, take a trip to the computer lab. Lead your writers to use a word processing program to create three text boxes onscreen. Then, depending on the type of writing you want students to practice, have them label each box and start planning as described below.

- **Opinion writing (W.2.1; W.3.1):** The student uses the top box to introduce his opinion, the middle box to supply supporting reasons, and the bottom box to provide a conclusion.

- **Informational/explanatory texts (W.2.2; W.3.2):** The student uses the top box to introduce the topic, the middle box to list facts and definitions to develop points, and the bottom box for a conclusion.

- **Narratives (W.2.3; W.3.3):** The student uses the top box to plan the beginning of his story, the middle box for the middle, and the bottom box for the end.

April Parker, St. Pius X School, Greensboro, NC

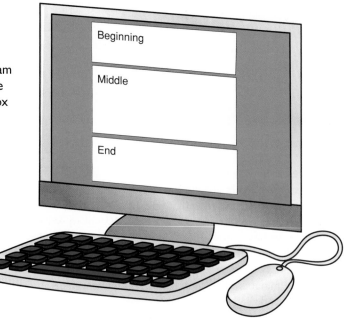

Beginning

Middle

End

---

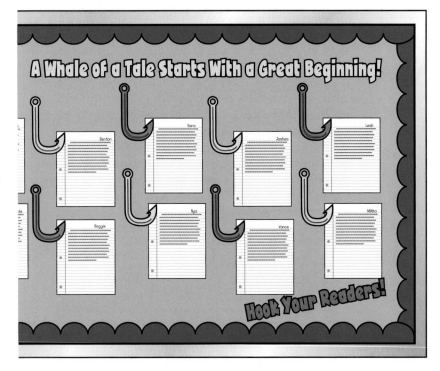

# Whale of a Tale!

**Writing introductions (W.2.3; W.3.3a)**

No need for students to fish around for a great story beginning—this display serves as an easy reference! To prepare, set up a display with the title shown and make a supply of hook patterns from page 68. Each time you or your students come across a great beginning such as in a class reading or when reading a child's draft, write it on a hook, cut it out, and post it on the display. Then, when students write, encourage them to refer to the beginning statements to inspire their own. As they become more proficient with writing introductions on their own, have each child copy her introduction onto a hook and post her final draft next to the tip of the hook.

April Parker

# Writing Tips & Tools

## Twist on a Favorite
**Subject-verb agreement (L.3.1f)**

This version of Heads Up, Seven Up provides plenty of grammar practice. Before playing, have each child write on separate paper strips two phrases: one showing subject and verb agreement and the other showing incorrect subject and verb use. Collect the strips and write on the board the headings shown. To play, direct students to put their heads down on their desks and their thumbs up. Then choose seven students as players by tapping their thumbs. Give each player a strip and direct him to stand at the front of the room. Each player reads the phrase and then calls on a classmate to tell if the phrase is correct or incorrect. Then the player places the phrase under the corresponding heading on the board. Have the students sit down; then repeat the process until everyone has had a chance to play.

adapted from an idea by April Parker, St. Pius X School, Greensboro, NC

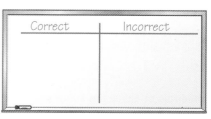

## Planning Ahead
**Writing: informational (W.2.2; W.3.2)**

Help students guide their writing with this handy organizer. To make one, a child cuts apart the booklet pages from a copy of page 69. He stacks the pages in order and staples them together across the top. He uses reference materials to complete each page, using the back for additional writing space as needed. After his booklet is complete, the student uses its contents to write a report or other informational piece.

## A Trio of Tasks
**Writing: imagined narratives (W.2.3; W.3.3)**

Build off your study of folklore (RL.2.2; RL.3.2) and get students excited to write their own tall tales. Share examples of hyperbole from well-known tall tales and lead students to understand the role of exaggeration in such stories. Next, roll two dice three times and have each child write the resulting numbers at the top of a sheet of paper. Then project page 70 onto the board. Instruct each student to write the matching nouns on her paper and then use them in examples of hyperbole in her tall tale. Provide time for volunteers to read their stories aloud for the whole class.

Andrea O'Donnell, Pittsburgh Urban Christian School, Pittsburgh, PA

# Writing Tips & Tools

## Brilliant Stories
**Writing (W.2.1–3; W.3.1–3, 10)**

Come rain or shine, this sunny manipulative provides plenty of writing inspiration. Give each student a copy of the wheel patterns on page 71 and direct him to cut them out. Next, have him place the circular cutout atop the sun ray cutout and push a brad through each dot to attach them. The child turns the wheel to reveal a desired writing prompt title, copies it onto his paper, and starts writing. Whether he writes at school or uses it for inspiration during the summer, he's sure to get a variety of writing practice.

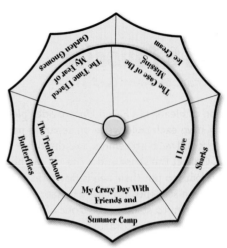

## Ways to Begin a Sentence

| | | |
|---|---|---|
| The | A | An |
| They | Their | She |
| Her | He | His |
| Earlier | Before | Yesterday |
| Now | Soon | Meanwhile |
| After | Just when | First |
| Second | Next | Once |
| Then | Finally | Lastly |
| In conclusion | On the other hand | Furthermore |
| However | Although | |

## Avoid *I* Overload
**Sentence variety**

Young writers tend to lean on common strategies when writing, and that includes starting each sentence with *I*. To avoid this pronoun overload, enlist the help of your writing experts to create an authentic writing reminder. First, program a sheet of chart paper as shown; then provide students with colorful paper, scissors, and markers. Guide students to think about their own writing samples as well as the work of their favorite authors to generate words or phrases that work as sentence starters. Instruct students to write their response or responses on the paper and cut around them. Group related sentence starters (articles, adverbs, temporal words, etc.) and glue them to the chart paper. Hang the list where it is easily accessible, and encourage students to refer to it when writing to avoid stories and reports that are full of the word *I*.

Lienna Dickens, Mark Twain Elementary, Houston, TX

## Say the Word
**Adverbs (L.2.1e)**

> I'd like the red group to line up quietly.

Make the most of transition times while exposing students to real-life examples of adverbs. As you direct students to another activity, to another location, or to line up, make statements that use adverbs. For example, say, "I'd like the red group to line up quietly" or "I need the yellow group to quickly return their math materials to the table." Then ask students to identify the adverb in the directions. Follow up the directions with a statement based on the students' actions, such as "The red group can do a better job of lining up quietly" or "Thank you, yellow group, for responding quickly."

Beth Pallotta, Eden Christian Academy, Pittsburgh, PA

 Find **prompts and more** on pages 72–86.

# Memories of

_____

**Note to the teacher:** Use with "Monthly Memories" on page 54.

THE MAILBOX **63**

# Circle Pattern

Use with "Knowing Their Way Around" on page 55.

I Can Run Circles Around

_____

_____
name

TEC43068

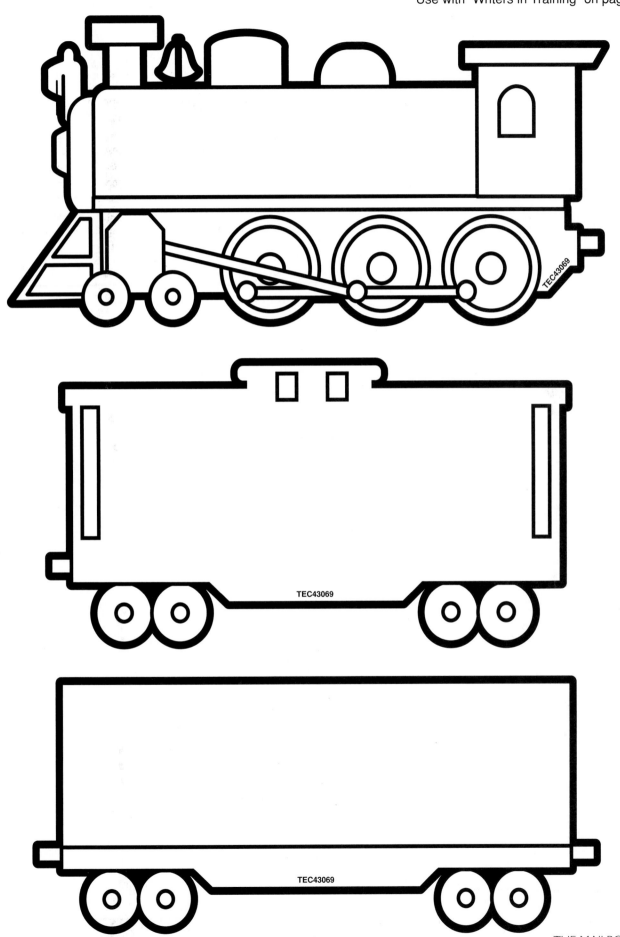

TEC43069

TEC43069

TEC43069

**Super**

name _____

| Superhero Status | Everyday Me |
|---|---|
| | |
| | |
| | |
| | |
| | |

**Note to the teacher:** Use with "Save the Day!" on page 56.

_____'s Character Planner

name

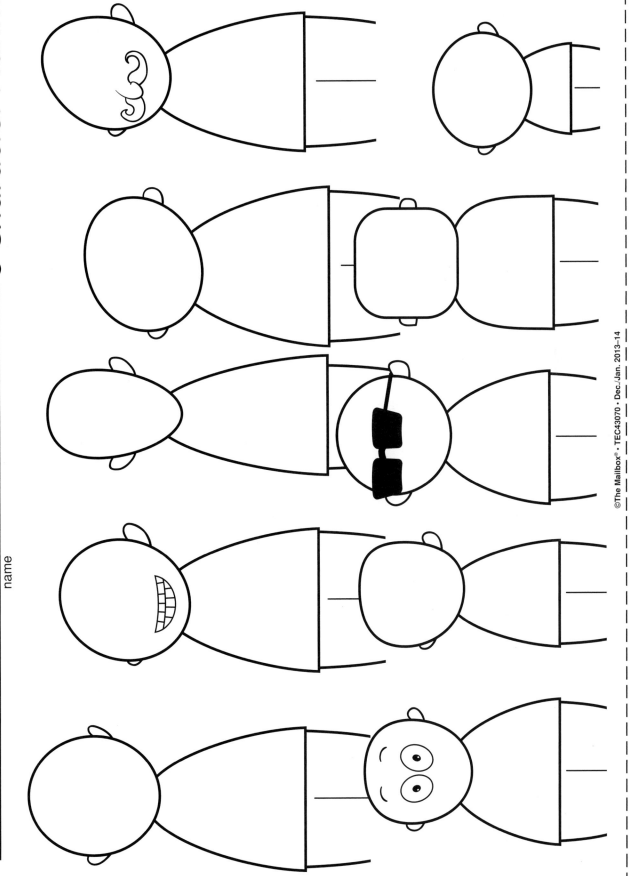

**Note to the teacher:** Use with "Check the Lineup" on page 58.

THE MAILBOX | **67**

# Hook Patterns

Use with "Whale of a Tale!" on page 60.

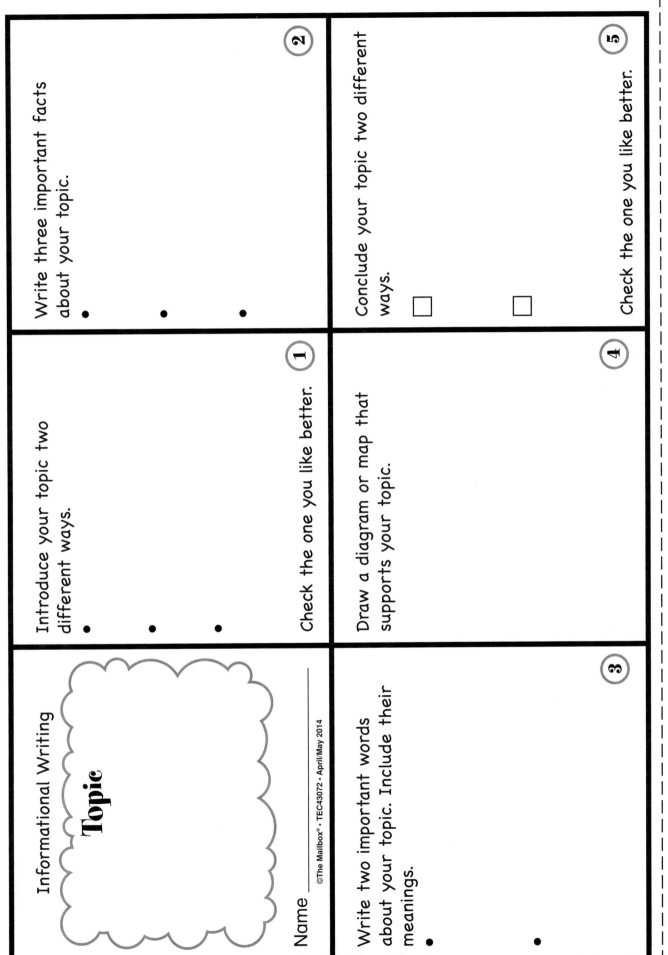

**Informational Writing**

## Topic

Name _____

©The Mailbox® • TEC43072 • April/May 2014

① Introduce your topic two different ways.

- 
- 
- 

Check the one you like better.

② Write three important facts about your topic.

- 
- 
- 

③ Write two important words about your topic. Include their meanings.

- 
- 

④ Draw a diagram or map that supports your topic.

⑤ Conclude your topic two different ways.

☐

☐

Check the one you like better.

Note to the teacher: Use with "Planning Ahead" on page 61.

| (2) elephants | (3) pizzas | (4) the Internet |
|---|---|---|
| (5) school buses | (6) milk shakes | (7) children |
| (8) trees | (9) cheetahs | (10) skyscrapers |
| (11) sharks | (12) books | A **tall tale** is a story set in fairly modern times. It is a funny story that exaggerates the traits or actions of the main character (hero). |

©The Mailbox® • TEC43072 • April/May 2014

**70** THE MAILBOX **Note to the teacher:** Use with "A Trio of Tasks" on page 61.

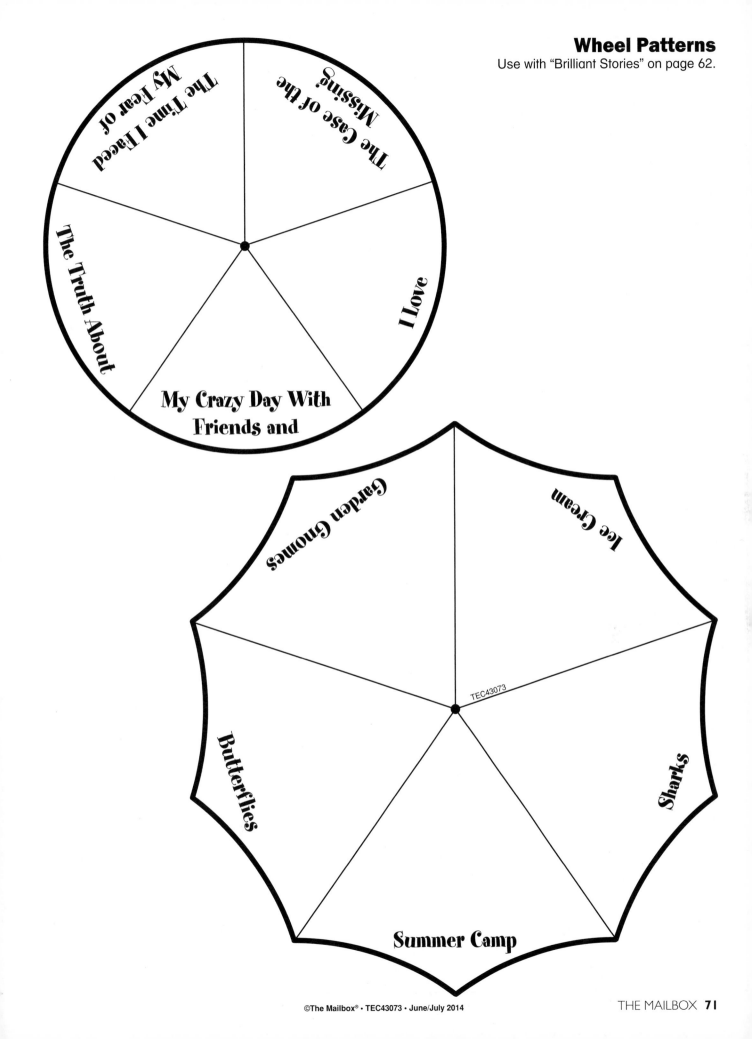

My Fear of

The Time I Faced

The Case of the Missing?

The Truth About

I Love

My Crazy Day With Friends and

Garden Gnomes

Ice Cream

Butterflies

Sharks

Summer Camp

TEC43073

# Back-to-School Prompts

 Pretend you can bring only one school supply to school this year. What will you bring? Why?

 Write a story about a new student joining your class. Include the words "Just when it seemed like things couldn't get any better,..."

 Describe the routine you follow to get ready for school each morning.

 Should students at your school wear uniforms? Why or why not?

 What are three things your new teacher should know about you?

 How do students in your class or school borrow books? Write to explain each step.

 If you could add one rule to your class or school rules, what would it be? Why?

Explain why your classroom has rules.

TEC43068

---

# September Prompts

 Write a story that takes place in an apple tree.

 Is it more important for kids to learn sports or music? Explain.

 Write a story about spending a day with a grandparent.

 Tell about a time when you felt nervous. Describe your actions and feelings.

 Write a thank-you letter to a helper in your school or community.

 What does "practice makes perfect" mean to you?

 Pretend the water fountain now spurts apple juice instead of water. How do you feel? Why?

Write a story with this title.

The Best Weekend Ever

Describe what you usually do after school.

TEC43068

---

**How to Use** Have each child staple a copy of this page in his writing journal. Or cut copies in half and distribute only one month's prompts at a time to students. When a student uses a prompt, he colors its shape.

Name _____

# November Prompts

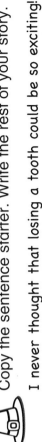 How might a person show that he or she feels thankful?

If you could invite a famous person to your Thanksgiving Day meal, who would you choose? Why?

In honor of Veterans Day (November 11), write a letter or poem thanking a veteran.

Copy the sentence starter. Write the rest of your story.
I never thought that losing a tooth could be so exciting!

Write a story that takes place on a turkey farm.

The animals of the forest need to elect a new leader. Who would do the best job? Tell why.

Pretend a new friend has never heard of corn. Tell your friend everything he needs to know about it.

How do you feel about eating leftovers? Explain.

---

Name _____

# October Prompts

 Write directions for someone who has never carved a pumpkin.

List your top ten favorite sweet treats. Tell why you like your number one better than number ten.

Is it better to have Halloween events on Halloween or the weekend before Halloween? Write three reasons to support your opinion.

Write a story that ends with the main character learning that it is best to tell the truth.

A science magazine asks you to write a report about the fall leaves where you live. What important facts do you include?

Would you like to travel a long distance on a ship? Why or why not?

Write a true story about a time when you felt proud.

Choose a title. Write its story.
The Creepy Hayride     The Mystery of the Key

**How to Use** Have each child staple a copy of this page in his writing journal. Or cut copies in half and distribute only one month's prompts at a time to students. When a student uses a prompt, he colors its shape.

Name _____

# December Prompts

 Copy and complete. Then give reasons.

_____ is the month with the best holidays.

 Write a song or poem about a holiday that is important to you.

 Write a make-believe story about a character who opens an unusual present.

 Should children be paid an allowance? Why or why not?

 Write a true story about a time you helped someone. Use words like *first, next,* and *then* in your story.

 Pretend you have a classmate from another country. Tell everything he needs to know about eating lunch at your school.

 Describe someone you know who has a gift for telling jokes.

 Write a story that takes place somewhere cold.

TEC43070

Name _____

# January Prompts

 Do you think it is a good idea to make New Year's resolutions? Why or why not?

 Write a letter thanking someone for a gift they've given you.

 A big snowstorm closes school. How do you spend your day?

 Write a story with this title:

Footprints in the Snow

 Think of a favorite story. Write its sequel, telling what the characters do next.

 Copy and complete.

It's easy to make *your own breakfast. First....*

A snowpal comes to life. Tell the story.

January is Oatmeal Month. What is your opinion of oatmeal? Give reasons.

TEC43070

**How to Use** Have each child staple a copy of this page in his writing journal. Or cut copies in half and distribute only one month's prompts at a time to students. When a student uses a prompt, he colors its shape.

## Name _____

# February Prompts

- A new groundhog will start predicting the start of spring. Write the groundhog a letter telling what it needs to know about how to do this job.

- Write a sentence about each student in your class. Be kind and use a different adjective in each sentence.

- Write a true story about someone or something you love.

- Should a box of candy be filled with only one kind of chocolate or different kinds of chocolate? Give reasons to support your opinion.

- If you could go back in time, would you rather spend a day with President Washington or President Lincoln? Why?

- Choose a US president. Tell what you know about his life.

- Write a make-believe story about a time you traded places with an animal for one day.

- In some schools, all the boys are grouped in classes together and all the girls are grouped together. Would you like to be in a school like this or one where boys and girls are in the same class? Explain.

TEC43071

## Name _____

# March Prompts

- Tell about a time when your plans had to change because of the weather.

- In honor of Dr. Seuss's birthday, write a review of a Dr. Seuss book you know well. Tell why you did or did not like it.

- Write a true story with this title.
  My Luckiest Day

- Explain the best way to catch a leprechaun and find his gold.

- Write a make-believe story that takes place in your classroom.

- Tell what you know about rainbows. Use facts.

- Copy a sentence. Provide reasons and a concluding sentence.
  - ☐ I am so glad spring is finally here.
  - ☐ I'd be happier if winter stuck around a while longer.

- Write a how-to guide for kids who are new to your school. Tell how to have fun in spring.

TEC43071

©The Mailbox® • TEC43071 • Feb./Mar. 2014 • (W.2.1–3; W.3.1–3)

**How to Use** Have each child staple a copy of this page in his writing journal. Or cut copies in half and distribute only one month's prompts at a time to students. When a student uses a prompt, he colors its shape.

# April Prompts

Name _____

Choose a title. Write the story.

☐ The Magic Umbrella    ☐ Rain, Rain, Go Away!

What is your opinion of rain? Give reasons to support your idea.

What do you know about storm safety? Use facts.

Should children be allowed to eat whatever they want? Why or why not?

Write a true story about a time when you couldn't stop laughing.

April is Mathematics Awareness Month. Explain how you use math when you are not at school.

What are the three best things about this time of year? Tell why you think so.

What would be a fun place away from school to take your class for recess? Explain why you think so and tell what you would do there.

TEC43072

# May Prompts

Name _____

Write a story titled "Surprise!"

Choose an opinion. Write to support it.

☐ Growing a garden is a great idea.
☐ Growing a garden is too much work.

What do you know about how plants grow? Use facts.

Write a make-believe story from a butterfly's point of view.

Name an important lady in your life. Then describe a party you would throw for her.

Think about a place you would like to visit. Use facts to explain why you want to go there.

A person who is a ray of sunshine is someone who makes you feel happy. Write a story about someone who you think of as a ray of sunshine.

Write a true story about a time when you were either too big or too small to take part in something you wanted to do.

TEC43072

**How to Use** Have each child staple a copy of this page in his writing journal. Or cut copies in half and distribute only one month's prompts at a time to students. When a student uses a prompt, he colors its shape.

# June Prompts

 June is National Iced Tea Month. What is your opinion of iced tea? Give reasons.

 "My Best Memory of This School Year"

 Write a true story about a time you felt both happy and sad.

 All of a sudden, you are weightless! Write a story about what happens next.

 Write a letter giving advice to a student who will be in this class next year.

 Father's Day falls on the third Sunday in June. Write a poem for someone who is a father.

 Write a story titled "My Teacher's Secret Life." Tell what your teacher does after school or on weekends.

 Choose one task you perfected this year. Explain how to do it from start to finish.

TEC43073

---

# Summer Prompts

 Is summer break important for students? Tell why you think so.

Use facts to tell about summer in the southern hemisphere.

Tell about a time you had fun with water.

Write a make-believe story with the title "The Unusual Ice Cream Truck."

Explain how to build the perfect sand castle.

Write a story that takes place during summer and has a lifeguard as a character.

 How do you like to spend your summer days: with a lot to do or free to relax? Explain.

 If you go the extra mile, it means you do more than you have to do. Write about a time you went the extra mile.

TEC43073

---

©The Mailbox® • TEC43073 • June/July 2014 • (W.2.1–3; W.3.1–3)

**How to Use** Have each child staple a copy of this page in his writing journal. Or cut copies in half and distribute only one month's prompts at a time to students. When a student uses a prompt, he colors its shape.

Name _____

Date _____

# Up, Up, and Away

**Prompt** Imagine you take a trip in a spaceship. Write a story about your adventure.

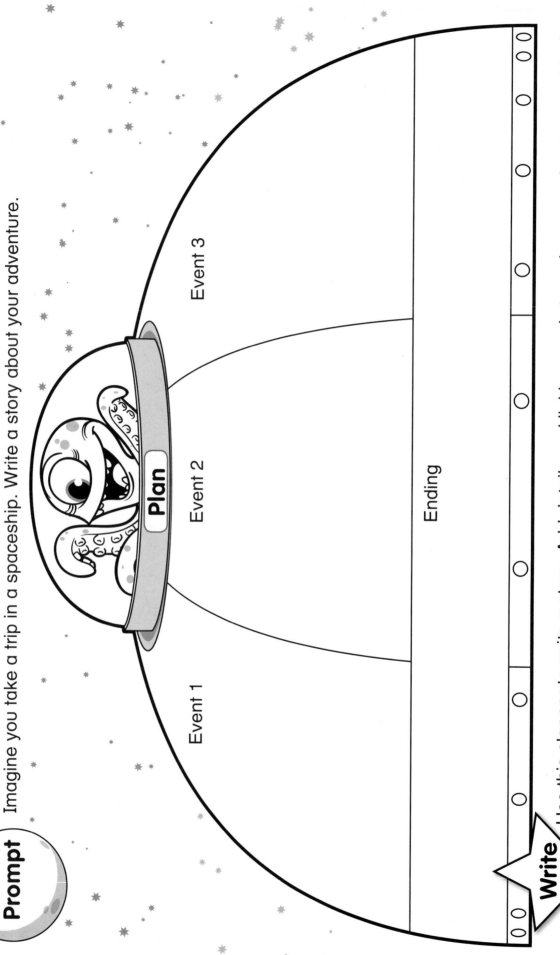

Plan

Event 1

Event 2

Event 3

Ending

**Write** Use this planner to write a story. Add details and linking words to make your adventure exciting!

©The Mailbox® • TEC43069 • Oct./Nov. 2013 • (W.2.3; W.3.3)

# Student Superhero

**Prompt**

If you could have a superpower for one day, what would you want to have and why?

**Plan**

In my opinion, the best superpower to have would be _____ .

**Reason 1**

**Reason 2**

**Reason 3**

**Write**

Tell which superpower you think would be the best to have for one day. Include three reasons to support your opinion. Then write a conclusion.

©The Mailbox® • TEC43072 • April/May 2014 • (W.2.1; W.3.1)

Name _____

Date _____

# Soak Up the Savings

**Prompt**

Many places face droughts in the summer. Even if droughts are not a problem where you live, how can you save water?

**Plan**

Use research materials to answer the questions.

What is a drought?

What can you do to save water?

1.

2.

3.

**Write**

Tell what a drought is and use facts to explain what you can do to save water.

©The Mailbox® • TEC43073 • June/July 2014 • (W.2.2; W.3.2)

**Note to the teacher:** Give each child a copy of "In Short Supply" on page 148 to use as a reference for this writing task.

Name_____ Date_____

# Holiday Happenings

Decide where capital letters are needed in the word bank.
Then draw ⹀ below those letters.
Use the word bank to correctly write each holiday in the
   matching sentence.

**Word Bank**

☺ april Fools' day    🎄 christmas    🥚 easter    👔 father's day

🐻 groundhog day    🍬 halloween    hanukkah    🎉 Independence day

🌸 mother's day    🎉 new year's eve    ☘ st. patrick's Day    🎩 thanksgiving Day

♡ valentine's day    🏴 Veterans day

1. The shamrock is a symbol for ☘ _____.

2. Children might hunt for eggs on 🥚 _____.

3. A candle is lit each of the eight nights of _____.

4. People celebrate 🎉 _____ on December 31.

5. Moms get cards and gifts on 🌸 _____.

6. Silly tricks are played on friends on ☺ _____.

7. Some boys and girls go trick-or-treating on 🍬 _____.

8. Fireworks sparkle in the sky on 🎉 _____.

9. 🎩 _____ is when people eat turkey and give thanks.

10. You might see a lot of hearts on ♡ _____.

11. Men and women who fought for our country are remembered on

    🏴 _____.

12. 🐻 _____ is when
    some folks believe a groundhog predicts how long
    winter will last.

> **Bonus:** Use each unused
> holiday from the word bank
> in a different sentence.

Name_____  Date_____

# Taking a Hike

Complete each sentence by writing the plural of each word.

1. Our scout troop takes _____ every fall.
   hike

2. We bring our _____ with us.
   lunch

3. It is chilly today, and even though we are wearing coats and _____,
   hat
   our _____ chatter.
   tooth

4. Our guide hands us trail _____ and water _____.
   map                                           bottle

5. There are lots of _____, _____, and _____
   man                        woman                        child
   on this trail today.

6. Many _____ have their _____ with them.
   family                        dog

7. _____ crunch under our _____ as we walk.
   Leaf                              foot

8. We see wild _____ and _____ through the trees.
   turkey                    deer

9. Two _____ slither under the _____.
   snake                              bush

10. _____ and other _____ fly overhead.
    Goose                        bird

11. We all rest on _____ at the top of the mountain.
    bench

12. We laugh and tell _____ before heading back.
    joke

**Bonus:** Write the plural words from sentences 2 and 3. Next to each word, write the rule you used to make it plural.

©The Mailbox® • TEC43069 • Oct./Nov. 2013 • Key p. 308 • (L.3.1b)

Name _____

Date _____

# Meet Max, Extreme Explorer!

Would you like to visit the planet _____ ? Or is a trip to _____
                                    planet                                    country

more your speed? My pal Max has been exploring new places all his life. Not long after he was born in

_____ , _____ , his parents took him along on a top secret mission to
city               state

_____ . When they came back, they sold their house on _____ and
planet                                                           street name

_____ . 
moved to _____ .
         continent

Max learned to swim. He loved it! He talked his parents into going to the _____ and the
                                                                          river

_____ . You'd think he was a fish! For a while, he even talked his parents into visiting all the
ocean

water parks in _____ and _____ .
               state                state

Now that he is older, Max prefers to see the sights in the United States.

He has been to the Grand Canyon, the Statue of Liberty, and the

_____ . Max loves to go to new places!
US landmark

Use capital letters to write place names.

©The Mailbox® · TEC43069 · Oct./Nov. 2013 · (L.2.2a)

**How to Use** Project this page and complete it with students as a whole-group activity. Or have each child complete a copy of this page using an atlas, a science book, or a social studies book to help him fill in the blanks.

# Game Time

Complete each sentence.
Cross off each word from the word bank as you use it.

1. My dad won basketball tickets, _____ he is taking me to the game.

2. My mom is looking forward to it, _____ my sister is not very excited.

3. We don't go to many games _____ the tickets cost a lot of money.

4. We have an extra ticket, _____ I invite a friend to go with us.

5. I have to choose either Luke _____ Hunter.

6. I choose Hunter _____ Luke has been to many games.

7. Hunter has never been to a basketball game _____ has he watched one on TV.

8. We may have free tickets, _____ we still have to pay for parking.

9. We arrive early, _____ the players have already warmed up.

10. That player is tall, _____ he moves faster than the speed of light!

11. He shoots foul shots well _____ not layups.

12. I eat candy _____ Hunter eats popcorn during the game.

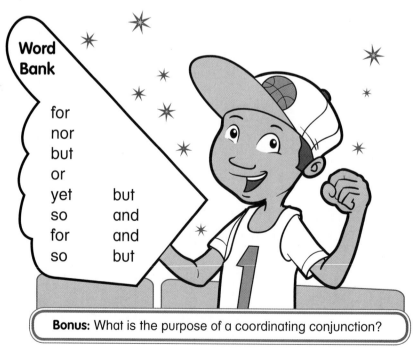

**Word Bank**

for
nor
but
or
yet     but
so      and
for     and
so      but

**Bonus:** What is the purpose of a coordinating conjunction?

       ©The Mailbox® • TEC43070 • Dec./Jan. 2013–14 • Key p. 308 (L.3.lh)

# Time to Clean Up Her Act

Underline the subject in each sentence. Circle the verb.
Decide if the verb and subject agree.
Shade the letter in the matching column.

| | Yes | No |
|---|---|---|
| 1. Ima Robber rides into town. | B | N |
| 2. She tie up her horse, Lightning. | O | L |
| 3. They makes a good team. | H | G |
| 4. She spots the town bank. | U | E |
| 5. Ima cover her face. | W | D |
| 6. She grabs her empty money sack. | M | C |
| 7. Lightning neighs loudly. | F | K |
| 8. Ima walk into the bank. | T | L |
| 9. She take all the money. | A | I |
| 10. The bankers chases after her. | Y | R |
| 11. Ima jumps on Lightning. | K | M |
| 12. Swiftly, they ride out of town. | W | D |
| 13. The bankers tells the sheriff where Ima goes. | G | Y |
| 14. The sheriff quickly catches up to Ima. | N | S |
| 15. Ima give all the money to the sheriff. | L | A |

**Bank**

**Bonus:** For each sentence in which the subject and verb did not agree, write the correct verb.

## Why did the bandit bathe before robbing the bank?
To answer the riddle, write each uncolored letter on its matching line or lines.

___ ___ ___   ___ ___ ___ ___ ___ ___   ___ ___   ___ ___ ___ ___   ___
14  3   4     5   9   1   8   4   12    8   2    11  9   7   4     9

___ ___ ___ ___ ___   ___ ___ ___ ___ ___ ___ ___.
6   15  4   9   1     13  4   8   9   5   9   10

# She's Going to Be a Star!

Combine each clause on the left with its matching clause on the right.
Write the complex sentence on its line below.

**Independent Clause**

☆ she never performs for lots of people

✪ she tries out for *Talent Stars*

▢ Kat is nervous

✪ people always listen

△ she will be a star in her parents' eyes

✪ they will invite her to perform on the show

✪ Kat checks the mailbox every day

◯ Kat sends in a tape of her singing

**Dependent Clause**

☆ Whenever Kat sings

✪ Since Kat wants to be a rock star

◯ before she gets on the show

✪ If the judges like Kat

✪ Although Kat sings at home

✪ even though she just sent in her tape

▢ when her letter arrives

△ As long as Kat sings

1. ☆ _____

2. ✪ _____

3. ◯ _____

4. ✪ _____

5. ✪ _____

6. ✪ _____

7. ▢ _____

8. △ _____

**Bonus:** Complete this definition. A complex sentence is made of an _____ clause and at least one _____ clause.

©The Mailbox® • TEC43073 • June/July 2014 • Key p. 308 • (L.3.1h)

# MOVING IN THE "WRITE" DIRECTION

## Writing Process Ideas

### PREWRITING
*(W.2.3; W.3.3a–c)*

Use this analogy to emphasize the importance of planning a story. Place a long strip of masking tape on the floor (tightrope). Explain that a good writer starts with an interesting beginning—like when an acrobat steps onto a tightrope—and then uses a variety of connected steps to get to a satisfying ending—like when the acrobat gets off the tightrope. A writer, just like the acrobat, must make sure that all the steps go together so he doesn't go off topic—or fall off the tightrope. Model the parts of a story by starting at one end of the tape and naming an interesting beginning, moving across the tape as you name related events, and continuing until you reach the end of the tape and name a satisfying ending. Remind students that the planning phase is just for the basic parts of the story and details can be added during the drafting stage.

Cheryl Rayl, Mayville Elementary, Mayville, MI

### DRAFTING AND REVISING
*(W.2.5, 6; W.3.5, 6)*

When students are ready to write drafts, send them to the computer. After a child keys in his draft, enlarge the font and increase the line spacing. Help the student save his document; then print the draft and discuss areas for improvement. Direct the child to capture his new ideas on the printout; then have him add the changes to his saved document. Since the draft is saved, inserting additions and making needed corrections will be a snap (and less intimidating than rewriting the whole piece)! As an added bonus, students will practice using digital tools to produce their writing.

Cheryl Rayl

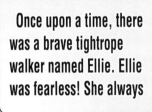

Once upon a time, there was a brave tightrope walker named Ellie. Ellie was fearless! She always

### EDITING
*(W.2.5; W.3.5)*

Here's a fun way of reminding students how to critique their classmates' writing. Simply post a copy of page 88. Then, each time students peer-edit, point to the mini poster and say, "Remember 'tutu.'" Each child will tell her partner two things she likes about the writing and suggest two ways to improve it.

Melissa R. Ashbaugh, Almont Community School, Almont, MI

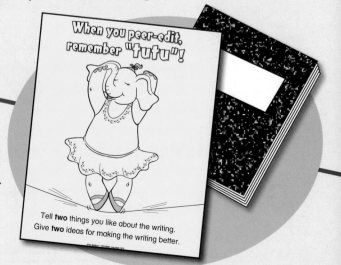

When you peer-edit, remember "tutu"!

Tell **two** things you like about the writing.
Give **two** ideas for making the writing better.

# When you peer-edit, remember "tutu"!

Tell **two** things you like about the writing.

Give **two** ideas for making the writing better.

**Note to the teacher:** Use with "Editing" on page 87.

# MATH

# MATH
## Tips & Tools

## I Say, You Say
### Add within 20 (2.OA.B.2)

Have a few minutes to spare? That's all you need to complete this quick activity. Name a sum less than 20, such as ten. Then lead students to an addend by saying, "When I say [six], you say…" and have them respond with the appropriate number *(four)*. Repeat your addend and have students repeat theirs two more times. Then, as time allows, announce a different sum and repeat the exchange of information.

Sheila Jurss, Elmhurst, IL

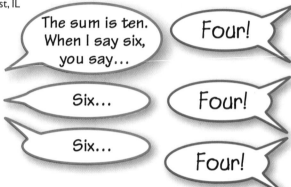

## Mystery Sum
### Add within 1,000 (3.NBT.A.2)

Revisit computation skills with this whole-class game. Out of students' sight, draw a tic-tac-toe grid and number each section with a different digit from 1 to 9. Circle any two rows, columns, or diagonals; then add the resulting three-digit numbers as shown. Next, have each child draw a grid on his dry-erase board and number it with the digits 1 to 9 as he chooses. Direct him to circle any two rows, columns, or diagonals and then add the resulting three-digit numbers. When everyone has finished, project your grid and problem on the board. Invite any child with the same sum to retrace his solving steps for the class and, if his sum does match your sum, award him a small prize. If an exact match is not made, award the prize to the student with the closest sum. Repeat the activity as time allows.

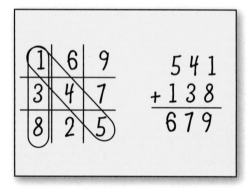

## Learning From Laundry
### Odd and even numbers (2.OA.C.3)

No need to work students' socks off—this simple idea will have them making quick work of odd and even numbers! In advance, place 20 or fewer socks, gloves, or mittens in a basket. Invite a child to count the items; then explain that an even number of items will result in pairs of two with no leftovers and an odd number will always have one left over. Have another child pair the items and announce the total as odd or even. If an even pairing is made, invite the child to write a number sentence showing it as a sum of two addends. Add or remove items to the basket and repeat.

Isobel Livingstone, Rahway, NJ

$$12 = 6 + 6$$

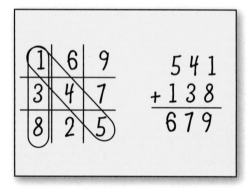

Go to page 119 for an independent skill sheet on odd and even numbers.

# It's a Pileup
**Skip-count (2.NBT.A.2)**

Small group or whole class, this activity works either way! To practice skip-counting by fives, give each child Unifix cubes or base ten bits (in multiples of five); then have students sit in a circle. Designate a child as the starter and announce a number. The starter places five cubes or bits in the center of the circle and says the next number in the series. Then the student to the left of the starter puts five more manipulatives on the pile and says the next number. Students continue until each child has added to the pile of manipulatives, until all the manipulatives are used, or until a desired number is reached. To practice counting by tens, distribute base ten rods; to count by hundreds, pass out base ten flats. If desired, have a student write each number of the pattern on the board or a sheet of paper as it's announced.

Heidi Kobs, Scales Technology Academy, Tempe, AZ

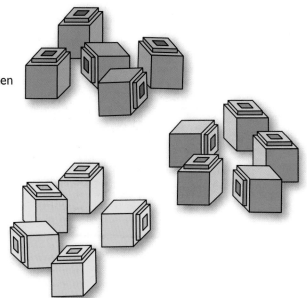

Cara started her snack at 10:05. It took her ten minutes to eat. What time did Cara finish her snack?

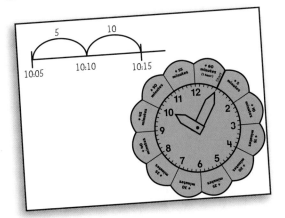

# Little by Little
**Elapsed time (3.MD.A.1)**

Build on students' understanding of time to five minutes as you lead them toward elapsed-time work. First, have each child cut apart the clock face, clock hands, and elapsed-time wheel from a tagboard copy of page 101. Instruct her to place the clock atop the wheel and the hands atop the clock. Help her insert a brad through the layers of paper and fasten it. Share an elapsed-time problem, like the one shown, and direct students to move the clock hands to show the start time. Next, have her move the wheel so the bold start line is next to the minute hand. Then have her find the answer. Lead students to use the start time, interval, and end time to demonstrate the problem on a number line, using the same curved lines on the wheel on the diagram. As students become more familiar with elapsed-time problems, introduce problems that address time to the minute and have them demonstrate their thinking on a number line.

# MATH
## Tips & Tools

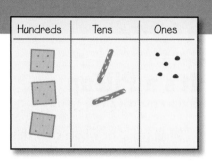

| Hundreds | Tens | Ones |
|---|---|---|

## Mmmm...Math!
**Modeling numbers**
**(2.NBT.A.1)**

Make hands-on learning even more engaging with edible base ten manipulatives. Give students individual saltine crackers to use as hundred flats, pretzel sticks to use as ten longs, and mini chocolate chips to use as one units. Also give each child a place value chart. Announce or display a number less than 1,000; then lead students to model the number with the manipulatives on the chart. When practice time is up, invite your mathematicians to nibble on their manipulatives. **To extend the activity,** challenge students to create subtraction problems based on what they eat (2.NBT.B.7).

Jessica Womack, Finley-Oates Elementary, Bonham, TX

## Works Like Magic
**Interpret products (3.OA.A.1)**

Your students will be multiplication magicians who are able to turn arrays into factors by the end of this activity. To start, tell students that they are magicians. Assign each child a different letter and have him write it on his paper. Next, remind students that a good magician never reveals his secrets, so students must keep the cards you give them a secret. Give each student two numbered playing cards and direct him to use the values on the cards to draw an array. When all the arrays are completed, collect the cards and give each child a copy of page 102. Then, on your signal, direct students to visit each classmate's desk and write on the matching row of his paper an equation that reflects the array drawn. Also, guide the child to use the factors in the equations to determine which numbers were on the cards originally given to each student.

Elizabeth Gaglio, Chamberlayne Elementary, Richmond, VA

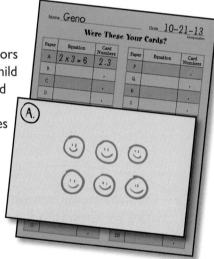

## The Big Picture
**Place value (2.NBT.A.2)**

Invest a little time now, and students will reap the benefits of this portable grid all year long. Use masking tape to make a 10' x 10' grid on a 10' x 12' tarp. Next, label a supply of tagboard cutouts, each with a different number from 1 to 100. When you're ready for students to use the grid, take it to your multipurpose room. Place the 1 and 100 card on the grid; then have students add the remaining cards to complete the chart. If time allows after completing the chart, invite individual students to stand on the tarp and act out the solutions to addition problems involving up to four two-digit numbers (2.NBT.B.6).

As the year progresses, prepare more cards in sets of one hundred (101–200, 201–300, and so on) for students to organize on the chart. Not only will students get the big picture of how numbers are arranged, but this sturdy, tear-resistant material will last throughout the year (and then some!).

Catherine Kinzel, Munroe Elementary, Tallmadge, OH

**tip** → Color-code each set of cutouts and store each set in a separate resealable plastic bag.

# Getting Closer
## Rounding to the nearest ten (3.NBT.A.1)

To help your students locate the nearer ten when hundred charts are not available, give this idea a try. Start by writing a number on the board, such as 23, and tell students you want to round it to the nearest ten. Underline the digit in the tens place and write the value of the digit below. Next, ask students what the next highest ten would be and write that value above the number. Have students count on or count back to determine which value the number in the middle is closer to and circle it. Explain to students that since 23 is closer to 20, you will round 23 to 20. (Lead them to understand that numbers with a five in the ones place are always considered closer to the larger value.) As your learners become more proficient in rounding, introduce larger numbers and demonstrate that the strategy still works. Later, when students solve word problems that involve estimation, remind them of this strategy to help them determine the answer.

Amy Payne, Clara J. Peck Elementary, Greensboro, NC

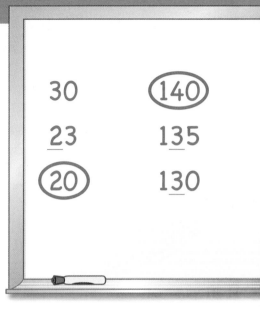

# Hungry for More
## Comparing numbers (2.NBT.A.4)

Thankfully, the alligator in this activity doesn't bite, but it does serve as a simple visual reminder for comparing numbers. To make one, open a pair of safety scissors and attach masking tape to keep the blades in a safe, open position. (For extra fun, draw teeth on both sides of the tape.) Set out the alligator with a deck of cards, face cards removed.

**For an independent activity,** a student stacks the cards and then takes six cards off the deck, arranging them in sets of three, as shown. She decides which number is greater and places the alligator between the cards, remembering that the alligator's mouth will always open toward the larger amount. She writes the number sentence on a sheet of paper, clears away the cards, and continues as time allows.

**For a partner activity,** have students use the cards to play a variation of the game of War. Instead of revealing one card at a time, students pull three cards from the deck and place them facedown on the work space. One player says, "One, two, three, eat!" and then both students reveal their three-digit numbers. Together they determine how to place the alligator between their cards. After the player with the larger number reads the resulting inequality, she sets all six cards aside. The player with more cards wins.

adapted from an idea by Heather Aulisio, Tobyhanna Elementary Center, Pocono Pines, PA

# MATH
## Tips & Tools

## Quick Check
**Time (2.MD.C.7; 3.MD.A.1)**

Use this fun idea, and it will only be a matter of time before students show confidence and accuracy when reading a clock. Here's what to do. When students are working on a paper-and-pencil task, announce, "Time check!" Instruct each student to quickly look at your analog clock and write next to her name the time shown. Students will love the unexpected challenge, and you can get a better handle of students' time-telling skills. If desired, award a bonus point if the time is correct.

Deb Brun, Orlo Avenue School, East Providence, RI

**tip** If your classroom displays only a digital clock, have students write the time in words on their papers or draw a picture of the matching analog clock time.

## Works of Art
**Measurement (2.MD.A.1)**

With this easy-to-prepare idea, students practice measuring length and following directions while creating a mini masterpiece. In advance, label a copy of the directions on page 103 with various lengths, food items, and colors. Give each child a copy of the programmed page, two sheets of paper, and a ruler. Guide students to follow the directions, and once their projects are complete, have them add decorative details. If desired, revisit the activity at a later date, this time programming a copy of page 103 with school supplies or toys.

Sheri O'Quinn, Skyview Elementary, Lizella, GA

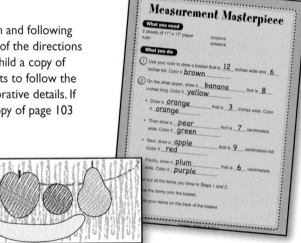

## Go Figure
**Geometry (2.G.A.1–3; 3.G.A.1)**

To help students' math vocabularies quickly take shape, write on separate paper strips geometry-related terms. Fold the strips and put them in a bag or container. Also set out a math textbook or dictionary. Divide the class into two teams; then direct a player from Team 1 to choose a paper. After he does so, start a timer for one minute. Instruct the child to refer to the textbook's glossary or dictionary if needed to clarify the word's meaning. Then have the child draw a picture that will best lead his teammates to name the word on his paper. If his teammates can identify the term before time expires, the team earns a point. If they cannot, Team 2 gets a chance to guess for a point before taking its own turn. The team with more points at the end of play wins.

Lynne Watters, Horizon Elementary, Sunrise, FL

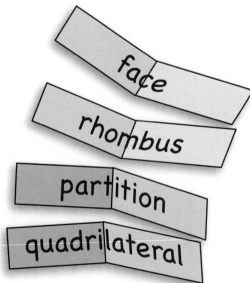

# Anything but Boring
**Solving word problems (2.OA.A.1; 3.OA.D.8)**

Forget about the same old word problem review—students are sure to love this practice activity! First, make a class supply of the word problem cards from page 104. (Use the top row for second grade and the bottom row for third grade.) Instruct each student to fill in the blanks on a card and then glue the problem to the top of a sheet of paper. Next, put students into groups of three and direct them to sit in a circle. At your signal, have each child pass his paper to the student on his right. The student solves her classmate's problem. At your next signal, have each student pass the paper again. This time, each child reads and checks the new problem she is holding. Finally, direct students to pass the papers back to their original owners.

Amy Satkoski, Orchard Park Elementary, Indianapolis, IN

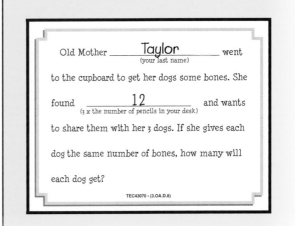

Old Mother ____Taylor____ went
(your last name)
to the cupboard to get her dogs some bones. She
found ____12____ and wants
(5 x the number of pencils in your desk)
to share them with her 5 dogs. If she gives each
dog the same number of bones, how many will
each dog get?

TEC43070 • (3.OA.D.8)

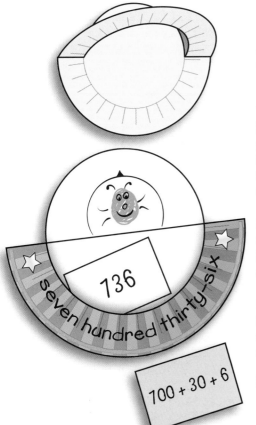

# Mission to Math
**Place value**

Send students to an out-of-this-world display after they make this fun spaceship. To make a spaceship, a student folds a six-inch paper plate in half and then unfolds it. Next, he cuts along the rim of one of the resulting semicircles. The child refolds the plate and glues the rim together. Then the student adds the details described below before decorating his spaceship to his liking. Collect the index cards (as described below) and store them near a display of the completed spaceships. Invite students to visit the display and put the cards in the matching spaceships.

**Read and write numbers (2.NBT.A.3):** The student writes the word form of a three-digit number along the base of the spaceship. Then the student cuts an index card in half. She writes the standard form of the number on one half and the expanded form on the other half.

**Rounding numbers (3.NBT.A.1):** The student writes a number on the spaceship as directed for "Read and write numbers" above; then he writes the number rounded to the nearest ten on one index card half and to the nearest hundred on the other half.

Debbie Ashworth, McLeansville, NC

# MATH
## Tips & Tools

## On the Money
### Solving problems with coins (2.MD.C.8)

Here's an idea you can take to the bank! To help students who struggle with relating coin values and problem solving, use a permanent marker to label the tails side of a set of plastic coins with the matching values. Distribute the coins to students and instruct them to use the manipulatives when solving word problems, using the heads side of the coins as they work and then flipping the coins over when they need a reminder of the value.

April LoTempio, Ben Franklin Elementary, Kenmore, NY

## Oopsie!
### Critiquing others' reasoning (2.MP.3; 3.MP.3)

Build students' mathematical proficiencies with Mistake Mondays. At the start of each week, display a problem with an incorrect solution. Guide each student to find the errors, tell what was done wrong, and explain why. Also have the child identify the correct solution. Used as a weekly warm-up, this task will help students build knowledge and understanding of math practices.

adapted from an idea by Colleen Dabney, Williamsburg, VA

## Who Will Operate?
### Word problems (2.OA.A.1; 3.OA.D.8)

Get ready to use this fun idea stat! To prepare, display a word problem and list on the board a plus and minus sign (second grade) or all four operation signs (third grade). Read the problem aloud and give a student a toy stethoscope to wear. Direct the child to place the stethoscope on the operation he would use to solve the problem and explain how he would do so. If the problem has more than one step, have him place the stethoscope on the sign for the first step and explain before moving to the sign for the second step. Get the rest of the class involved by having each child give a thumbs-up or a thumbs-down in response to each of the student's choices. **To vary the activity,** write possible answers on the board instead and have the student place the stethoscope on the correct one.

Heather Aulisio, Tobyhanna Elementary Center, Pocono Pines, PA

# Sweet Practice
**Place value (2.NBT.A.1)**

This whole-group review game is quite a treat! To prepare, give each child a copy of the bingo board on page 105 and direct her to write in each space a different number from a given range (such as 90 to 115). Supply students with conversation hearts to use as markers. To play, simply call out a letter and use place value terms to name a number from the range, such as "B, nine tens and five ones." Students play according to traditional rules, but, in order to be declared a winner, she must correctly read back all the covered spaces that led to her bingo. At the end of the game, invite students to munch on their markers. If desired, play all year long! Use such sweet treats as candy corn in the fall, red and green M&M's candies in the winter, and jelly beans in the spring.

Robyn Sincavage, Mahanoy Area Elementary, Mahanoy City, PA

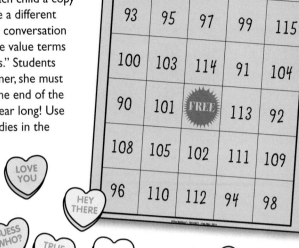

 Mount seasonal stickers on squares of paper and distribute them to students who have food allergies.

# Embrace This Earworm!
**Perimeter (3.MD.D.8)**

When students are presented with word problems that involve perimeter, this is just the ditty to remind them what it is. Introduce the whole song and, when students work independently, encourage them to focus on the first verse.

Nancy A. Silva, Indian Brook Elementary, Plymouth, MA

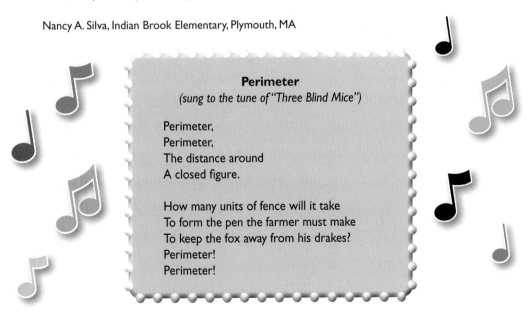

**Perimeter**
*(sung to the tune of "Three Blind Mice")*

Perimeter,
Perimeter,
The distance around
A closed figure.

How many units of fence will it take
To form the pen the farmer must make
To keep the fox away from his drakes?
Perimeter!
Perimeter!

## Pattern Block Puzzlers
### Shapes and attributes (2.G.A.1; 3.G.A.1)

Students use their geometry knowledge to write and solve these fun riddles. To start, give each child a pattern block and direct him to keep it hidden from his classmates. Also write the sentence starters, as shown, on the board. Direct each student to use the attributes of his pattern block as he copies and completes the sentences on a sheet of paper. Provide time for each child to share his clues aloud and then invite a classmate to guess the shape being described. Have the student confirm the correct answer by showing his pattern block to the class.

Karen E. Holzmann, Morgan L. Martin Elementary, Green Bay, WI

*I am a quadrilateral. I have parallel sides, but I am not a square. What am I?*

I am ____. I have ____, but I am not ____. What am I?

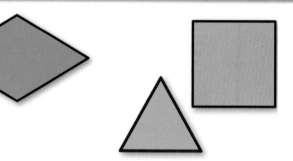

## Make a Splash
### Measuring length (2.MD.A.1)

Colorful pool noodles become math tools with this clever idea. Use a permanent marker and a yardstick to mark one-inch increments along the length of a pool noodle. Then use colorful tape and a permanent marker to label six-inch intervals. If desired, stop marking at three feet and cut off the remaining foam. Challenge students to use the labeled pool noodles to measure large items within the classroom and around the school.

Nancy A. Silva, Indian Brook Elementary, Plymouth, MA

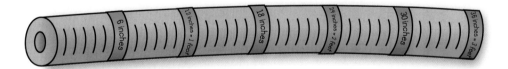

# Icing on the Cake
**Partitioning shapes (2.G.A.3)**

Give students a taste of equal parts with this small-group game. In advance, copy the gameboard on page 106 and laminate it. Next, cut sixteen 1⅜" x 1¾" paper rectangles (game pieces) and get a die. Divide students into two teams and assign each team a grid.

To play, a student from Team 1 rolls the die and chooses a partitioned shape on her team's grid. Depending on her roll, she names the shares as halves, thirds, or fourths; describes the whole as two halves, three thirds, or four fourths; or loses a turn. If the student's answer is correct, give the child a game piece to cover the corresponding grid section. If the answer is incorrect, her turn ends and a player from Team 2 rolls the die. The first team to cover all the shapes on its grid wins.

# Around the Clock
**Elapsed time (3.MD.A.1)**

To demonstrate understanding of using time intervals, have each child fold a copy of the booklet pattern on page 107 in half; then have him fold it in half two more times. The student unfolds the last two folds and cuts through the top layer along each fold. Next, the child draws on the top of the left flap a morning activity that he does that takes place at the top of the hour. On the next flap, he draws an activity that occurs two and a half hours later. On the third flap, he draws an activity that takes place four hours and 15 minutes after that, and finally, on the right flap, he draws an activity that happens five hours and 30 minutes after the previous one. The child writes the time on each flap; then he lifts the flap, draws the matching clock hands, and writes a statement that describes the activity.

Debbie Ashworth, McLeansville, NC

# MATH
## Tips & Tools

## Eager to Explore
**Attributes of plane shapes: angles (2.G.A.1)**

Students needn't go far to complete this geometry-based activity! To prepare, make student copies of the arrow patterns on page 108 and recording sheet. Direct each child to cut out the arrows and insert a brad through the dots to secure the arrows together. Explain to students that an angle is formed when two rays (like the arrows) share the same endpoint (the brad). Tell students that triangles have three angles, quadrilaterals have four, pentagons have five, and hexagons have six. Then provide time for each child to visit objects around the room, manipulate the arrows to match the angles on the objects, and record his findings on a copy of the recording sheet.

Cheryl Rayl, Mayville Elementary, Mayville, MI

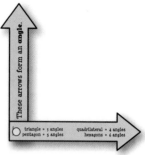

These arrows form an angle.

triangle = 3 angles      quadrilateral = 4 angles
pentagon = 5 angles      hexagons = 6 angles

## Partitioned for Place Value
**Read and write numbers (2.NBT.A.3)**

Repurpose part of a glass pack kit (used for packing and protecting glassware in boxes) into a handy math tool that is perfect for small-group instruction. Here's how! First, copy page 109 onto card stock and then cut apart the cards. Glue each place value term to the bottom of a glass pack divider and attach a paper clip to the top of each one (display). Stand the display as shown. When leading a small group, say or model a three-digit number or show one written in expanded form. Then have a child use the digit cards to make the matching number on the display. **As an alternative**, put a number on the display and have students use base ten pieces to model it or write its value in expanded form.

Colleen Dabney, Williamsburg, VA

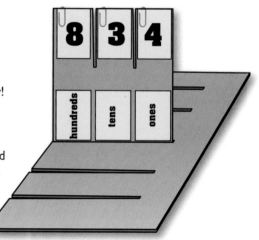

## Surface Size
**Area (3.MD.C.7a)**

Prepare a few simple materials, and this step-by-step center is ready to use! Copy page 110 and put it in a plastic page protector. Next, cut five or more paper rectangles, each with whole-inch side lengths, and label each rectangle with a different letter. Set out the activity card and rectangles with a supply of one-inch tiles. A child follows the steps on the card to complete the activity on her own paper. **To extend the activity**, have the child explain the relationship between the number of tiles used on each rectangle and its corresponding multiplication equation.

**Need more math practice?** No problem! Turn to pages 113–134.

# Clock Face, Clock Hands, and Elapsed-Time Wheel

Use with "Little by Little" on page 91.

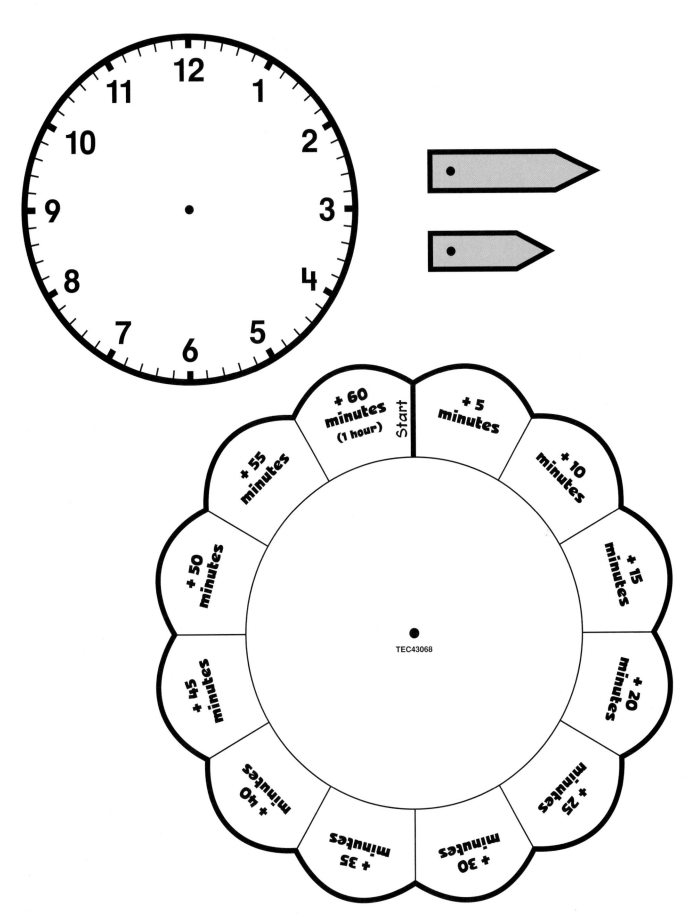

# Were These Your Cards?

| Paper | Equation | Card Numbers | Paper | Equation | Card Numbers |
|-------|----------|--------------|-------|----------|--------------|
| A | | , | P | | , |
| B | | , | Q | | , |
| C | | , | R | | , |
| D | | , | S | | , |
| E | | , | T | | , |
| F | | , | U | | , |
| G | | , | V | | , |
| H | | , | W | | , |
| I | | , | X | | , |
| J | | , | Y | | , |
| K | | , | Z | | , |
| L | | , | AA | | , |
| M | | , | BB | | , |
| N | | , | CC | | , |
| O | | , | DD | | , |

©The Mailbox® • TEC43069 • Oct./Nov. 2013

102 THE MAILBOX  **Note to the teacher:** Use with "Works Like Magic" on page 92.

# Measurement Masterpiece

## What you need

2 sheets of 11" x 17" paper     crayons

ruler     scissors

## What you do

1. Use your ruler to draw a basket that is _____ inches wide and _____ inches tall. Color it _____.

2. On the other paper, draw a _____ that is _____ inches long. Color it _____.

   - Draw a _____ that is _____ inches wide. Color it _____.

   - Then draw a _____ that is _____ centimeters wide. Color it _____.

   - Next, draw a _____ that is _____ centimeters tall. Color it _____.

   - Finally, draw a _____ that is _____ centimeters wide. Color it _____.

3. Cut out all the items you drew in Steps 1 and 2.

4. Glue the items onto the basket.

5. Write your name on the back of the basket.

©The Mailbox® • TEC43070 • Dec./Jan. 2013–14

# Word Problem Cards

Use with "Anything but Boring" on page 95.

---

I know the best cookie baker in the world. _____ (woman you know) made a huge batch of my favorite kind, _____ (kind of cookie), for my birthday. There were _____ (number between 30 and 60) cookies to start. They tasted so good I ate _____ (double your age) more. How many cookies are left?

TEC43070 • (2.OA.A.1)

---

Old Mother _____ (your last name) went to the cupboard to get her dogs some bones. She found _____ (3 x the number of pencils in your desk) and wants to share them with her 3 dogs. If she gives each dog the same number of bones, how many will each dog get?

TEC43070 • (3.OA.D.8)

---

_____ (favorite male TV character) is loved by his fans! On _____ (today's day of the week), he got _____ (the number of students in your class) tweets from his fans. The next day, he got _____ (days in this month) more tweets! How many tweets did he get in all?

TEC43070 • (2.OA.A.1)

---

_____ (man's name) spent 2 hours today making snowballs. He made _____ (your age) snowballs the first hour. He made the same number the second hour. Yesterday, he made _____ (number of kids in your house) more snowball(s) than today. How many snowballs did he make yesterday?

TEC43070 • (3.OA.D.8)

©The Mailbox® • TEC43070 • Dec./Jan. 2013–14

# B I N G O

|   |   |   |   |   |
|---|---|---|---|---|
|   |   |   |   |   |
|   |   |   |   |   |
|   |   | FREE |   |   |
|   |   |   |   |   |
|   |   |   |   |   |

**Note to the teacher:** Use with "Sweet Practice" on page 97.

# Icing on the Cake

## Partitioning shapes

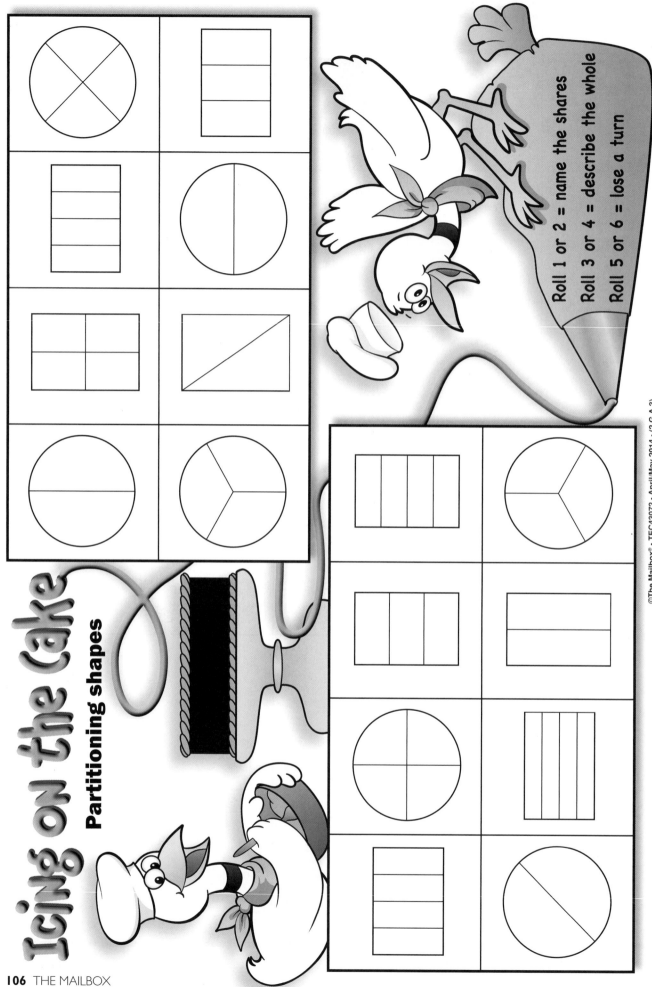

Roll 1 or 2 = name the shares
Roll 3 or 4 = describe the whole
Roll 5 or 6 = lose a turn

©The Mailbox® · TEC43072 · April/May 2014 · (2.G.A.3)

**Note to the teacher:** Use with "Icing on the Cake" on page 99.

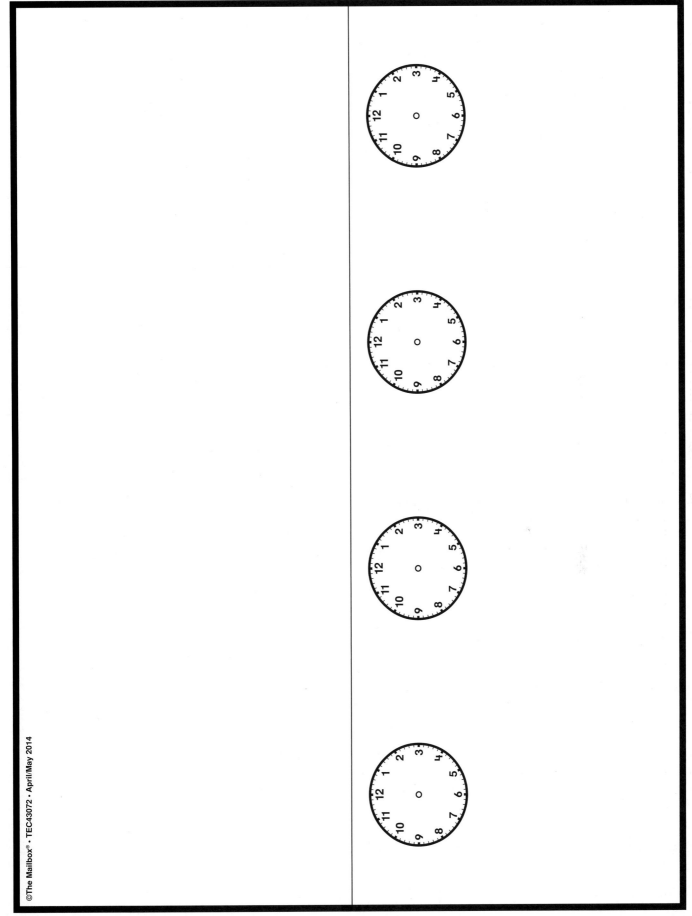

## Arrow Patterns and Recording Sheet

Use with "Eager to Explore" on page 100.

• These arrows form an **angle**.

TEC43073

• triangle = 3 angles
pentagon = 5 angles
quadrilateral = 4 angles
hexagons = 6 angles

Name ______________________ Date ______________

Recording sheet

# Angles Everywhere!

| Object | Number of Angles | Name of Shape |
|---|---|---|
| | | |
| | | |
| | | |
| | | |
| | | |
| | | |

| 4 | 9 | ones |
|---|---|---|
| TEC43073 | TEC43073 | TEC43073 |
| 3 | 8 | tens |
| TEC43073 | TEC43073 | TEC43073 |
| 2 | 7 | hundreds |
| TEC43073 | TEC43073 | TEC43073 |
| 1 | 6 | |
| TEC43073 | TEC43073 | |
| 0 | 5 | |
| TEC43073 | TEC43073 | |

# Surface Size

**What You Need**
- paper rectangles
- one-inch tiles

① Choose a rectangle. Write the letter on your paper.

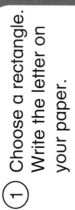

② Cover the rectangle with tiles.

Do this.

Don't do this.

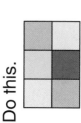
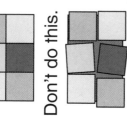

③ Count the tiles used.

*1, 2, 3...*

④ Write the total.

Ⓑ 6 tiles

⑤ Write a multiplication equation for the area. (Hint: Use the two different side lengths.)

Ⓑ 6 tiles
3 x 2 = 6 square units

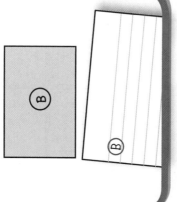

⑥ Remove the tiles.

Ⓑ

⑦ Repeat Steps 1–6 two or more times. Use a different rectangle each time.

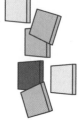
Ⓔ

©The Mailbox® • TEC43073 • June/July 2014 • (3.MD.C.7a)

**Note to the teacher:** Use with "Surface Size" on page 100.

# Make Yourself at Home!

**What You Need**
- addition flash cards
- unlined paper

① Draw 6 house shapes.

② Take a flash card.

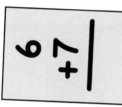

③ Write and solve the problem inside the first house shape. Make sure the numbers go across (horizontally).

6 + 7 = 13

④ Write a related subtraction fact. Make sure the numbers go down (vertically).

6 + 7 = 13
− 7
  6

⑤ Repeat Steps 2–4 for each house shape.

6 + 7 = 13
− 7
  6

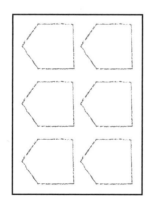

⑥ On the back of your paper, tell why knowing addition facts helps you solve subtraction problems.

Knowing addition facts helps me solve subtraction facts because _____

©The Mailbox® • TEC43068 • Aug./Sept. 2013 • (2.NBT.B.5)

**Step-by-step activity:** Copy this activity card and put it in a plastic page protector for durability. Then put the activity card and needed materials at a center.

# Measurement

# Ready to Restock!

## What You Need

centimeter ruler

Unifix cubes

container of school supplies

---

① Make your paper look like this.

| Item | Cubes | Centimeters |
|------|-------|-------------|
|      |       |             |
|      |       |             |
|      |       |             |

---

② Choose 4 school supplies. List each item in the first column.

| Item | Cubes | Centimeters |
|-------|-------|-------------|
| pencil |     |             |
|      |       |             |
|      |       |             |

---

③ Measure each item with the cubes.

Write.

| Item | Cubes | Centimeters |
|--------|-------|-------------|
| pencil | 7     |             |

---

④ Measure each item with the ruler.

Write.

| Item | Cubes | Centimeters |
|--------|-------|-------------|
| pencil | 7     | 18          |

---

⑤ Explain why you have two different numbers for each item's measurements.

| Item | Cubes | Centimeters |
|------|-------|-------------|
|      |       |             |
|      |       |             |
|      |       |             |

I have

---

©The Mailbox® • TEC43071 • Feb./Mar. 2014 • (2.MD.A.2)

Copy this activity card and put it in a plastic page protector for durability. Gather school supplies—such as an unsharpened pencil, a highlighter, a crayon, a pink bar eraser, a packaged bandage, and a glue stick—and place them in a container. Then put the activity card and the materials at a center.

**Step-by-Step Activity**

# MATH
# Mind-Builders

**1** Write four different number sentences that each have a sum of 16.

____ + ____ = 16

____ + ____ = 16

____ + ____ = 16

____ + ____ = 16

**2** Describe two different ways to solve each problem.

A. 9 + 7 =

B. 13 − 5 =

**3** Make each equation true.

A. 120 = ____ ones

B. 60 + 100 + 7 = ____

C. 2 hundreds = ____

D. ____ = 5 ones + 2 hundreds

E. 15 tens = ____ hundred + ____ tens

**4** Use the data in the tally chart to make a picture graph. Draw a ☺ to show each student vote.

*Students' Favorite Lunches*

| Pizza | ┼┼┼ |
|---|---|
| Chicken Strips | II |
| Cheeseburger | III |

**5** There are 30 students in Ms. Apple's class. There are 6 more boys than girls. How many boys and girls are in Ms. Apple's class?

**6** Students at Walker School have a 6-hour school day. If school ends at 2:30 PM, what time does school start? Draw an analog clock to show the start time.

**7** Ryder uses 5 sheets of notebook paper on Monday. If he uses the same amount each day for the rest of the school week, how many sheets of paper will he have used in all? Explain how you found the answer.

**8** Mr. Wise bought a 10-liter fish tank for his classroom. He poured 1,000 milliliters of water into the empty tank. Can he pour more water into the tank? Explain how you know.

©The Mailbox® · TEC43068 · Aug./Sept. 2013 · Key p. 308

**How to Use** Give each student a copy of this page to work on during free time. Or, to use it as morning work or a math warm-up activity, project a copy of the page and color the number of each task you want students to complete.

# MATH
# Mind-Builders

**1.** What number goes in the box to make the equation true? Tell how you solved for the missing number.

$$7 + \square = 16 - 3$$

**2.** Draw two different shapes that each have four sides. Write the name for each shape. Then tell something they have in common other than the number of sides.

**3.** Hazel, Jett, and Casper count their Halloween treats. Hazel has one hundred seventy-eight treats. Jett has two hundred eight treats. Casper has one hundred eighty-seven treats. Write each treat amount as a number. Circle the largest number. Underline the smallest.

**4.** Luis solved 38 + 40 by adding 30 + 40 + 8. Will this strategy work? Why or why not?

**5.** Ella needs 30 minutes to put her costume on. If she wants to leave for the Halloween parade at 4:30 PM, what is the latest time she can start putting on her costume?

It turns out Ella didn't start putting on her costume until 4:10. If it took her 30 minutes to get dressed, what time did she leave for the parade?

**6.** Ms. Webb's class made ten bags of popcorn for the fall festival. If each bag weighs 5 pounds, how many pounds of popcorn did the class make?

**7.** There are 18 ears of corn. If you put 3 ears on each plate, how many plates will you fill? Show your work with pictures.

**8.** How is a *factor* like an *addend?* How are they different?

©The Mailbox® • TEC43069 • Oct./Nov. 2013 • Key p. 308

**How to Use** Give each student a copy of this page to work on during free time. Or, to use it as morning work or a math warm-up activity, project a copy of the page and color the number of each task you want students to complete.

# MATH
# Mind-Builders

**1** Evan went holiday shopping. He bought these items. How much did he spend in all?

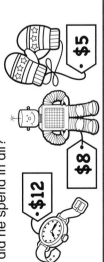

· $12
$8
· $5

**2** There are 40 mini candy canes in a box. Ms. Berry needs 100 candy canes. How many boxes should she buy? Tell why you think so.

**3** Cindy built a snow fort that was 56 inches tall. Amy's snow fort was 67 inches tall. How much taller is Amy's snow fort? Show how you know.

**4** Dr. King's birthday is January 15. Al's birthday is five days after Dr. King's. Keira's birthday is ten days before Dr. King's. Todd's birthday is two days before Keira's. When is each child's birthday?

**5** Adam put up some holiday lights. Of these, 54 burned out. That left Adam with 686 working lights. How many lights did Adam start with?

**6** Show the different ways you can partition this shape into parts with four equal areas. (Redraw the shape for each new arrangement.)

**7** Shape A has 3 side lengths, and each is 4 inches long. Shape B has 4 side lengths, and each is 3 inches long. Which shape has the larger perimeter? Use pictures, words, or numbers to show your work.

**8** What number completes the equation? Explain how you know.

$$36 \div \boxed{\phantom{0}} = 9$$

**How to Use** Give each student a copy of this page to work on during free time. Or, to use it as morning work or a math warm-up activity, project a copy of the page and color the number of each task you want students to complete.

## MATH
# Mind Builders

**3** Rewrite each value in number form. Order the numbers from least to greatest.

8 tens 5 ones      12 tens      1 hundred 12 ones

**4** Collin finds 5 four-leaf clovers. How many leaves does he have in all? Draw a picture to show your work. Then write the answer.

**6** Write the greatest three-digit number whose digits add up to 15.

Write the smallest three-digit number whose digits add up to 15.

**7** What is wrong with this fact family? Tell how to correct it.

$3 \times 5 = 15$

$15 \div 3 = 5$

$3 \div 15 = 5$

$5 \times 3 = 15$

**1** Show 10 different ways to make **100**. Use pictures, words, and equations.

**2** For each box, write the item that does not belong. Explain your choice.

A.     16   2   7   12

B.     8 + 9      3 + 5
       5 + 6      8 + 7

C.

**5** A leaky faucet is wasting 100 milliliters of water every hour. How long will it take to lose 1 liter of water?

**8** A leprechaun finds a pot of gold. It has 25 gold coins in it. Each time the leprechaun blinks, the number of coins doubles. If he blinks 5 times, how many coins will be in the pot?

©The Mailbox® · TEC43071 · Feb./Mar. 2014 · Key p. 308

**How to Use** Give each student a copy of this page to work on during free time. Or, to use it as morning work or a math warm-up activity, project a copy of the page and color the number of each task you want students to complete.

# MATH Mind Builders

**1.** Choose a topic. Quietly survey ten classmates. Record your survey results on a bar graph.

**Eye Color**

**Hair Color**

**Right Handed or Left Handed?**

**2.** When Rip Van Winkle wakes, he sees this clock. He doesn't know what time it shows. Draw an analog clock that shows this time. Then draw another analog clock that shows the time 30 minutes later.

10:45

**3.** Write and solve an addition word problem using the two numbers shown. Then write and solve a subtraction word problem using the numbers.

## 53

## 48

**4.** Copy and complete.

o o o o o
o o o o o

**If** o o o o o shows $2 + 2 + 2 + 2 + 2 = 10$, **then** o o o o o / o o o o o **shows** _____.

Draw an array that shows $3 + 3 + 3 = 9$.

**5.** Birds are sitting in a tree. If $\frac{1}{8}$ are blue jays, $\frac{4}{8}$ are cardinals, $\frac{2}{8}$ are doves, and $\frac{1}{8}$ are robins, which kind of bird represents half of the birds in the tree? Explain how you know.

**6.** Use the data to make a line plot.

### April Rainfall

| Inches | Number of Days |
|--------|----------------|
| 0 | ‖‖‖ |
| $\frac{1}{2}$ | ‖‖‖ ‖‖ |
| 1 | ‖‖‖‖ |
| $1\frac{1}{2}$ | ‖‖‖ ‖ |
| 2 | ‖‖ |
| $2\frac{1}{2}$ | ‖‖‖ |
| 3 | ‖‖ |

**7.** Rich has 10 nickels in his pocket. Each nickel weighs 5 grams. How much do Rich's nickels weigh? Is this more or less than a kilogram? How do you know?

**8.** Mr. Farmer removed 40 peas from some pea pods. He forgot to track how many pea pods he picked and how many peas were in each pod. If each pod had the same number of peas, how many pods could he have picked? Show two or more possible solutions.

**How to Use** Give each student a copy of this page to work on during free time. Or, to use it as morning work or a math warm-up activity, project a copy of the page and color the number of each task you want students to complete.

# MATH
# Mind-Builders

**1** The water at the shallow end of the pool is 36 inches deep. If the pool is labeled in feet, which measurement should be used? Explain.

**6 feet   36 feet   3 feet**

**2** Some numbers read the same left to right and right to left, like 11 and 55. List all the two-digit numbers like this that are less than 100. Add them all. Is the sum greater or less than 500? Explain.

**3** How is a ruler like a number line?

**4** Which shape is equally partitioned into fourths? Explain why the other shapes are not.

A. 

B. 

C. 

**5** What numbers come next in the pattern? What is the pattern rule?

**2, 4, 8, 10, 20, 22, ___, ___**

**6** Find the multiplication problem in each row. Write the x and = signs.

| A. | 3 | 6 X 1 = 6 | 8 |
|----|----|----|----|
| B. | 4 | 5 | 3 | 1 | 5 |
| C. | 9 | 7 | 2 | 1 | 4 |
| D. | 4 | 2 | 3 | 2 | 6 |
| E. | 6 | 0 | 0 | 6 | 9 |
| F. | 3 | 8 | 2 | 4 | 7 |

**7** Jamie, Myra, Seth, and Bo swim in a race. Jamie does not finish first. Myra places after Jamie but before Bo. Who wins the race? Copy and complete the chart to find out.

| | 1st | 2nd | 3rd | 4th |
|----|----|----|----|----|
| Jamie | x | | | |
| Myra | | | | |
| Seth | | | | |
| Bo | | | | |

**8** Principal Stern buys 6 boxes of freezer pops. Each box holds 50 freezer pops. If there are 355 students at her school, will she have enough freezer pops for each child to have one? If not, how many more boxes will Principal Stern need to buy?

**How to Use** Give each student a copy of this page to work on during free time. Or, to use it as morning work or a math warm-up activity, project a copy of the page and color the number of each task you want students to complete.

# Leaping Lily Pads!

Circle *odd* or *even*.
Draw a picture to support your answer.

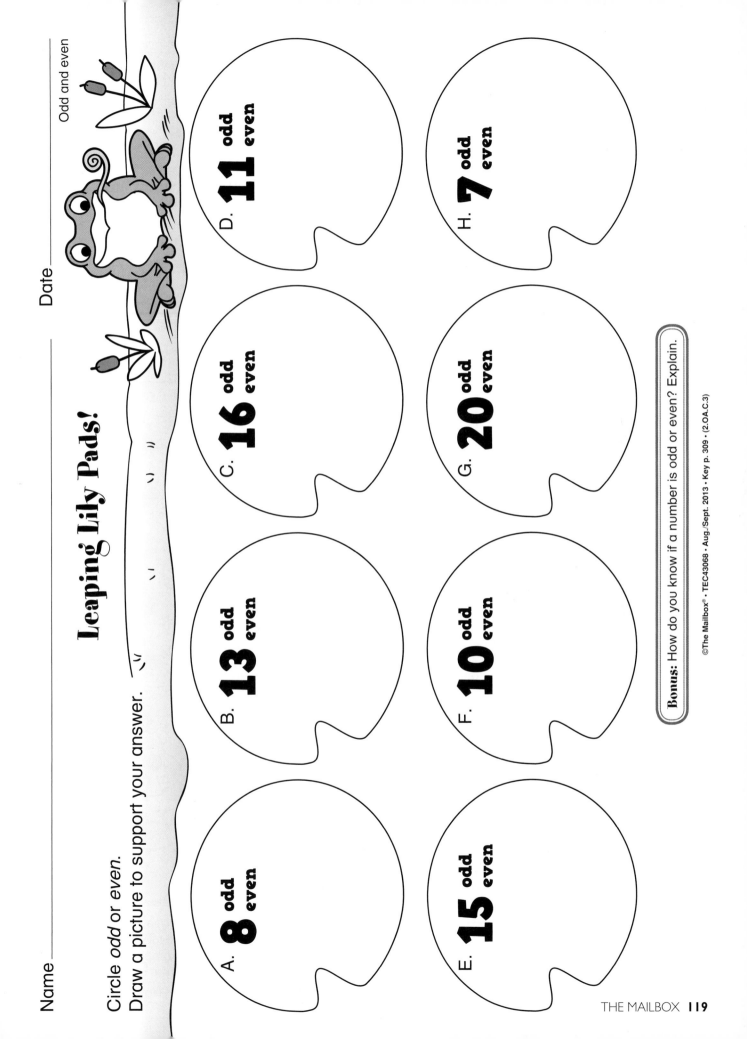

A. **8**   odd
             even

B. **13**   odd
              even

C. **16**   odd
              even

D. **11**   odd
              even

E. **15**   odd
              even

F. **10**   odd
              even

G. **20**   odd
              even

H. **7**   odd
             even

**Bonus:** How do you know if a number is odd or even? Explain.

Name _____  Date _____

# Sips and Slurps

Use the tally chart to complete the bar graph.
Then answer the questions below.

| Juice Flavors | |
|---|---|
| apple | ЖЖ ЖЖ ЖЖ ЖЖ |
| berry | ЖЖ |
| lemon-lime | ЖЖ ЖЖ ЖЖ |
| orange | ЖЖ ЖЖ |
| grape | |
| cherry | ЖЖ |

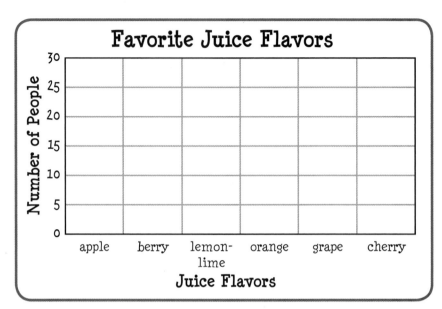

**Favorite Juice Flavors**

1. How many people voted for their favorite juice flavor? _____

2. What scale is shown on the *y*-axis of the graph? (Circle.)

   1 person          5 people          10 people

3. How many more people chose lemon-lime juice than orange? _____

4. Which juice flavor did people choose least? _____

   Which did they choose most? _____

5. How many more people voted for apple juice than berry? _____

6. When added together, which two flavors have more
   votes than apple? _____

   _____

7. Which pair received more votes? (Circle.)

   orange and berry          lemon-lime and cherry

8. Based on the data, which two flavors would you buy
   if you were planning a party for these people? Why?

   _____

   _____

**Bonus:** Use the information from the tally chart to make a picture graph. Include a key that shows ☐ = 5 people.

Add and subtract within 1,000

# The Fastest to Five

| | | | |
|---|---|---|---|
| $\begin{array}{r} 257 \\ + 345 \\ \hline \end{array}$ | $\begin{array}{r} 741 \\ - 362 \\ \hline \end{array}$ | $\begin{array}{r} 679 \\ + 238 \\ \hline \end{array}$ | $\begin{array}{r} 431 \\ + 229 \\ \hline \end{array}$ | $\begin{array}{r} 420 \\ - 275 \\ \hline \end{array}$ |
| $\begin{array}{r} 736 \\ - 119 \\ \hline \end{array}$ | $\begin{array}{r} 562 \\ + 312 \\ \hline \end{array}$ | $\begin{array}{r} 737 \\ - 228 \\ \hline \end{array}$ | $\begin{array}{r} 309 \\ - 221 \\ \hline \end{array}$ | $\begin{array}{r} 458 \\ + 386 \\ \hline \end{array}$ |
| $\begin{array}{r} 583 \\ - 356 \\ \hline \end{array}$ | $\begin{array}{r} 291 \\ - 456 \\ \hline \end{array}$ | $\begin{array}{r} 382 \\ + 178 \\ \hline \end{array}$ | $\begin{array}{r} 625 \\ - 332 \\ \hline \end{array}$ | $\begin{array}{r} 665 \\ + 261 \\ \hline \end{array}$ |
| $\begin{array}{r} 746 \\ + 147 \\ \hline \end{array}$ | $\begin{array}{r} 598 \\ - 159 \\ \hline \end{array}$ | $\begin{array}{r} 389 \\ + 497 \\ \hline \end{array}$ | $\begin{array}{r} 972 \\ - 254 \\ \hline \end{array}$ | $\begin{array}{r} 240 \\ - 131 \\ \hline \end{array}$ |
| $\begin{array}{r} 801 \\ - 343 \\ \hline \end{array}$ | $\begin{array}{r} 418 \\ + 134 \\ \hline \end{array}$ | $\begin{array}{r} 264 \\ - 187 \\ \hline \end{array}$ | $\begin{array}{r} 817 \\ + 179 \\ \hline \end{array}$ | $\begin{array}{r} 143 \\ + 478 \\ \hline \end{array}$ |

## Directions for two players:

1. Each player takes a different-colored crayon.

2. When it is your turn, use your pencil to solve a problem.

3. Have your partner check your answer on the calculator.
   - If it is correct, shade the box with your crayon.
   - If it is incorrect, erase your answer.

4. The first player to shade five boxes in a row horizontally ($\leftrightarrow$), vertically ($\updownarrow$), or diagonally ($\diagdown$) wins!

©The Mailbox® · TEC43068 · Aug./Sept. 2013 · (3.NBT.A.2)

**Partner Game** Make a copy of this page for each pair of students. Give the players two different-colored crayons and a calculator.

Comparing numbers

# Far Out!

Decide whether the number sentence is true.
Color the star in the matching column.

How will the astronaut get clean while he is in outer space?

| | | Yes | No |
|---|---|---|---|
| 1. | 2 hundreds + 5 tens + 3 ones > 235 | B | O |
| 2. | 649 = 6 tens + 4 hundreds + 9 ones | M | K |
| 3. | 3 tens + 7 hundreds + 2 ones = 732 | C | R |
| 4. | 1 hundred + 8 ones < 180 | I | A |
| 5. | 289 > 2 hundreds + 9 tens + 8 ones | E | R |
| 6. | 4 tens + 3 hundreds + 1 one > 314 | N | E |
| 7. | 9 hundreds + 5 tens < 905 | T | A |
| 8. | 468 = 8 ones + 4 hundreds + 6 tens | H | S |
| 9. | 712 < 2 hundreds + 7 tens + 1 one | R | D |
| 10. | 2 ones + 6 hundreds + 3 tens > 263 | W | K |
| 11. | 4 tens + 7 ones + 5 hundreds = 547 | E | T |
| 12. | 9 tens + 8 ones + 1 hundred = 981 | W | G |
| 13. | 153 < 5 hundreds + 1 ten + 3 ones | M | O |
| 14. | 6 tens + 7 hundreds + 8 ones < 768 | H | L |
| 15. | 431 > 5 tens + 4 hundreds + 3 ones | E | S |

To answer the riddle, write each uncolored letter on its matching line or lines.

He will __ __ __ __   __   __ __ __ __ __ __   __ __ __ __ __ __.
          7  4  10  15   4   2  5  11  6  13  3   8  14  1  12  5  9

**Bonus:** For each number sentence that was untrue, change the symbol to make it true.

# Showtime!

Write the time beneath each clock.
Cross off the time as you use it.
Hint: Three times will not be crossed off.

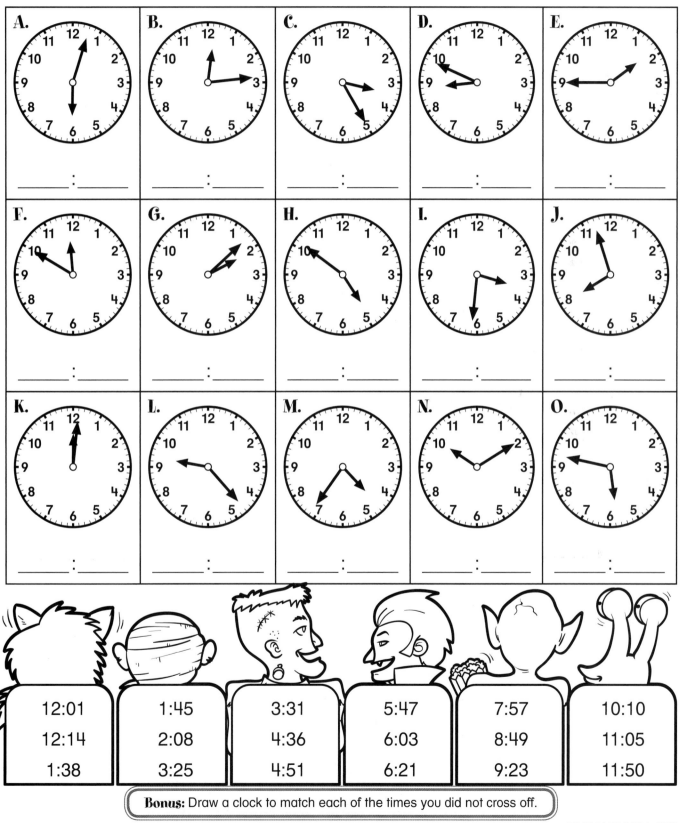

**Bonus:** Draw a clock to match each of the times you did not cross off.

Name _____ Date _____

Word problems: length

# Leaps and Bounds

| Leap Lengths | |
|---|---|
| Grasshopper | Length |
| Gretta | 6 inches |
| Gomer | 8 inches |
| Grammy | 5 inches |
| Gunter | 7 inches |
| Gwen | 9 inches |

Every member of the Grasshopper family can leap great distances. They want to find out which one of them can leap the farthest, so Gramps plans a contest. He makes a sandpit that is 18 inches long. Then Gramps invites family members to see how far they can leap from the starting line. He keeps a table of the results.

Use the story above and the number line to find each answer.
Then write an equation to support your answer.

1. How far from the end of the sandpit was Gretta's leap?

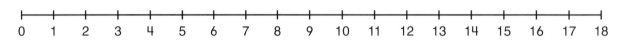

Answer: _____     Equation: _____

2. How much farther was Gwen's leap than Grammy's leap?

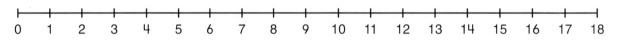

Answer: _____     Equation: _____

3. How much farther would Gomer need to leap to reach the end of the sandpit?

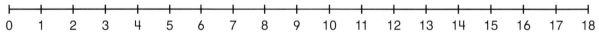

Answer: _____     Equation: _____

4. How far did Gunter and Gomer leap in all?

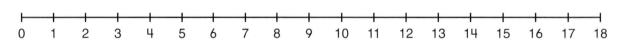

Answer: _____     Equation: _____

5. How far did Gretta and Gwen jump in all?

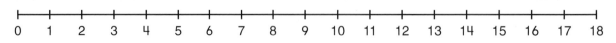

Answer: _____     Equation: _____

**Bonus:** When combined, which three grasshoppers' jumps equal the length of the sandpit? Draw and use a number line to solve. Then write an equation that supports your answer.

©The Mailbox® • TEC43069 • Oct./Nov. 2013 • Key p. 309 • (2.MD.B.5)

# Chow Time

Write the time each teacher's class starts lunch.

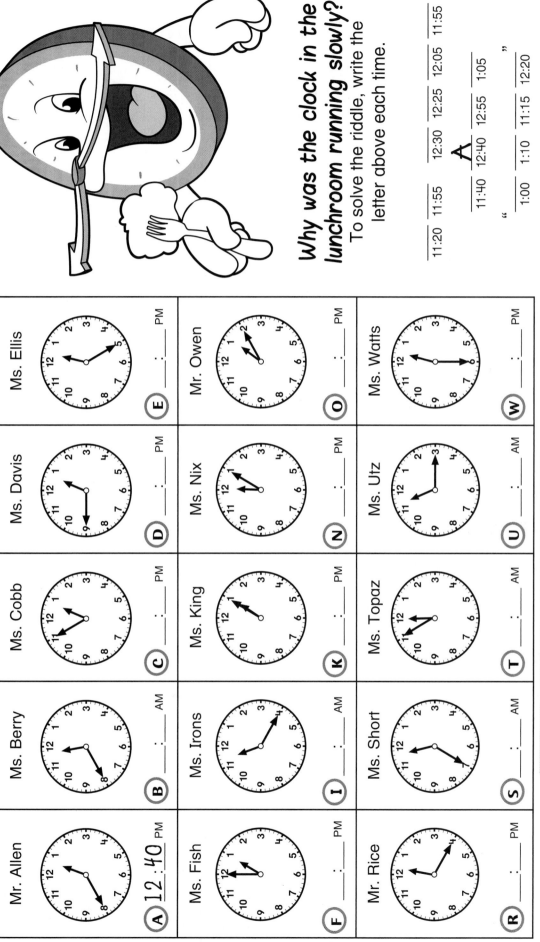

**A** 12:40 PM  Mr. Allen

**F** __:__ PM  Ms. Fish

**R** __:__ PM  Mr. Rice

**B** __:__ AM  Ms. Berry

**I** __:__ AM  Ms. Irons

**S** __:__ AM  Ms. Short

**C** __:__ PM  Ms. Cobb

**K** __:__ PM  Ms. King

**T** __:__ AM  Ms. Topaz

**D** __:__ PM  Ms. Davis

**N** __:__ PM  Ms. Nix

**U** __:__ AM  Ms. Utz

**E** __:__ PM  Ms. Ellis

**O** __:__ PM  Mr. Owen

**W** __:__ PM  Ms. Watts

## Why was the clock in the lunchroom running slowly?

To solve the riddle, write the letter above each time.

" __ __ __ __ __
11:20  11:55  12:30  12:25  12:05  11:55

__ __ A __ __ __
11:40  12:40  12:55  12:05  1:05

__ __ __ __ __ "
1:00  1:10  11:15  12:05  12:20

__ __ __ __ __ __ __ .
11:35  12:25  12:55  1:10  12:05  12:45  11:35

**Bonus:** Order the lunch times from earliest to latest.

# Pouring Shapes

Draw an X on each shape that is not a quadrilateral.
Then color the remaining shapes by the code.

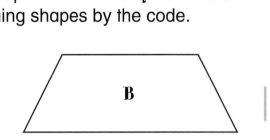

A

B

C

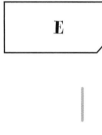
D

E

F

G

I

J

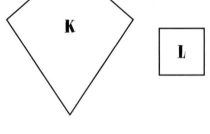
K

L

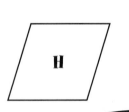
H

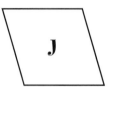

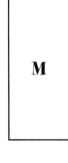
M

N

**Color Code**
square = red
rectangle = blue
rhombus = yellow
other quadrilaterals = green

O

P

Q

R

S

T

©The Mailbox® • TEC43070 • Dec./Jan. 2013–14 • Key p. 309 • (3.G.A.1)

# Snowball Fight!

Read.

The Penguins are having a snowball fight with their neighbors. Paula Penguin can make 10 snowballs from one bucket of snow. Her brother Pete can throw 5 snowballs every minute.

Skip-count to solve each problem.
Show your work. Label your answers.

1. Paula has 4 buckets of snow. How many snowballs can she make?


2. How many snowballs can Pete throw in 5 minutes?


3. Paula makes a total of 90 snowballs. How many buckets of snow did she scoop?


4. If Paula had 5 buckets of snow, how many snowballs could Pete throw?


5. How many buckets of snow would Paula need to make 100 snowballs?


6. How long would it take Pete to throw 100 snowballs?


**Bonus:** There are 35 inches of snow in the Penguins' yard. If it melts at a rate of 5 inches per day, how many days will it take to melt away?

# Shape Smash

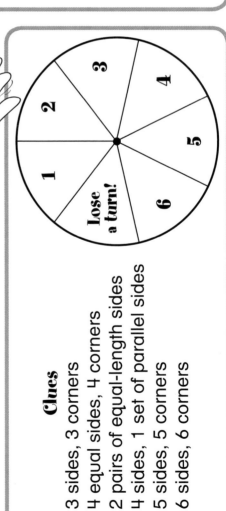

## Directions for two players:

1. Choose a crayon. Pick a different color than your partner.

2. When it's your turn, use the paper clip and a pencil to spin the spinner. Read the matching clue.

3. Say the name of the shape that matches the clue. Point to a matching shape on the gameboard.

4. Have your partner check your answer on the key.
   If it is correct, color the space.
   If it is incorrect, your turn is over.

5. The player with more colored shapes at the end of play wins.

### Clues
1 = 3 sides, 3 corners
2 = 4 equal sides, 4 corners
3 = 2 pairs of equal-length sides
4 = 4 sides, 1 set of parallel sides
5 = 5 sides, 5 corners
6 = 6 sides, 6 corners

©The Mailbox® • TEC43071 • Feb./Mar. 2014 • Key p. 310 • (2.G.A.1)

**Partner Game** Make a copy of this gameboard as well as a copy of the key on page 310 for each pair of students. Each student pair will need two different-color crayons and a paper clip.

# Sweet Slices

Name _____  Date _____

Shade the shape to show the fraction.
Write the fraction of the unshaded part.

**A** shaded = $\frac{3}{4}$

unshaded = _____

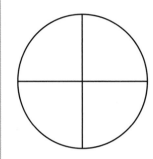

**B** shaded = $\frac{1}{2}$

unshaded = _____

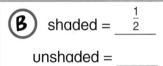

**C** shaded = $\frac{2}{4}$

unshaded = _____

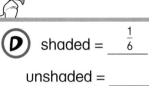

**D** shaded = $\frac{1}{6}$

unshaded = _____

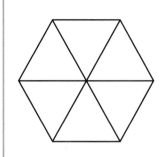

**E** shaded = $\frac{2}{3}$

unshaded = _____

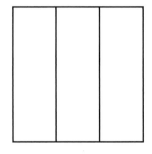

**F** shaded = $\frac{3}{8}$

unshaded = _____

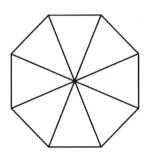

**G** shaded = $\frac{2}{6}$

unshaded = _____

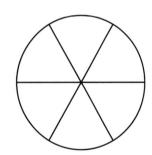

**H** shaded = $\frac{4}{6}$

unshaded = _____

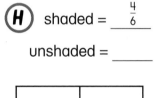
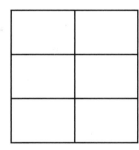

**I** shaded = $\frac{7}{8}$

unshaded = _____

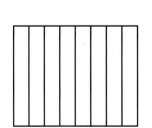

**J** shaded = $\frac{1}{4}$

unshaded = _____

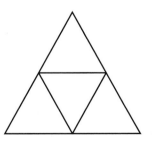

**K** shaded = $\frac{1}{2}$

unshaded = _____

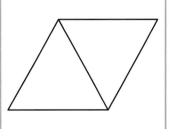

**L** shaded = $\frac{4}{8}$

unshaded = _____

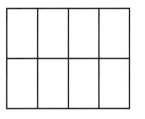

**Bonus:** Show three different ways to partition same-size rectangles into four equal sections.

# Hunting for Measurements

Measure each object.

| Object | Name of Object | Length (    ) |
|--------|----------------|---------------|
| A |  |  |
| B |  |  |
| C |  |  |
| D |  |  |
| E |  |  |
| F |  |  |
| G |  |  |
| H |  |  |

Use the table to answer the questions.

1. Which object is the longest? _____

2. Which object is the shortest? _____

3. Are any objects the same length? _____ If so, which ones?
   _____

4. Which object is longer, A or C? _____ How much longer is it?
   _____

5. Which object is shorter, D or H? _____ How much shorter is it?
   _____

6. Compare objects B and G. Write two sentences to describe how their lengths
   compare. _____
   _____
   _____

> **Bonus:** Choose two objects from the table that have not been compared. Write
> the letters. Then tell which object is shorter and by how much.

**How to Use**  Program the table above with classroom objects and a measurement (inches or centimeters). If desired, put a labeled sticky note on each object to make it easier for students to locate. Make student copies of this page; then provide each child with a ruler.

# Animals Everywhere

Read.

Today, I went to Mr. McFinkle's zoo. He has the strangest collection of animals, so I made sure to visit all five habitats. I noticed that Mr. McFinkle keeps the same kind of animal in each habitat.

In the first habitat, I saw 24 legs but only 3 animals. In the second habitat, I saw 32 legs but only 8 animals. In the third habitat, I saw 18 legs but only 9 animals. In the fourth habitat, I saw 30 legs and only 5 animals. In the last habitat, I saw 12 legs but only 4 animals.

**Mr. McFinkle's Zoo**
Be sure to see...

Zorax    Wapag

Beezle    Tricaden

Oclet

Use the passage and chart to answer the questions.
Complete the equations to support your answers.

1. Which kind of animal is in the first habitat?

   _____ ÷ ? = _____. To solve, I can use _____ x _____ = _____.

   Each animal has _____ legs, and the animal is an _____.

2. Which kind of animal is in the second habitat?

   _____ ÷ ? = _____. To solve, I can use _____ x _____ = _____.

   Each animal has _____ legs, and the animal is a _____.

3. Which kind of animal is in the third habitat?

   _____ ÷ ? = _____. To solve, I can use _____ x _____ = _____.

   Each animal has _____ legs, and the animal is a _____.

4. Which kind of animal is in the fourth habitat?

   _____ ÷ ? = _____. To solve, I can use _____ x _____ = _____.

   Each animal has _____ legs, and the animal is  a _____.

5. Which kind of animal is in the last habitat?

   _____ ÷ ? = _____. To solve, I can use _____ x _____ = _____.

   Each animal has _____ legs, and the animal is a _____.

**Bonus:** A new habitat is planned for the zoo. If it will hold 5 animals and you will see 25 legs, how many legs will each animal have? Explain how you got your answer.

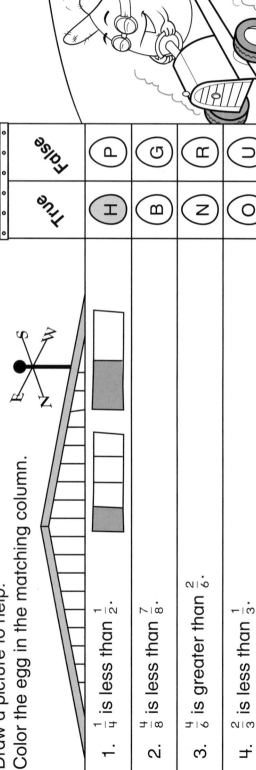

# Down on the Farm

Read. Decide whether the statement is true or false.
Draw a picture to help.
Color the egg in the matching column.

| | True | False |
|---|---|---|
| 1. $\frac{1}{4}$ is less than $\frac{1}{2}$. | H | P |
| 2. $\frac{4}{8}$ is less than $\frac{7}{8}$. | B | G |
| 3. $\frac{4}{6}$ is greater than $\frac{2}{6}$. | N | R |
| 4. $\frac{2}{3}$ is less than $\frac{1}{3}$. | O | U |
| 5. $\frac{1}{2}$ is the same as $\frac{1}{3}$. | S | C |
| 6. $\frac{2}{8}$ is greater than $\frac{6}{8}$. | E | O |
| 7. $\frac{3}{6}$ is less than $\frac{1}{6}$. | R | D |
| 8. $\frac{1}{4}$ is not the same as $\frac{3}{4}$. | T | L |
| 9. $\frac{5}{8}$ is greater than $\frac{1}{8}$. | M | E |
| 10. $\frac{2}{3}$ is not the same as $\frac{1}{3}$. | F | G |

## What do you call an egg that goes on adventures?

To solve the riddle, write each uncolored letter on the numbered matching line.

An

"__ __ __ __ __ __ __ __ __ __ - __ __ __ __ __ __"
6  2  10  5  1  8  4  7  9  3

**Bonus:** Rewrite each false statement to make it true.

Name _____  Date _____

# Shooting Marbles

Write an addition equation for each array.
Color the marble with the matching sum.

(25) (10) (20) (4) (8)

(12) (8) (5) (6) (20) (9)  (15)

| A.  | B. | C. |
|---|---|---|

_____  _____  _____

| D.  | E.  | F. |
|---|---|---|

_____  _____  _____

| G. | H. | I. |
|---|---|---|

_____  _____  _____

| J. | K. | L. |
|---|---|---|

_____  _____  _____

**Bonus:** For each array in A–C, write a different addition sentence.
(Hint: The new sums should match the answers you wrote above.)

# All Around the Farmer's Market

Use the measurements from each problem to write the known side lengths. Solve for the unknown side length.

1. A rectangular table has a perimeter of 146 inches. If each of the long sides measure 48 inches, what is the length of each short side?

_____ Ⓐ

2. A fruit stand has 6 sides. It has a perimeter of 162 inches. Two sides are each 15 inches long, another two sides are each 27 inches long, and one more side is 64 inches long. What is the length of the sixth side?

_____ Ⓒ

3. A rectangular ice cream stand has a perimeter of 114 inches. If the short sides are 21 inches each, what is the length of each long side?

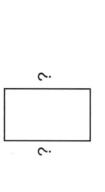

_____ Ⓔ

4. There is a table with a perimeter of 228 inches. If the five short sides are 18 inches long and two other sides are 30 inches each, what is the length of the longest side?

_____ Ⓡ

5. A table of strawberries has a perimeter of 104 inches. It is shaped like a trapezoid. One side is 24 inches long. Another side is 48 inches long. If the remaining sides are the same length, how long is each side?

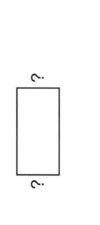

_____ Ⓨ

6. A farmer sells tomatoes. His table has 5 sides. The distance around it is 209 inches. Two of its sides are each 32 inches long. Another two sides are each 56 inches long. What is the length of the fifth side?

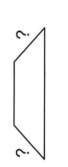

_____ Ⓛ

Bonus: Write a word problem for a shape that has a perimeter of 115 inches. Then solve it.

## Farmer Rick thinks one vegetable tastes best when it is eaten in a basement. What is it?
To find out, write each letter on its matching line or lines below.

" __  __  __  __  __  __  __ - __  __ "
  14  36  33   33  25  78   16

# A TREASURE TROVE OF
# Multiplication and Division Practice

The beauty of these ideas is that you can use them to reinforce just multiplication or division skills or to help students see the relationship between both operations.

## Movable Models

The only manipulatives you need for these activities are eager students!

**Multiplication** (3.OA.A.1; 3.OA.B.5) Lead student volunteers to a location where they can easily be seen; then instruct them to form an array, such as three rows of two. Call on another child to name the product. Redirect the same students to stand in two rows of three, and have another child name the product. Lead students to understand that the product of given factors is the same even if the order is not (commutative property).

**Division** (3.OA.A.2) Invite student volunteers to stand together where they can easily be seen. Have a child tell how many total students are standing; then instruct the students to split into a certain number of equal groups. Guide students to understand that division involves a whole group split into equal parts.

**Relating Multiplication and Division** (3.OA.A.4; 3.OA.B.6) After modeling the commutative property of multiplication as described above, tell students that the same values can be used to describe division problems. Have a child tell how many total students are standing; then instruct the students to split into a certain number of equal groups (such as two or three). Lead students to understand the same three numbers are involved in both tasks, which makes the numbers related (fact family), and knowing one problem can help them solve for the others in the set.

*adapted from an idea by Heather Malin, Stanley M. Koziol Elementary, Ware, MA*

**tip** Write the problems on the board so students see how the numbers are related.

## Merry Multiples

These small-group activities result in decorative references for your math wall. To make them, divide students into ten groups. Have each group cut out a smiley pattern from a copy of page 136 and write a different number from 1 to 10 where the nose would go.

**Multiplication** (3.OA.C.7) Have each group write a column of 11 multiplication signs down the left side of the strip, the numbers 0 to 10 in the middle of the strip, and then an equal sign and each product on the right. Display the projects on a math wall as a reference.

**Division** (3.OA.C.7) Have each group write the product of one times the number on the left side of the strip. Then have them list the remaining products (up to times ten) down the left side of the strip. The students write ten division signs in the middle of the strip and then the numbers 1 through 10 down the right side. Display the projects.

**Relating Multiplication and Division** (3.OA.C.7) After students complete the project based on the multiplication steps above, explain to them that they can use the problems to find the quotients. Tell them to start at the product and read the problem right to left, saying "divided by" in place of "equals" and "equals" in place of "times." So 9 x 1 = 9 will also show that 9 ÷ 1 = 9 when read in reverse.

9

x 0 = 0
x 1 = 9
x 2 = 18
x 3 = 27
x 4 = 36
x 5 = 45
x 6 = 54
x 7 = 63
x 8 = 72
x 9 = 81
x 10 = 90

*adapted from an idea by April Parker, St. Pius X School, Greensboro, NC*

TEC43071

TEC43071

# SCIENCE

# simply science

Science tools

# Hands-On Introductions

Teach students about various science tools while sparking an interest in upcoming science activities. Gather tools students will use during the next grading period, such as rulers, tape measures, platform scales or balance scales, and magnifying glasses. Set up stations of like materials and place a card at each station directing students to complete a simple task with the tool. Provide time for students to rotate to each station to get familiar with the tools and complete a log of the materials like the one shown. Repeat the activity at the beginning of each grading period so students will be familiar with the tools when the time comes to use them.

*Cheryl Rayl, Mayville Elementary, Mayville, MI*

| Tool | What It Looks Like | What It Does |
|------|--------------------|--------------|
| measuring tape | | finds the length of things that aren't flat |
| magnifying glass | | helps me see up close |
| platform scale | | tells me how much something weighs |
| computer | | allows me to draw diagrams and record observations |

Parts of a plant, plant life cycle

# Grown With Love

Engage students in the growth cycle of an easy-to-propagate plant, and the result will be Mother's Day gifts grown with love. To start, bring a large coleus plant to school. Refer to the plant as you guide students to identify its parts. Next, lead students to understand that one way this plant can grow is by being clipped and replanted. To demonstrate, clip a length of stem just below the leaves and put the stem in water to root. Make enough clippings for each child to have one, plus a few extras. When roots appear, transfer the plants to disposable cups filled with potting soil. Continue to make observations of the plants' growth. Then, in May, send home a plant with each child for a lovely Mother's Day gift.

*Sherry Darby, Mill Stream Elementary, Norridgewock, ME*

 tip For a decorative touch, use dollar store coffee mugs instead of disposable cups.

# simply science

Echolocation, cycles

# Go-To Games

Science is fun, and these activities prove it!

**Echolocation:** Choose one student to be a bat. Have him stand blindfolded in the center of a room (such as the multipurpose room). Direct the rest of the class (prey) to stand around the perimeter. Choose one student to be the targeted food source by silently tapping her on the shoulder. The bat says "echo" and the food source repeats him. The bat and food source continue in this manner, with the bat moving toward the sound until the bat locates its food. Choose a new bat and play again.

*Lori Anderson Terkeurst, Roscommon, MI*

**Earth's Cycles:** Play a game of Simon Says to familiarize students with the difference between rotation and revolution. To start, name yourself as Simon and have students stand. When you say "Rotation," students should spin in place. When you say "Revolution," they should walk around their desks. When you say "Rotate while revolving"—just like Earth does—the students do both.

*Ashley Thompson, Bowling Green Elementary, Bowling Green, VA*

| Candy | Mass | Shape | Sink or Float? |
|---|---|---|---|
| Snickers | 17 g | rectangle | sink |
| Milky Way | 17 g | rectangle | sink |
| 3 Musketeers | 15 g | rectangle | float |
| Kit Kat | 14 g | rectangle | float |

Sink or Float

# Dive Into Displacement

Students will be eager to dive into this sweet investigation! Gather a variety of fun-size candy bars and a balance scale; then fill a clear tub half full of water. Draw on the board a table like the one shown, choose a candy, and write its name on the first row. Unwrap the candy and use the balance scale to find its mass. Record the mass and the candy's shape on the table; then place the candy in the water. Wait and observe the candy; then complete the last column. Repeat with the other candies and use the data to determine why the candies sank or floated. **To extend the activity,** gather another supply of items (larger or smaller candies or math manipulatives) and have students use what they've learned from this activity to predict which will sink or float. Then test them to find out.

*Marjorie Archer, Nova Blanche Forman Elementary, Davie, FL*

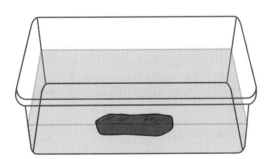

Mass and shape affect displacement. Displacement explains why an object sinks or floats.

# simply science

## Matter

# All Shapes and Sizes

To introduce matter to students, write the word *matter* on an index card. Tape the card to something in the classroom and tell students that matter is anything that takes up space and has mass. Give each child an index card and a loop of tape. Direct him to write "matter" on the card; then have him place the card on something in the classroom. Provide time for each child to tell where he placed his card and why he selected it, using the definition you shared earlier in his response. The repeated explanations will surely shape students' understanding of this new concept.

*Alison Walsh*
*St. Ignatius Loyola School*
*New York, NY*

## Adaptations: camouflage

# Under Wraps

Here's a fun and easy way to teach students about animals that disguise their appearance. In advance, make student copies of various black-line animal pictures. Also gather printed wrapping paper or scrapbook paper (the larger the pattern, the better). A student cuts out her animal and glues it to a piece of paper. Next, the child draws and colors the pattern from her paper on the animal cutout. With the animal hidden on its paper background, students will have a visual reminder of what this adaptation means.

*Liz Colton, Eagle Hills Elementary, Eagle, ID*

## Water cycle

# Go With the Flow!

Watch the water cycle in action with this mini model. To make one, fill a small paper cup halfway with water. Use a marker to draw the waterline on the outside of the cup. Carefully place the cup in a resealable plastic bag and seal the bag; then tape the bag to a window. Have students observe when condensation is present and how changes in the waterline indicate evaporation. As a follow-up activity, direct each child to make a diagram like the one shown, using glitter to indicate the water and cotton balls for clouds.

*Joslyn Matelski, Boyne City, MI, and*
*Krystal Larson, Walla Walla, WA*

## Habitats

# Divide and Conquer

Take students on a trip to multiple habitats without leaving your school. Have each class at your grade level become experts on the animals and environment of a different habitat. After gathering the important facts and building a thorough understanding of the habitat, guide students to make a 3-D display, such as a physical replica or an oversize diorama. Instruct the class to include details such as where in the world the habitat can be found, examples of plant and animal life, and how the plants and animals there depend on each other. After the display is complete, schedule time with the other classes to visit each room and learn more about the habitats studied!

*Lisa Ballard, West Elementary, Ft. Worth, TX*

## Life cycles
# Around and Around

Help students visualize an animal's growth and change by using a pinwheel. To make one, give a child a copy of page 144. Working in a counterclockwise manner around the pattern, he draws and labels in each unshaded section a different stage of a desired animal's life cycle. (For animals with life cycles of three stages—such as a grasshopper, spider, or bird—the student writes a title in the first section before drawing and labeling the others.) Next, he cuts out the pattern and cuts along the bold inside lines, stopping at the center circle. Then he pokes a hole through each dot and through a plastic straw, about half an inch from the top. The student brings the corners of the pattern toward the center so the holes overlap. Then he inserts a pushpin through the holes and the straw. (Provide assistance as needed.) Finally, the child adds his pinwheel to a display titled "Life Cycles Go Around and Around."

*Laura Johnson, South Decatur Elementary, Greensburg, IN*

## Plants
# Waterworks

Since April showers won't likely nourish May flowers in your classroom, give this quick watering tip a try. Poke holes in the lid of a clean plastic beverage container. Fill the container with water and put the cap on. Invite a student to use the container to water your classroom plants. With this no-mess solution, you're sure to keep your classroom plants in peak condition for observation.

*Heather Aulisio, Tobyhanna Elementary Center*
*Pocono Pines, PA*

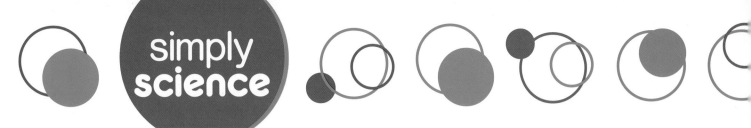
Force and motion

# Tissue Racers

From start to finish, this hands-on activity has students engaged and learning. In advance, collect an empty rectangular tissue box for each small group of students and a variety of objects that can be made into wheels (bathroom cups for tracing, cardboard, etc.). Next, poke two small holes on opposite sides of each box, as shown. Help students insert a thick straw though each pair of holes and then insert a dowel through each straw. Lead students to investigate and test which materials make the best wheels. After they secure the wheels onto their cars, have students determine whether any other details, such as rear spoilers, need to be added to help the cars go faster. Provide time for students to race their cars; then discuss why the winning model won. Encourage students to think about how any differences in box size may have influenced the winner, how the wheels may have helped, and how any added details affected the car's speed.

April Parker, St. Pius X School, Greensboro, NC

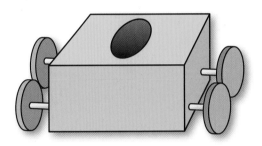

Environmental impacts on animals

# Polluted Water

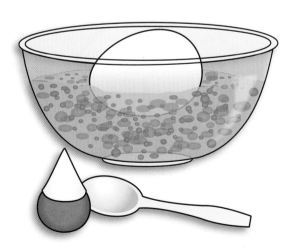

This demonstration helps students understand how humans have affected some animals and their habitats. To begin, fill a small glass bowl half full of vegetable oil. Tell students this represents the sea. Next, stir in a generous amount of red food coloring and tell students that it represents an oil spill. Place a hard boiled egg in the mixture. Repeatedly spoon the mixture atop the egg; then let the egg float for 30 or more minutes. Remove the egg and pat it dry. Invite students to share their observations about the egg; then peel the shell from the egg. When students see the discolored egg, ask them to share additional observations. Lead students to understand that because eggshells are naturally *porous* (having small holes that allow air or liquid to pass through), oils and other dangerous poisons can threaten the unborn animals inside.

 **Don't stop here!** Find science-based **skill sheets** on pages 145–148 and four ideas for **simple machines** on pages 149 and 150.

# Pinwheel Pattern

Use with "Around and Around" on page 142.

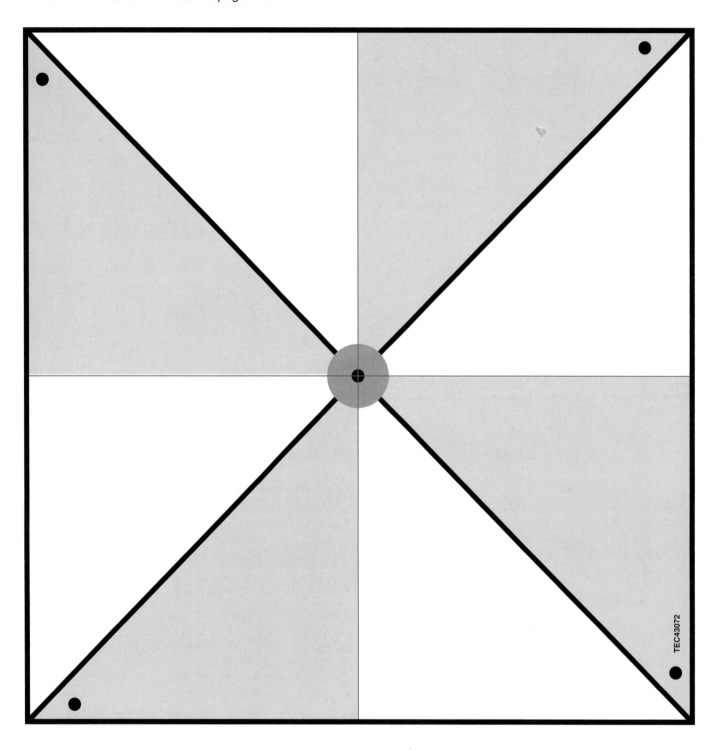

TEC43072

# Pumpkin Particulars

Read each set of sentences.
Write the matching main idea.
Circle the details that led you to each main idea.

**1**

Pumpkins can grow on vines. The vines often spread across the ground. Flowers sprout from the vines. Some of these flowers grow into pumpkins. It takes most pumpkins about four months to grow.

_____

**2**

Your body needs the vitamins and fiber found in pumpkins. Pumpkin pulp can be cooked. The pulp can be used for baked goods. The seeds can be roasted to make a healthy snack.

_____

**3**

Most pumpkins weigh less than 30 pounds, but some can grow to be over 1,000 pounds! Pumpkins can be orange, white, or even red. They can be tall or short. Some have smooth shells. Others have bumpy shells.

**4**

Bees drink nectar from pumpkin plants' flowers. Here, a bee gets orange pollen grains on its body. When a bee flies to a new flower, it carries the pollen. The bee leaves some pollen on the next flower. This new pollen helps the flower grow into a pumpkin.

## Main Ideas

☐ Pumpkins need bees to grow.

☐ Not all pumpkins look the same.

☐ Pumpkins are a healthy food choice.

☐ Pumpkins go through stages as they grow.

**Bonus:** Which paragraphs' details tell *why?* Which paragraphs' details tell *how?*

# A Restful Winter

**Prompt** What happens when an animal hibernates?

**Plan** What does *hibernate* mean?

Choose an animal.
☐ bat  ☐ bear  ☐ bumblebee  ☐ garter snake  ☐ raccoon  ☐ snail

How does this animal prepare to hibernate?

Where does it go when it hibernates?

What happens to the animal while it hibernates?

How long does this animal hibernate?

**Write** To start your writing, give the meaning of *hibernate*. Then use facts to tell what happens when your chosen animal hibernates. End your writing with a sentence or question about the animal you chose.

©The Mailbox® • TEC43070 • Dec./Jan. 2013–14 • (W.2.2; W.2.7; W.3.2; W.3.7)

**How to Use** Provide access to reference materials. Have students work in small groups (second grade) or independently (third grade) to complete a copy of this organizer. Then have them write an informational piece about hibernation.

# Every Little Bit Helps

Look at the photo. Read the caption.
Then answer the questions.

© Can Stock Photo Inc. / aspenrock / csp2652201

This squirrel enjoys an acorn. An acorn is
the seed of an oak tree.

1. Where is the squirrel? What is it doing?
_____
_____

2. How does the plant (oak tree) help the squirrel?
_____
_____

3. How does the squirrel help the plant (oak tree)?
_____
_____

4. The squirrel and plant (oak tree) are *interdependent*. What does that mean?
_____

**Bonus:** Give another example of a plant and an animal that are interdependent. Explain your choice.

©The Mailbox® • TEC43071 • Feb./Mar. 2014 • Key p. 310

# In Short Supply

Storms bring rain. Sometimes they bring too much rain. Then there is flooding. Other times storms bring strong winds. But what happens when there are no storms and rain doesn't fall? A period of time when the amount of rainfall is much less than normal is called a **drought.**

A drought can occur when the temperatures are hot. With the extra heat and lack of rain, problems can occur. Crops can die. Forest and grass fires are more likely to pop up. Streams and lakes can dry out, and the soil below can be blown away. People are often asked to reduce the amount of water they use.

There are many ways adults can **conserve**, or save, water. There are many ways you can help too. You may already know to turn off the water when you brush your teeth. The same is true when you wash your hands. By turning off the faucet as you lather your hands, you help save water. What else can you do? Choose one cup as your cup for the day. Use only that cup. This way, you cut back on the number of items that need to be washed. If you drop ice cubes on the floor or have leftover ice cubes after having a drink of water, put them in a houseplant's pot. The plant gets water as the ice melts. Take a shower instead of a bath and keep your shower under five minutes to reduce the water you use. Since flushing the toilet uses water, drop used tissues in the trash instead of the toilet. There are so many easy ways to conserve water.

©Can Stock Photo Inc./513569neotakezo

**When there is little rain, lakes like this one can dry out.**

Use the passage to answer the questions.
Write your answers on another sheet of paper.

1. What is a **drought**?

2. What are three problems that can result from a drought?

3. What does **conserve** mean?

4. How can you help save water? List three ways.

**Bonus:** Should you conserve water even if there isn't a drought? Why or why not?

©The Mailbox® • TEC43073 • June/July 2014 • Key p. 310 • (RI.2.1; RI.3.1)

# The Ruler Trick

**Lever**

### What You Need

wooden ruler          textbook          tabletop

### What You Do

1. Put a ruler on a tabletop so one end hangs over the edge.
2. Lay the textbook atop the ruler.
3. Try to lift the book by pressing on the ruler where it hangs over the tabletop.
4. Repeat many times, each time moving the book closer to the table's edge before pressing.
5. Stop when the book is at the edge of the table.

### Think and Answer

A *lever* was used in this task. Was it easier to lift the book with a long or a short lever? Why?

TEC43073

# Want to Race?

**Inclined plane**

### What You Need

5 stacked textbooks          medium-size toy car
2 paper clips          yardstick
medium-size rubber band

### What You Do

1. Hang the rubber band from a paper clip.
2. Slide the paper clip onto one end of the yardstick.
3. Attach the other paper clip to the car. Then connect it to the rubber band.
4. Lift the yardstick straight up. Record the length of the rubber band.
5. Place the yardstick on the books to make a ramp. Record the length of the rubber band.

### Think and Answer

**1** Why was the rubber band stretched farther when the yardstick was standing straight up? **2** Which simple machine reduced the stretch of the rubber band?

TEC43073

# Winding Down

## What You Need

right triangle cut from a 9" paper square

pencil          marker          tape          tabletop

## What You Do

1. Use a marker to outline the diagonal side of the triangle.
2. Hold the triangle perpendicular ($\perp$) to the tabletop. Say the name of the machine this shape looks like.
3. Place the triangle on the tabletop.
4. Put the pencil atop one leg of the triangle.
5. Roll the paper around the pencil. Tape the loose end in place.

## Think and Answer

**1** What simple machine was made by Step 5? **2** What are some real-life examples of this simple machine?

TEC43073

# Give Me a Lift

## What You Need

2 brooms          length of soft rope

## What You Do

1. Have one student hold a broom parallel (=) to the floor.
2. Have another student hold the other broom parallel to the floor about 18 inches away from the first broom.
3. Tie one end of the rope to the first broom handle.
4. Loop the rope around both brooms three times.
5. Slowly pull the loose end of the rope while the other two students try to keep the brooms apart.

## Think and Answer

**1** Why was it hard to keep the brooms apart? **2** What type of simple machine works like this one?

TEC43073

# SOCIAL STUDIES

# Exploring Social Studies

## Ready to Help
### Roles of community citizens

Put students' strengths on display as you build your classroom community. To begin, explain that a local community can be strong if its citizens work together and build on each other's strengths. Share examples of citizens in your community who use their strengths at their jobs—such as doctors, hairdressers, and chefs—and how other citizens of the community benefit from their work. Next, tell students that their classroom community will benefit from each child sharing his own skills and recognizing other students' strengths. Instruct each child to copy and complete the sentences shown on an index card. Then take a picture of each student performing the special skill he wrote about. Print the photos and post each one next to the corresponding index card on a display titled "Every Community Has Helpers—Even Ours!" Encourage students to refer to the board to get to know their new classmates and when they need help.

Cheryl Rayl, Mayville Elementary, Mayville, MI

My name is [Ryan]. I can make our classroom community stronger by helping others [tie their shoes superfast].

## State Stats
### Reading maps

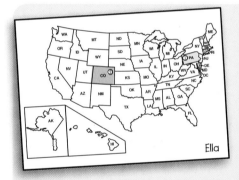

Ella

Students will surely be game for this sports-themed activity! As a class, choose a collegiate or professional sports team to follow for the season; then get a copy of the team's schedule. Next, have each child find your state on a copy of a US map, write the number "1" in its outline, and color it. Then share the location of the first opponent and direct students to find that team's home state, label it "2," and color it a different color. If desired, follow up with questions such as "In what direction will our team travel to play its next game?" or "Will our opponents travel east or west this weekend?" Before each game, locate the next opponent's home state.

Amy Hart, Saint Sylvester School, Pittsburgh, PA

tip → If the class can't agree on a team to follow, allow each student to be part of a group that follows its chosen team on a map.

## Words and Pictures
### Holidays

To explain the history related to Constitution Day and Citizenship Day (September 17), have each child complete a copy of page 156. Then, to dig a little deeper, share *We the Kids: The Preamble to the Constitution of the United States* by David Catrow. Use the illustrations to help reinforce the meaning of the phrases. Then give each small group of students a sentence strip programmed with a phrase from the preamble and direct the students to make an illustration that shows what the phrase means to them. If desired, order the sentence strips and illustrations on a display titled "How We See the Preamble."

Kelli L. Gowdy, High Point, NC, and Megan Campoli, Country Trails Elementary, Elgin, IL

provide for the common defense

# Exploring Social Studies

## Informative Shields
### Native American cultures

This one-of-a-kind project makes an interesting follow-up activity to Native American studies. To start, a child cuts a large circle from a paper grocery bag. He divides the paper into sections, making one section for each region or group studied. Next, the student labels each section and draws pictures that represent characteristics unique to each group. Then the child cuts feathers from construction paper and glues them to the back of his shield, so they hang down as shown. **As an alternative,** the student divides his shield into sections representing different topics studied about one particular group, such as location, housing, family life, and food. Then he completes his shield as described above.

Jeri Gramil, Emmitsburg, MD

 tip  Use the feather pattern on page 275 to make a template for students to trace.

## Where Are We?
### Geography

The destination of this activity is clear—a better understanding of how each of the communities students live in fit together on Earth. To start, use a mapping program, such as Google Earth, to show the view of Earth. Next, zoom in on the North American continent. Remind students that this large landform is one community they are part of. Zoom in again to view the United States. Note that even though lines appear in the computer program to show country and state boundaries, they do not physically appear on Earth. Continue to zoom in on your state, county, and city. If desired, zoom in on the exact location of your school. Reverse the activity to help students put together the smaller parts of the whole Earth community.

Cheryl Rayl, Mayville Elementary, Mayville, MI

## All Over Town
### Community

This eye-catching display shows what students have learned about a specific community during the year. To start, have each child program a copy of page 157 with a community name, such as your town's name, and instruct him to complete the organizer with examples for each category. Next, prepare a display with the title shown and make student groups based on the three categories on the organizer. Then direct students in each group to use the information from their category of the organizer to draw, color, and cut out the examples and post them in the matching section on the display.

Jennifer Bell, Toccoa Elementary, Toccoa, GA

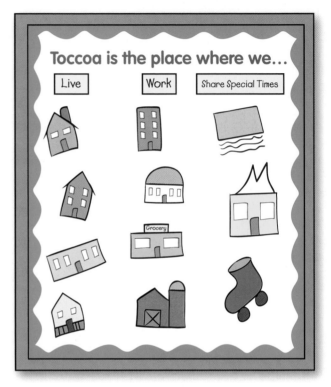

Toccoa is the place where we...
Live  Work  Share Special Times
Grocery

## Claim to Fame
### Influential people

Help students keep tabs on the important historic figures they study with an easy-to-make journal. To make one, stack several sheets of unlined paper and fold the stack in half. Staple the booklet along the fold and write the title shown. Each time a new figure is introduced, a child draws a picture of the person at the top of a page, labels the picture with the person's name, and writes the accomplishments that made the person famous or important. She keeps the journal at her desk as a handy reference.

Barbara Duran, Dorris Jones Elementary, Rockwall, TX

**tip →** Provide photocopied images of each figure for the child to cut out and glue inside her journal.

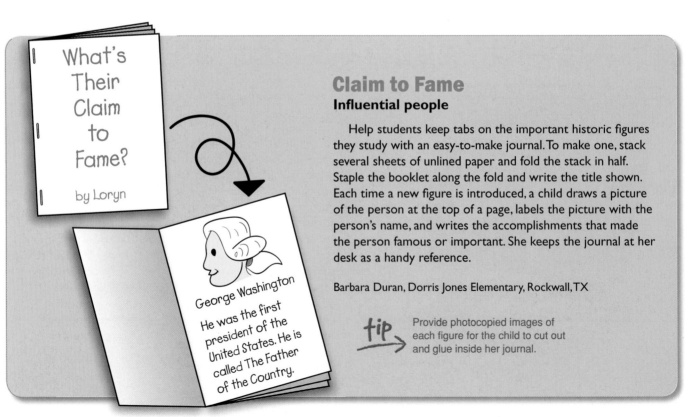

What's Their Claim to Fame? by Loryn

George Washington
He was the first president of the United States. He is called The Father of the Country.

# Exploring Social Studies

## Perfect Puzzles
### Geography

Piece together geography skills using old atlas maps. Remove the maps and mount them on construction paper. Laminate the maps; then puzzle-cut each one into sections. Place the pieces of each map in a separate labeled plastic bag. Set out the puzzles for students to complete during free time.

Julie Laney, Acworth, GA

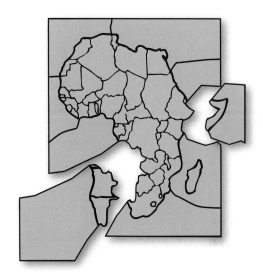

## Think About It
### Displays

Here's a social studies display that you can easily change out. Simply take a photo of each child looking pensive. Present a question, such as one of the ones shown, and have students write a reply on a sheet of paper. Next, instruct each child to cut around his writing to make a thought bubble as well as two smaller circles. Write the question on a sentence strip and post it on a display with students' photos and replies. When you start a new unit, pose a different question and replace students' thought bubbles with their new responses. So easy!

Carolyn Milford, Stockwell Place Elementary, Bossier City, LA

How would life be different if the telephone had never been invented?

**Influential people:** Of the people we studied, who had the greatest impact on his or her community? Why?

If you could meet one of the people we studied, who would it be? Why?

**Important inventions:** How would life be different if the [invention] had never been invented?

What product do you think should be invented?

**Community:** What is our community's greatest strength?

How is our classroom like a community?

**Economics:** What is the difference between wants and needs? What are your wants? What are your needs?

What does interdependent mean? Give examples.

**Geography:** If you could go anywhere in the world, where would it be? Why?

# One Long Meeting

Read.

In 1787, the United States was still very young. There were only 13 states. Each state had its own government. It had its own way of doing things. Many people were poor and unhappy. The new country needed to come together as one. So in May of that year, men from 12 states met to plan a new government. Great leaders such as George Washington, James Madison, and Benjamin Franklin were there. They wanted to share their ideas and help the young country.

During the meeting, 55 men shared ideas. They talked about what a strong government should look like. They planned laws that would help people in every state.

There were many disagreements among the men, and the meeting went on for four months. Finally, a plan was written. On September 17, 1787, the men who agreed on the country's new laws and aims signed the plan. This plan is known as the Constitution. It is still the basis of our government today.

Answer the questions.

1. Who were some of the leaders who met to plan a new government for the United States? _____

   _____

2. When did the meeting start?_____

3. Why did the men meet? _____

   _____

4. What did the men do during the meeting? _____

   _____

   _____

5. What is the Constitution? _____

   _____

   _____

> **Bonus:** How long did the meeting last? Why did it last that long?

©The Mailbox® • TEC43068 • Aug./Sept. 2013 • Key p. 311 • (RI.3.1)

**156** THE MAILBOX   **Note to the teacher:** Use with "Words and Pictures" on page 152.

Name _____

Graphic organizer: community

# is the place where we...

(community)

**Live**

**Work**

**Share Special Times**

©The Mailbox® • TEC43072 • April/May 2014

**Note to the teacher:** Use with "All Over Town" on page 154.

# Another Day to Say Thanks

Read the facts.

| | | |
|---|---|---|
| Veterans Day is a holiday in the United States. It is on November 11. | On Veterans Day, people thank the men and women who served in the armed forces. | The armed forces include the Army, Navy, Air Force, Marine Corps, and Coast Guard. |
| In the United States, parades are held and speeches are given on Veterans Day. | In 2011, there were more than 21 million veterans in the United States. | Other countries have holidays like Veterans Day. |
| People in Canada, Australia, and New Zealand observe Remembrance Day on November 11. They honor those who died in war. | Remembrance Sunday is held in the United Kingdom. It is held on the second Sunday in November. | Memorial Day also honors men and women who served in the armed forces, but it remembers those who died while serving. It is observed by Americans in May. |

Complete the tasks.

1. Use a red crayon to outline the section that tells what Veterans Day is and when it is celebrated in the United States.

2. Draw a star in the section that gives details about the armed forces.

3. Use a blue crayon to outline the sections that tell what happens on Veterans Day.

4. Use a black crayon to outline the section that compares Veterans Day to another US holiday. Then underline the name of that holiday.

5. Underline the name of a holiday that is also held on November 11 in other countries. Use a yellow crayon to color the section that tells about this holiday.

**Bonus:** Write a paragraph about Veterans Day in the United States. (Hint: Use the red and blue outlined sections to help you.)

# Honoring Dr. King

Read.

In Washington, DC, you will find many places that honor important people. One such place is the Martin Luther King Jr. National Memorial. This structure was built to remember the life and struggles of a man who fought for civil rights, Dr. King.

**Mountain of Despair**

To enter the memorial, a person walks between two large **boulders**. They are known as the Mountain of Despair. These boulders were once one big rock. They were split to reveal the Stone of Hope ahead.

**The Stone of Hope**

A 30-foot **statue** sits in the center of the monument. Dr. King's image is carved on this huge stone. On one side of the statue, the words "Out of the mountain of despair, a stone of hope" are carved.

Dr. King's image faces the very place where he gave his famous "I Have a Dream" speech many years ago. Now, his memorial reminds everyone about fairness and equality.

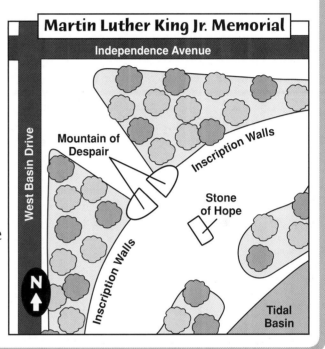

Answer the questions.

1. What is the Mountain of Despair made of? _____

_____

Where in the memorial are they found? _____

2. What is the Stone of Hope?_____

_____

3. What body of water does the Stone of Hope overlook? _____

4. What is important about the placement of the Stone of Hope? _____

_____

5. Where in Washington, DC, is the Martin Luther King Jr. National Memorial located? _____

**Bonus:** What are civil rights? Use reference materials to help you.

# Here, There, and Everywhere
## Engaging Activities to Reinforce Map Skills

## Headed in the Right Direction
### Cardinal and intermediate directions

To set up this classroom compass, put two long strips of painter's tape on the center of your classroom floor as shown. Label each strip with the corresponding cardinal direction and abbreviation. Familiarize students with the directions by naming different classroom objects and having them name the corresponding direction where each one is found. Then lead students on a scavenger hunt by having them follow cardinal directions to a classroom item.

After students are familiar with the cardinal directions, put two more strips of tape diagonally atop the existing tape. Label them with intermediate directions. Revisit the activities and direct students to incorporate the additional directions as well.

April Parker, St. Pius X School, Greensboro, NC

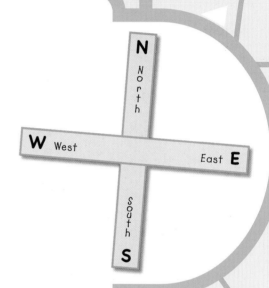

## Draw Some Interest
### Map keys and symbols

Build excitement for maps by turning your students into mapmakers. After exposing students to a variety of map keys and their symbols, put students in groups of four. Assign each group a location—such as a park, zoo, town, or classroom—and have each group member create a different symbol for a map of that location. Next, direct each student to draw and label the symbol on each of four small sticky notes. Group members exchange sticky notes so each child has one of each symbol. Each student organizes the sticky notes on a large sheet of construction paper to make a map key; then he draws a map that uses the symbols. Provide time for students within each group to share and compare their maps.

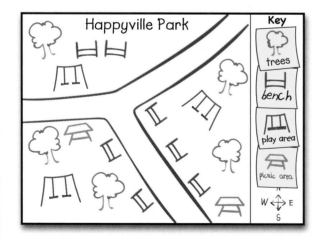

# Around Town
## Map scale

This activity makes using maps personal! Use a mapping website to make a map of the community that includes your school and print it. Then make student copies of the map. Show students how to use a ruler and the scale on the map to determine the distances between your school and locations around town. For an added challenge, tell students the principal has decided to consider all field trips to locations within a predetermined distance from school. Have each child list as many places of interest that are found within that distance as she can. Then have her choose a place from the list and write a letter to the principal telling why a field trip there should be approved.

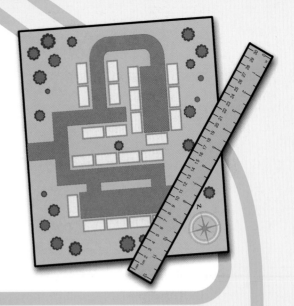

# A Coordinated Effort
## Grid map

Introduce students to the ABCs and 123s of using coordinates to make reading a grid map easier. First, make and label a grid with coordinates, like the one shown. Draw shapes, write letters or numbers, or put different stickers in some of the grid sections; then project the grid onto the board. Explain to students that some maps use this format and coordinates are used in order to read them. Then name an image on the grid. Show students how to track the letter and number from the image to find its coordinates. After having students name the coordinates of other images, reverse the task, giving students the coordinates and having them name the images found there. **For a follow-up activity**, give each child a grid and have him label the coordinates. Then provide a series of coordinates and instructions, such as those shown, and have each student complete the tasks on his grid.

Go to A1. Write your initials.
Go to B5. Color the square your favorite color.
Go to E3. Draw a happy face if you like to sing. Draw an unhappy face if you do not.
Go to C2. Write the abbreviation for the month when you were born.
Go to D4. Draw a star if you would travel to outer space. Draw an arrow if you would rather stay on Earth.

Turn to page 162 for a **practice page** on reading a grid map.

# Errands Under the Sea

Write the location of each place on Goldie's list.
Use the grid.

## To Do Today!

1. Return overdue books to Sunken Treasure Library. _____
2. Go for a ride at the Seahorse Ranch. _____
3. Eat lunch at Crabby Café. _____
4. Get groceries at Fish and More Foods. _____
5. Take out some cash from Sand Dollar Bank. _____
6. Have a laugh at Clownfish Comedy Club. _____
7. Visit Great Aunt Nessie at the Nurse Shark Hospital. _____
8. Get Grandma's pearl necklace fixed at Shell Jewelry. _____
9. Pick up some new plants at Stu's Seaweed Nursery. _____
10. Go to Oli Octopus Inc. to meet my new handyman. _____

| | A | B | C | D | E | |
|---|---|---|---|---|---|---|
| **1** | | bank | | grocery | | **1** |
| **2** | | | jewelry | | café | **2** |
| **3** | ranch | | | | | **3** |
| **4** | nursery | | | library | | **4** |
| **5** | handyman | | comedy club | | hospital | **5** |
| | A | B | C | D | E | |

**Bonus:** The gym where Goldie works out is missing from the grid.
Draw it on an open grid space. Then write its location.

# LEARNING CENTERS

# Learning Centers

## Building Meaning
**Compound words (L.2.4d)**

Materials:
list of compound words
unlined paper
scissors
crayons

A student folds a sheet of paper in half and then cuts three slits through the top layer to make flaps. The child chooses a word from the list and then writes the first part of the word on the left flap. He lifts the flap, writes the word again, and draws a picture. Next, the child draws a plus sign and writes the second part of the word on the middle flap. Then he lifts the flap, writes the word again, and draws a matching picture. On the right flap, the student draws an equal sign and writes the whole compound word. He lifts the flap and illustrates the meaning of the compound word.

Stacy Schriever
Prairie Lincoln Elementary
Columbus, OH

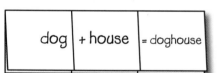

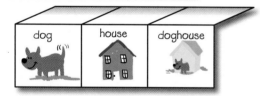

### Compound Words

| | | |
|---|---|---|
| airplane | bedroom | caveman |
| doghouse | earthworm | flagpole |
| grasshopper | hilltop | inchworm |
| jellyfish | keyhole | lunchbox |
| moonbeam | notebook | overflow |
| ponytail | rattlesnake | sandpaper |
| toothbrush | upstream | wheelchair |

## Go on Safari
**Parts of speech (L.3.1a)**

Materials:
student copies of page 176
reading material (such as a book or textbook)

To prepare, program a copy of page 176 with page numbers from the reading material you will provide. (Use a pencil to number pages that are unmarked in the reading material.) Then make student copies of the recording sheet. A child uses the book to complete each task. For a fun twist, select reading material based on animals.

Andrea O'Donnell
Pittsburgh Urban Christian School
Pittsburgh, PA

## Words to Grow On
### Vocabulary (RF.2.3; RF.3.3c)

**Materials:**
copy of page 177
current story or text
plastic page protector
overhead pen
wet wipe (eraser)

In advance, program a copy of page 177 with five current vocabulary words and two or more cloze sentences that, when completed, use the words. Then place the sheet in a plastic page protector. A child completes the page as directed, referring to the current story or text as needed. When he's finished, he clears the page protector for the next student.

Kristin Priola
Hickory Day School
Hickory, NC

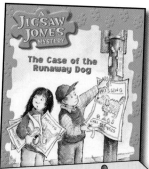

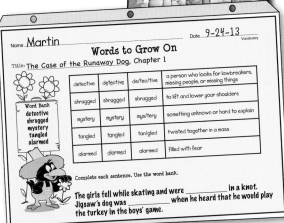

## Dear Teacher,...
### Writing (L.2.2b; W.2; W.3)

**Materials:**
large mailing envelope
letter-writing paper

A student writes a letter to you in narrative form or as an informational piece, detailing an important event that has recently happened. After she writes her letter, she folds it in half and places it inside the envelope. For students who want to share but need prompting, write one of the questions or prompts from below on a paper strip and include it with the center materials.

Cheryl Rayl
Mayville Elementary
Mayville, MI

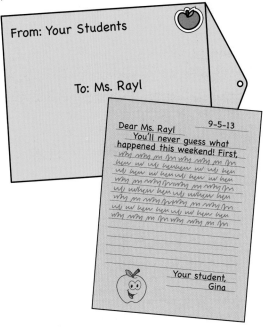

Tell me about something you learned yesterday.
Write a story about something that happened over the weekend.
What is your big news?
How will you spend your [holiday] vacation?

## Here, Fishy, Fishy!
### Missing addends

Materials:
copy of the direction and sum cards from page 178, cut apart
copy of the addend cards from page 179, cut apart
sentence strip, labeled as shown (mat)
calculator

For this partner center, students place the addend cards facedown in rows of four. Then they stack the sum cards facedown. Students follow the directions on the direction card, playing as time allows or until cards are unavailable to play.

adapted from an idea by Amanda Koth, Linden, VA

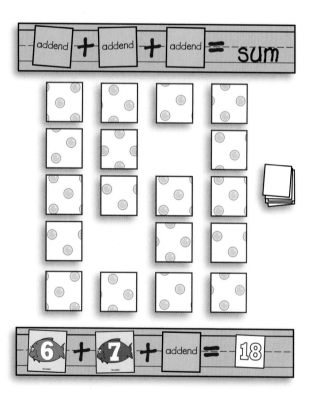

Use this center to prepare students for word problems with unknown numbers (2.OA.A.1).

## Math Matchup
### Graphs and line plots (3.MD.B.3, 4)

Materials:
copy of page 180, cards cut apart

A student studies the data on each card and determines which pairs of cards represent the same information. He writes the letter and number pairs on his paper. Then he chooses a graph or line plot, draws a star next to its pairing, and writes observations about the data.

**To vary the center,** remove the graphs and line plots. Direct the student to create a graph or line plot for each set of data. Or, as another option, remove the cards that list only data. Have the child write and answer questions about each graph and line plot.

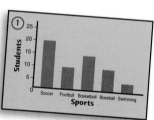

Jay
A. 3
B. 4
C. 1 ⭐
D. 2

From this graph, I know that five students chose soccer as their favorite sport. Basketball was the sport chosen the most, while football was chosen the least. There were 60 students involved with this data.

## Setting the Scene
**Narrative writing (W.2.3; W.3.3)**

Materials:
magazine pictures
glue
crayons

A student chooses two pictures she wants to incorporate into a story and glues them to the top of her paper. Next, she draws additional pictures to represent story elements not represented in the pictures. The child uses the pictures to write a story that addresses the five Ws.

To provide practice with other types of writing, put two pictures in each of a supply of bags. Also put in each bag a slip of paper with a type of writing (personal story, make-believe story, opinion, explanation). A child chooses a bag, glues the images and paper slip to her paper, and completes the writing task.

Kristin Priola, Hickory Day School, Hickory, NC, and Mary Davis, Keokuk Christian Academy, Keokuk, IA

Rex was so happy to be at the park. He played basketball with his friend Eric. He ran from place to place. Just when he thought his day couldn't get any better.

## Wanted!
**Past-tense irregular verbs (L.2.1d)**

Materials:
list of irregular verbs like the one shown
drawing paper
crayons

A child makes a "Wanted!" poster by titling his paper as shown and then drawing in the top half a simple picture of a story character or a seasonal mascot, such as a trick-or-treater; a turkey; or, later in the year, Santa Claus or Cupid. Then the child chooses three or more words from the list. He changes the words to the past tense as he writes sentences that tell what the character did that made her wanted by the authorities. (Remind students that the character could be sought after to reward her for good behavior, not just negative behavior.) After proofreading his sentences, the student underlines each irregular verb with a crayon.

| Irregular Verbs | | |
|---|---|---|
| become | give | make |
| break | hide | ride |
| feel | keep | see |
| find | know | throw |
| forget | lose | |

WANTED!
Monster Max

Max made little kids cry on Halloween night.
He rode up and down the street on his bike, roaring at the trick-or-treaters.
He found a bag of candy and kept it for himself.
If you see Monster Max, call 555-MEAN.

# Learning Centers

## In My Opinion

**Introduction and conclusion statements (W.2.1; W.3.1a, d)**

**Materials:**
copy of the sentence strips from page 181, cut apart

A child reads the sentences and matches each introductory sentence with its conclusion. If desired, have the student choose a pair of sentences and use them to write a complete paragraph. **As an alternative,** go online to get introductory sentence strips and fill-in-the-blank conclusion strips. A child cuts apart the strips, completes a conclusion for each introduction, and then glues the matching pairs to his paper.

adapted from an idea by Cheryl Rayl, Mayville Elementary, Mayville, MI

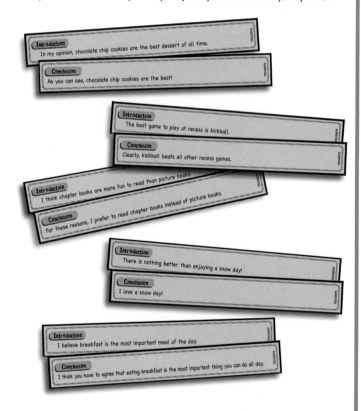

## Roll, Read, and Write

**Vocabulary (L.2.3; L.3.3)**

**Materials:**
word list like the one shown
2 dice

To prepare this center, make a numbered list of 12 words, such as seasonal words, recent vocabulary words, or—as an extra challenge—words that require students to use their dictionary skills. Set out the list with two dice. A student rolls the dice and copies onto her paper the word next to the corresponding number. She repeats this two or more times, until she has three different words listed. Then the student uses the words rolled in a series of sentences or in a story.

adapted from an idea by Cynthia Holcomb, San Angelo, TX

# Math in a Flash
**Fluently add (2.OA.B.2)**

**Materials:**
three-color paint chips, labeled as described below

In advance, make a supply of cards by labeling the top two strips of a paint chip with related facts. Then write the sum on the bottom strip and fold the bottom strip behind the paint chip. A student selects a paint chip, reads the related problem, and names the sum. Then he flips the bottom strip down to check his answer. **To make this a paper-pencil task,** write a different letter on each strip. After the child selects a strip, he writes the letter and writes the sum before checking his work.

Cheryl Lauer-Sciacca
Holtsville, NY

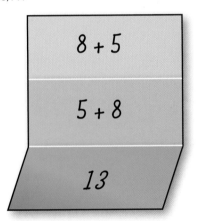

# Parking Lot Products
**Multiplication (3.OA.C.7)**

**Materials:**
car patterns from page 182, copied on two different-colored papers and cut out
11" x 17" poster board
permanent marker
multiplication flash cards

To prepare this center game for three, use the marker to draw a parking lot on the poster board. Label two spaces "No Parking" and each of the other spaces with a different number (product) from 0 to 100. Set out the parking lot, cars, and flash cards.

To play, one student serves as the caller. Each of the other two students chooses a set of cars and places one car at the parking lot entrance. The caller reads a problem. If the product is on the parking lot, players "drive" their cars to the corresponding parking space. The first child to reach the space gets to keep her car there while the other player must return his car to the entrance. If the product is not on the parking lot, the players move their cars to the "no parking" spaces. (After play begins, more than one car may be parked here.) To continue play, each player places a car at the entrance and the game continues until all the spaces are filled. The student with more parked cars in the numbered spaces at the end of play wins.

Heather Aulisio, Tobyhanna Elementary Center, Pocono Pines, PA

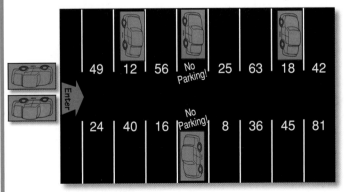

*tip* ➔ Set out toy cars in two different colors instead of using the car patterns.

## "Frooty" Fun

**Spelling-sound correspondence (RF.2.3b)**

Materials:
colored ring cereal
glue

A student makes as many *oo* words as he can, gluing ring cereal in place of the vowel team. If desired, a child includes a key that shows which cereal color(s) he used to represent the long *oo* sound and which he used to represent the short *oo* sound.

Amy Stokes, Lebanon Road Elementary, Charlotte, NC

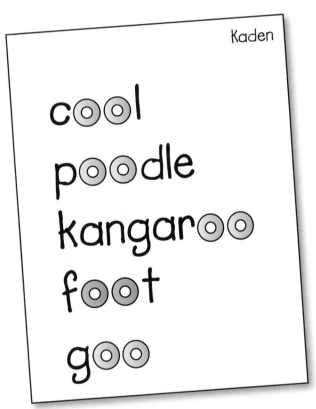

## The Magic Touch

**Handwriting**

Materials:
resealable plastic bags filled with tempera paint so they're almost full
alphabet strip
pencil

Using the eraser end of a pencil or her finger, a child refers to the alphabet strip and copies the letter formation in the paint. She squishes the bag to clear the letter and forms a different letter on the smooth surface. **To vary the center,** set out a list of spelling words. The child spells each word across the top of the bag.

Heather Aulisio, Tobyhanna Elementary Center, Pocono Pines, PA

*tip* → Double-bag the paint to avoid messes.

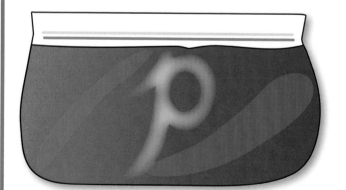

# Go Down the Line
**Measuring length (2.MD.A.1)**

**Materials:**
long piece of bulletin board paper
ruler
die
2 different-color markers

To complete this activity for two, each student chooses a marker. Player 1 rolls the die and uses the number rolled to draw a line in inches. He marks the end of the line with a dot and labels his line. Player 2 takes a turn in the same manner. Students continue rolling the die and extending their lines for ten rolls. The child with the longer line wins. **To vary the activity,** have students measure their lines with centimeters.

Heather Aulisio, Tobyhanna Elementary Center, Pocono Pines, PA

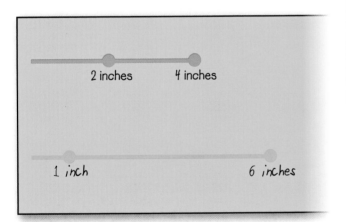

# All Shapes and Sizes
**Understanding fractions (3.NF.A.1)**

**Materials:**
student copies of the recording sheet from page 183
2 each of die-cut circles, squares, and rectangles
paper bag

In advance, divide one of each type of shape into halves and the other into thirds. Place all six shapes in the same bag. A child takes a shape from the bag and draws it four times on her recording sheet. If the shape can be partitioned into the amount shown, she draws the lines and shades one section. Then she writes the corresponding fraction. If the shape cannot be partitioned into the amount shown, she draws an X atop the shape. Then she answers the question at the bottom of the recording sheet.

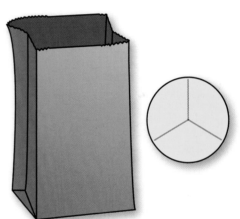

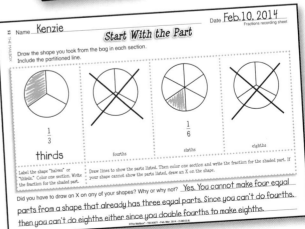

# Learning Centers

## Top-Ten List
### Capitalizing geographic names (L.2.2a)

**Materials:**
maps and atlases
fine-tip markers or colored pens

A student numbers a sheet of paper from 1 to 10. He uses the maps and atlases to write a top-ten list of interesting places. Then the child traces each capital letter with a marker or pen. **For a fun alternative**, put out a current Candy Land gameboard. Have each student rewrite ten of the locations and characters with correct capitalization.

adapted from an idea by Andrea O'Donnell, Pittsburgh Urban Christian School, Pittsburgh, PA

Tamer

1. Washington, DC
2. Mesa Verde National Park
3. Hawaii
4. Mexico
5. Ocean City, Maryland
6. Niagara Falls
7. Mount McKinley
8. Australia
9. Great Wall of China
10. Grand Canyon

## What's in a Name?
### Writing: informative (W.2.2; W.3.2)

**Materials:**
alphabet stampers
ink pad

A child stamps down the left side of her paper the letters of her name, a character's name from a recently read story, or a current topic studied. Then she writes facts about herself, the character, or the topic, using the letter stamped to start each description.

Christine Vohs, Olathe, KS

**S** weet and silly

**T** alkative but respectful

**A** lways ready to sing!

**R** eally into science and math

# Four to Explore
## Vocabulary (L.2.4; L.3.4)

**Materials:**
student copies of page 184
dictionary or access to online references

A child lists on his paper four words based on a personal interest, such as a sport or an activity. Then he completes the tasks, referring to the dictionary or online references as needed.

Barbara Duran, Dorris Jones Elementary, Rockwall, TX

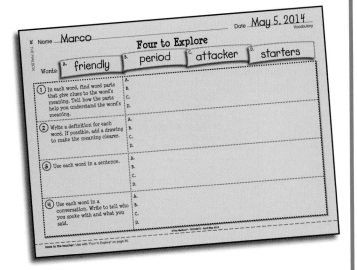

 Help indecisive students by leaving a list of suggested words at the center.

# Double Duty
## Spelling, multiplication (3.OA.C.7)

**Materials:**
student copies of page 185
10 current spelling or vocabulary words
2 dice

A student rolls the dice. If she rolls a number between 2 and 10, she writes it on a copy of page 41. If she rolls 11 or 12, she rolls again. Then the child copies each word from the list onto her paper. Then she counts the letters in each word and writes an equation using that number and the number rolled.

adapted from an idea by Debbie Vandrew, Porter Elementary, Paintsville, KY

Name Cora    Date April 8, 2014
Spelling, multiplication

### Two Times the Practice
Roll. Write.

X 4

| Word | Equation |
|------|----------|
| hurried | 4 x 7 = 28 |
| talked | 4 x 6 = 24 |
| settled | 4 x 7 = 28 |
| swimming | 4 x 8 = 32 |
| trying | 4 x 6 = 24 |
| liked | 4 x 5 = 20 |
| exploring | 4 x 9 = 36 |
| dyed | 4 x 4 = 16 |
| | |
| | |

## Take Another Look
**Alphabetical order**

**Materials:**
tagboard copy of page 186

In advance, cut the tagboard into ten strips. As you cut, program a word on the back of each strip, writing the words in alphabetical order from the top strip to the bottom. Store the strips in an envelope.

A child removes the strips and orders them so the words are in alphabetical order. To check his work, he turns over one strip at a time. If the words are correctly ordered, the complete picture will appear.

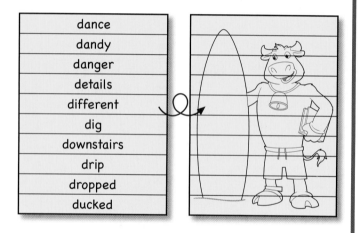

| |
|---|
| dance |
| dandy |
| danger |
| details |
| different |
| dig |
| downstairs |
| drip |
| dropped |
| ducked |

## Luck of the Draw
**Word relationships (L.2.5; L.3.5)**

**Materials:**
copy of the task cards on page 187, cut apart
playing cards, one of each numbered 2–9
dictionary (optional)

A student stacks each set of cards facedown and then takes the top card off each stack. Next, the child writes on her paper the letter from the task card and the number from the playing card. She uses the number on the playing card to determine her task and writes her responses on her paper. Then the student sets the cards aside and takes the next pair. She continues in this manner as time allows. If desired, direct the child to use the dictionary to clarify the meaning of the boldfaced words on the cards.

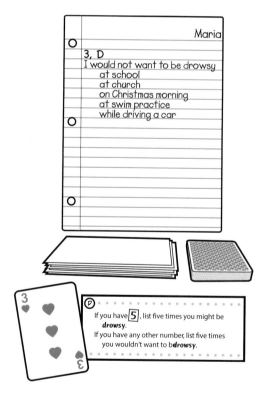

Maria

3, D
I would not want to be drowsy
   at school
   at church
   on Christmas morning
   at swim practice
   while driving a car

If you have 5, list five times you might be **drowsy**.
If you have any other number, list five times you wouldn't want to be **drowsy**.

## Time Out
**Time to five minutes (2.MD.C.7)**

**Materials:**
craft sticks
container
manipulative clock

To prepare this center for two, label each of a supply of craft sticks with times to five minutes. Also label four craft sticks with "Time Out." Put the sticks writing-side down in a container.

To start, Player 1 takes a stick from the container and reads the time. She manipulates the clock hands to show the matching time. If her partner agrees that the clock shows the correct time, she keeps the stick. If the time shown is incorrect, she puts the stick back in the container. If she selects a "Time Out" stick, she returns all her sticks to the container. Students alternate play. The child with more sticks wins.

Marie Tomkewitz, Sinclair Elementary, San Antonio, TX

## Which Way to Go?
**Division (3.OA.C.7)**

**Materials:**
10 or more division flash cards
paper circles labeled as shown
yellow-and-red counter

A child stacks the flash cards problem-side up in two equal piles; then she places a paper circle in front of each pile. She tosses the counter and draws a flash card from the corresponding pile (yellow or red). She writes the problem and answer on her paper; then she flips the card over to check her work. If her answer is correct, she makes a check on her paper and awards herself a point. If her answer is incorrect, she circles the answer and writes the correct quotient next to it. After she plays all the flash cards, the child totals her score. She repeats the activity as time allows, trying to improve her score with each round.

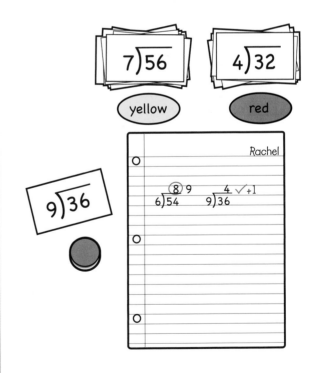

Find more center activities on pages 188–192. Then turn to pages 193–204 for activity cards.

# Word Safari

Title: _____

**①** Go to page _____. Write four nouns from this page. Tell what all these nouns have in common.

**②** Go to page _____. Write three verbs from this page. Circle the regular verbs. Underline the irregular verbs.

**③** Go to page _____. Write two pronouns from this page. Tell who or what each pronoun is replacing.

**④** Go to page _____. Write two adjectives from this page. Tell who or what each adjective is describing.

**Note to the teacher:** Use with "Go on Safari" on page 164.

# Words to Grow On

Title: _____

| Write the word. | Underline the vowels. | Draw lines to show syllables. | Write the meaning. |
|---|---|---|---|
| | | | |
| | | | |
| | | | |
| | | | |

Complete each sentence. Use the word bank.

**Word Bank**

©The Mailbox® • TEC43068 • Aug./Sept. 2013

**Note to the teacher:** Use with "Words to Grow On" on page 165.

# Here, Fishy, Fishy!

## Directions for two players:

1. When it's your turn, take a sum card and place it at the end of the mat.

2. Turn over two addend cards, and put them on your mat.

3. Say the missing addend that makes the equation true. If it is impossible to make the equation true, your turn ends.

4. Have your partner check your answer on the calculator.
   If it is correct, keep the addend cards and put the sum card in a discard pile.
   If it is incorrect, return the addend cards to the rows and put the sum card in a discard pile.

5. Play until there are no more addend or sum cards left. The player with more addend cards wins.

TEC43069

| 12 | 14 | 16 | 18 | 20 |
|----|----|----|----|----|
| 12 | 14 | 16 | 18 | 20 |
| 11 | 13 | 15 | 17 | 19 |
| 11 | 13 | 15 | 17 | 19 |

TEC43069 (on each card)

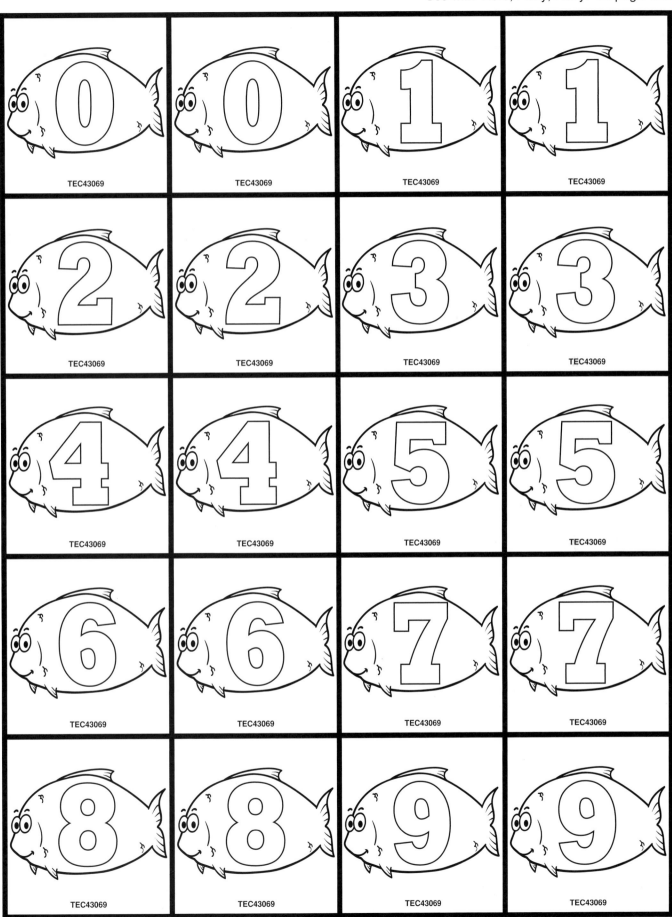

# Data and Graph Cards

Use with "Math Matchup" on page 166.

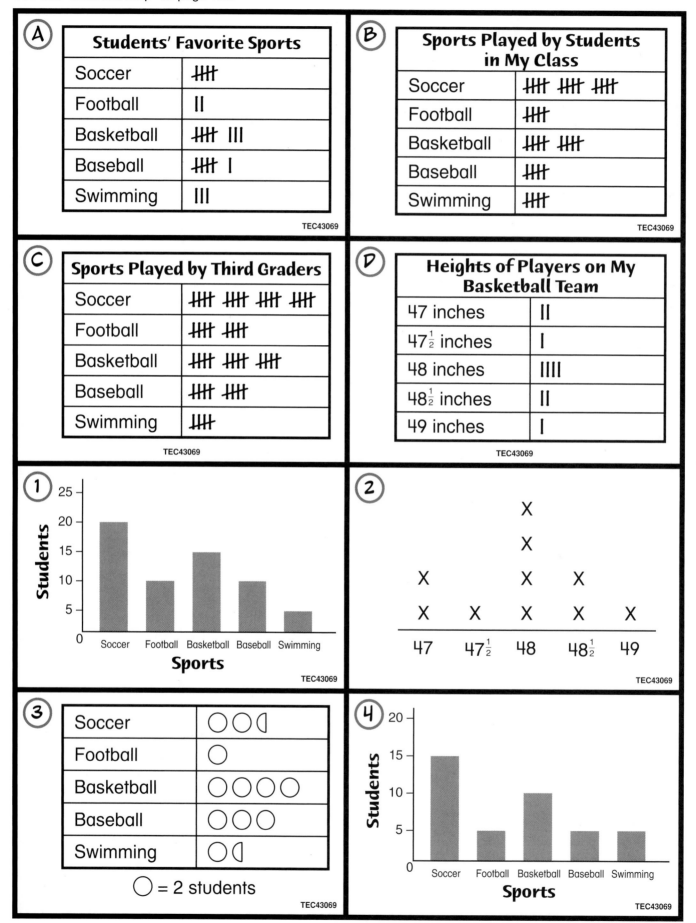

**A — Students' Favorite Sports**

| Soccer | IIII |
| Football | II |
| Basketball | IIII III |
| Baseball | IIII I |
| Swimming | III |

TEC43069

**B — Sports Played by Students in My Class**

| Soccer | IIII IIII IIII |
| Football | IIII |
| Basketball | IIII IIII |
| Baseball | IIII |
| Swimming | IIII |

TEC43069

**C — Sports Played by Third Graders**

| Soccer | IIII IIII IIII IIII |
| Football | IIII IIII |
| Basketball | IIII IIII IIII |
| Baseball | IIII IIII |
| Swimming | IIII |

TEC43069

**D — Heights of Players on My Basketball Team**

| 47 inches | II |
| $47\frac{1}{2}$ inches | I |
| 48 inches | IIII |
| $48\frac{1}{2}$ inches | II |
| 49 inches | I |

TEC43069

**1** — Bar graph: Students vs. Sports
(Soccer 20, Football 10, Basketball 15, Baseball 10, Swimming 5)

TEC43069

**2** — Line plot with X's over 47, $47\frac{1}{2}$, 48, $48\frac{1}{2}$, 49

TEC43069

**3** — Pictograph

| Soccer | ◯◯◖ |
| Football | ◯ |
| Basketball | ◯◯◯◯ |
| Baseball | ◯◯◯ |
| Swimming | ◯◖ |

◯ = 2 students

TEC43069

**4** — Bar graph: Students vs. Sports
(Soccer 15, Football 5, Basketball 10, Baseball 5, Swimming 5)

TEC43069

Use with "In My Opinion" on page 168.

**Introduction**

In my opinion, chocolate chip cookies are the best dessert of all time. TEC43070

**Introduction**

The best game to play at recess is kickball. TEC43070

**Introduction**

I think chapter books are more fun to read than picture books. TEC43070

**Introduction**

There is nothing better than enjoying a snow day! TEC43070

**Introduction**

I believe breakfast is the most important meal of the day. TEC43070

**Conclusion**

As you can see, chocolate chip cookies are the best! TEC43070

**Conclusion**

Clearly, kickball beats all other recess games. TEC43070

**Conclusion**

For these reasons, I prefer to read chapter books instead of picture books. TEC43070

**Conclusion**

I love a snow day! TEC43070

**Conclusion**

I think you have to agree that eating breakfast is the most important thing you can do all day. TEC43070

# Car Patterns

Use with "Parking Lot Products" on page 169.

# Start With the Part

Draw the shape you took from the bag in each section.
Include the partitioned line.

| | | |
|---|---|---|
| | | |

fourths | sixths | eighths

Label the shape "halves" or "thirds." Color one section. Write the fraction for the shaded part.

Draw lines to show the parts listed. Then color one section and write the fraction for the shaded part. If your shape cannot show the parts listed, draw an X on the shape.

Did you have to draw an X on any of your shapes? Why or why not? _____

©The Mailbox® • TEC43071 • Feb./Mar. 2014 • (3.MD.D.8)

**Note to the teacher:** Use with "All Shapes and Sizes" on page 171.

Name _____ Date _____

# Four to Explore

A. _____  B. _____  C. _____  D. _____

Words:

| | |
|---|---|
| **1** In each word, find word parts that give clues to the word's meaning. Tell how the parts help you understand the word's meaning. | A.<br>B.<br>C.<br>D. |
| **2** Write a definition for each word. If possible, add a drawing to make the meaning clearer. | A.<br>B.<br>C.<br>D. |
| **3** Use each word in a sentence. | A.<br>B.<br>C.<br>D. |
| **4** Use all four words in a conversation. Write to tell who you spoke with and what you said. | A.<br>B.<br>C.<br>D. |

©The Mailbox® · TEC43072 · April/May 2014

**Note to the teacher:** Use with "Four to Explore" on page 173.

Name _____  Date _____

Spelling, multiplication

# Two Times the Practice

Roll. Write.

X _____

| Word | Equation |
|------|----------|
|  |  |
|  |  |
|  |  |
|  |  |
|  |  |
|  |  |
|  |  |
|  |  |
|  |  |

# Surfer Pattern

Use with "Take Another Look" on page 174.

TEC43073

## Task Cards

Use with "Luck of the Draw" on page 174.

**A**

If you have **2**, list two places that make you feel ***cozy***.
If you have any other number, list two places that do not make you feel ***cozy***.

TEC43073

**B**

If you have **3**, list three places where it is okay to be ***noisy***.
If you have any other number, list three places where you should not be ***noisy***.

TEC43073

**C**

If you have **4**, list four people who are ***related*** to you.
If you have any other number, list four people who are not ***related*** to you.

TEC43073

**D**

If you have **5**, list five times you might be ***drowsy***.
If you have any other number, list five times you wouldn't want to be ***drowsy***.

TEC43073

**E**

If you have **6**, list six things that make you ***shiver***.
If you have any other number, list six things that do not make you ***shiver***.

TEC43073

**F**

If you have **7**, list seven animals that are ***fearsome***.
If you have any other number, list seven animals that are not ***fearsome***.

TEC43073

**G**

If you have **8**, list eight foods that are ***tasty***.
If you have any other number, list eight foods that are not ***tasty***.

TEC43073

**H**

If you have **9**, list nine book characters that are ***honest***.
If you have any other number, list nine people you know who are ***honest***.

TEC43073

# In the Word Lab
## Card 1

Write the word in each set that can be either a noun or a verb. Choose one word and write two sentences, using the word as a noun in one and a verb in the other.

TEC43073

# In the Word Lab
## Card 2

For each set, write the abstract noun. Then write another abstract noun that begins with the same letter. (Hint: An abstract noun names things like ideas, feelings, and concepts. You cannot see, hear, taste, smell, or touch it.)

TEC43073

# In the Word Lab
## Card 3

Write the word in each set that has a prefix. Circle each prefix and write a meaning for each word. Then write another word that has the same prefix as each circled prefix.

TEC43073

# In the Word Lab
## Card 4

Choose two sets of words. Write the six words in alphabetical order. Find each word in the dictionary and list the guide words found on the page.

TEC43073

**Learning Center** Copy this page; then cut apart the cards. Place a copy of the center mat on page 189 in a plastic page protector. Store the cards with the center mat.

# In the Word Lab

Choose a card.
Follow the directions.
Write your answers on a sheet of paper.

**A.**
impossible
loyalty
sock

**B.**
courage
preload
steps

**C.**
friendship
mislabel
watch

**D.**
dislike
stand
weakness

**E.**
beauty
uncork
water

# Claim the Names

Be the player who corrects and claims more squares.

**Materials:**
copy of page 191

### Directions for three students:

1. Decide who will play and who will judge. Write your name at the top of the gameboard.

2. Player 1 draws a line vertically or horizontally to connect two dots. Then Player 2 draws a line.

3. Players take turns drawing lines until one player boxes in a sentence. That player reads the sentence aloud and points out the word or words that should be capitalized.

4. If the judge agrees that the answer is correct, the player claims the space by writing his or her initials inside. Then that player takes another turn.

   If the judge disagrees with the answer, the other player can claim the box by giving the correct answer.

5. Players take turns until all the boxes have been claimed. The player who claims more boxes wins.

©The Mailbox® • TEC43071 • Feb./Mar. 2014 • (L.2.2a)

---

# Make a Match

Be the player who collects more pairs of matching cards.

**Materials:**
copy of the cards from page 192, cut apart
scrap paper

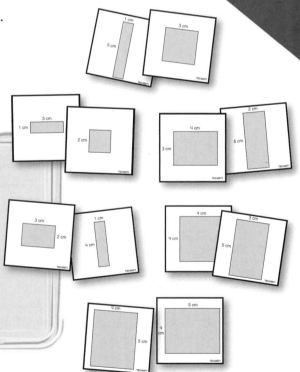

### Directions for two players:

1. Place the cards facedown in rows and columns.

2. When it's your turn, flip over two cards. Find the perimeter of each figure.

3. If the perimeters are equal, keep the cards. If not, flip the cards over.

4. Take turns until all the cards are played. The player with more cards wins.

©The Mailbox® • TEC43071 • Feb./Mar. 2014 • (3.MD.D.8)

---

**Center Games** Copy this page. Then cut apart the direction cards. Place each card in a separate plastic page protector with copies of the reproducible mentioned on the card.

Player 1_____ Player 2_____ Judge_____

I am ready for valentine's day!

I love sweetie's candy.

Have you been to ireland?

Gramps was excited to see the grand canyon.

Riley wore green on st. patrick's day.

Did the groundhog see its shadow on Groundhog day?

Dad is on a work trip in new York City.

I want a pair of Top speed brand sneakers.

Mom bought shiny Grin toothpaste.

It would be cool to go to mars.

I still have candy from halloween.

Do you play in oak Hill park?

When is flag Day?

Part of the pecos river is in Texas.

The largest continent is asia.

Will you buy me some tender care tissues?

My favorite food is cluck cluck chicken strips.

She was born in New jersey.

Last labor day, I went to the beach.

The pacific Ocean is so pretty.

**Note to the teacher:** Use with "Claim the Names" on page 190.

# Game Cards

Use with "Make a Match" on page 190.

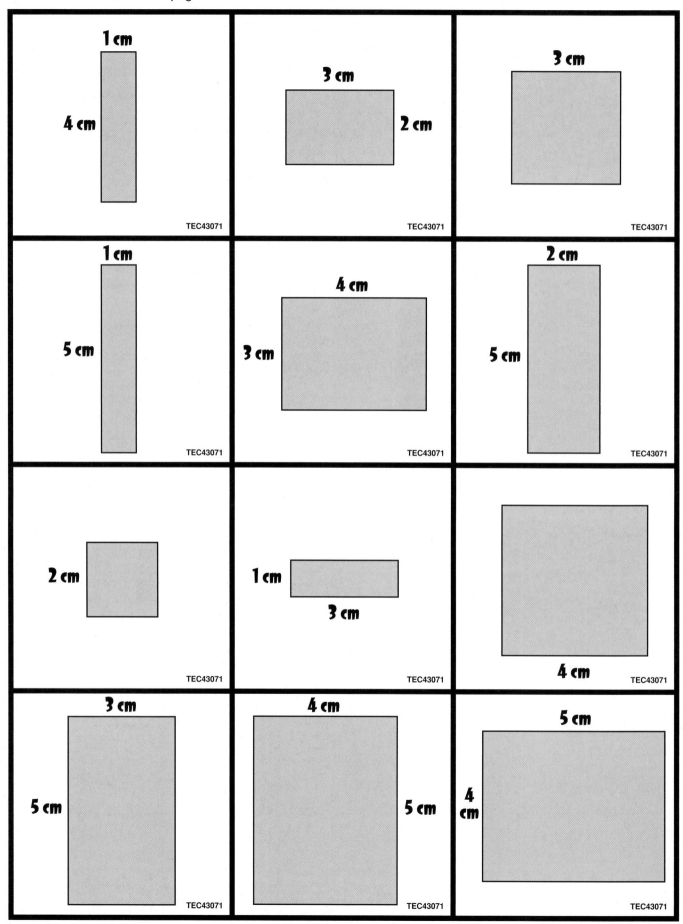

# Language Arts Activity Cards

**How to Use** Copy this page; then cut apart the cards. Use them as center or free-time activities.

Rearrange and expand simple sentences

# Good Times Ahead

Write two different sentences that each use all the words shown.

Then write another sentence with all the words shown plus new words.

**my** **over** **is**

**coming** **friend**

TEC43068 · (L.2.1f)

Write a narrative

# A Moment in Time

Write a story about an event that takes place in a short amount of time. (It can be true or make-believe.)
Use vivid details so the reader feels as if he or she is there for every second.

TEC43068 · (W.2.3)

Text features

# A Gigantic Home

Read the text.
Tell why a bold word is shown.
Then tell about other places you might see a bold word.

An ant is an insect. It lives in a nest. The nest has many **chambers**, or rooms. The queen ant has a chamber just for its eggs. Some chambers are for the young ants, and others store food.

TEC43068 · (RI.2.5)

Short and long vowels

# Word Chains

Make a chain of all the short-vowel words.
Make another chain of all the long-vowel words.
(Hint: Write the words from left to right and top to bottom.)

net
u
b

net      seem      big

gas      moan      nights      sleep

pail     laid      slip      plug

dream    gal       lips      mine

TEC43068 · (RF.2.3a)

# Language Arts Activity Cards

## Busy Words

Latin suffixes: -ation

The suffix -ation means "action or process."
Add -ation to each root word. (Hint: Drop the final e before adding the suffix.)
Then write the new word's meaning.

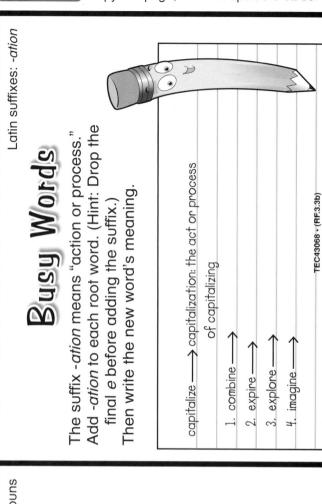

capitalize ———→ capitalization: the act or process of capitalizing

1. combine ———→
2. expire ———→
3. explore ———→
4. imagine ———→

TEC43068 • (RF.3.b)

## First Choice for Fun

Support an opinion

Choose an opinion and copy it.
Then write three reasons that support the opinion.

PE is always fun!

Nothing is better than spending time in the art room!

TEC43068 • (W.3.1b)

## My Family

Functions of nouns

Number your paper from 1–8.
If the **noun** is the subject of the sentence, write S.
If the **noun** answers who or what about the subject, write W.

1. My **mom** is a doctor.
2. My dad sells **cars**.
3. Grandpa ate **spinach** today.
4. Did you see my sister ride her **bike**?
5. My **brother** is loud.
6. Our **cousin** lives next door.
7. My cat bugs my **dog**.
8. My **dog** chews bones.

TEC43068 • (L.3.1a)

## Set to Sail

Use a dictionary

Copy Pirate Pete's travel supply list.
Use a dictionary to check his work.
Write the page number where each word is found.
Rewrite any misspelled words.

1. anker
2. biskits
3. compass
4. parrit
5. telescope
6. water

TEC43068 • (L.3.2g)

# Language Arts Activity Cards

**How to Use** Copy this page; then cut apart the cards. Use them as center or free-time activities.

---

Apostrophes in contractions

## Make New Words

Make contractions by matching words from the left with words from the right.
Write each contraction you make.

| | |
|---|---|
| not | is |
| is | they |
| are | we |
| will | do |
| | can |
| | was |
| | he |
| | she |

TEC43070 • (L.2.2c)

---

Common prefixes

## Break New Ground

Copy the tables.
Add the prefix to each base word.
Write the meaning of the new word.

| un can mean *not* | | |
|---|---|---|
| | unafraid | not afraid |
| afraid | | |
| checked | | |
| chewed | | |
| sent | | |

| re can mean *again* | |
|---|---|
| check | |
| freeze | |
| paint | |
| read | |

TEC43070 • (L.2.4b)

---

Text features: glossary

## Book It!

How are a glossary and a dictionary the same?
How are they different?

TEC43070 • (RI.2.5)

---

Reflexive pronouns

## People Placeholders

Divide your paper into four parts.
Choose four pronouns.
Use each pronoun in a different sentence.
Draw a matching picture.

I gave myself a pat on the back.

myself
yourself
himself
herself
themselves
ourselves

TEC43070 • (L.2.1c)

---

# Language Arts Activity Cards

**How to Use** Copy this page; then cut apart the cards. Use them as center or free-time activities.

Latin suffixes: -able, -ible

## On the Lookout

Copy the words that have the suffix *able* or *ible*.
Underline each suffix.

Fable
preventable
bible
resistible
sensible
agreeable
breakable
collectible
table
distractible
dribble
washable

TEC43070 • (RF.3.3b)

Words and uses

## Get Personal

Describe someone who is *friendly*.
Describe someone who is *helpful*.
Is a *friendly* person always *helpful*? Explain.

TEC43070 • (L.3.5b)

Text features: hyperlinks

## Use Your Noggin!

What is the hyperlink on this screen?
What happens when a reader clicks on a hyperlink?

The human brain is an amazing organ. It is your body's control center. It stores information and sends signals to other parts of your body. Your thoughts, moods, and emotions come from your brain. The brain, along with the spinal cord, are part of the body's **central nervous system**.

TEC43070 • (RI.3.5)

Punctuating dialogue

## A Little Mystery

Copy the story starter.
Add quotation marks to show what the characters say.
Then finish the story.

Sherlock Bones was very quiet. He looked closely at the evidence, snapped pictures, and took notes.
I will need just a little more time to gather these clues, Sherlock Bones said.
Is there anything I can do to help? the park ranger asked.

TEC43070 • (L.3.2c)

Collective nouns

# Grouped Together

Draw a picture to show each noun.
Tell what these nouns have in common.
Write two more nouns that could be in this group.

forest

family

team

TEC43072 • (L.2.1a)

Rearrange sentences

# The Old Switcheroo

For each sentence, change the order of the words to make a new sentence.

1. Whenever they get the chance, Gary and Harry play tricks on their friends!

2. These twins will exchange shirts and pretend to be the other.

3. Will Gary and Harry fool their friends again?

TEC43072 • (L.2.1f)

Closely related adjectives

# It's Your Choice

Tell your choices. Use a dictionary to help.
Then explain.

1. Would you rather it be *nippy* or *cold* outside?

2. Would you rather have a pet whose fur is *woolly, shaggy,* or *bristly*?

3. Would you rather eat a meal that is *warm* or *overheated*?

TEC43072 • (L.2.5b)

Apostrophes in possessives

# Explain the Rule

Why do some of the nouns in these sentences have an 's?

That boy's kite soars high in the sky.

My cat's tail is shorter than my dog's tail.

Your dress's sash is dragging on the ground.

TEC43072 • (L.2.2c)

# Language Arts Activity Cards

---

Capitalizing words in titles

## A Must-Read List

Add five book titles to the list.
Start each title with the last letter of the title above it.
Highlight each capital letter.

My Father's Dragon

No, David!

TEC43072 • (L.3.2a)

---

Latin suffixes: -ment

## Get to the Meaning

One meaning for *ment* is the act of doing something.
Add *ment* to each base word shown.
Write a meaning for each new word.

agree

equip

employ

move

pay

TEC43072 • (RF.3.3b)

---

Function of pronouns

## Rock On!

Copy each sentence.
Circle the pronoun.
Tell who or what each pronoun replaces.

1. Rita Rock Star thinks she has the best fans.
2. The fans come to Rita's shows in large numbers, and they get very loud!
3. The show is so good it often sells out.
4. My brother said he once waited in line for three days just to get a ticket!

TEC43072 • (L.3.1a)

---

Abstract nouns

## Senses Aside

Write the five abstract nouns from this list.
Then use each one in a different sentence.

You can't see, hear, touch, feel, or smell an abstract noun.

cackle        quicksand
kindness      growth
goodness      anger
rotation      lumber
luck          trousers

TEC43072 • (L.3.1c)

---

## Just for Giants

Number words

We fit giants from size ninety-two to one hundred ninety-five!

Write each shoe size in words.

A.  99

B.  107

C.  130

D.  165

E.  182

TEC43068 • (2.NBT.A.3)

## More Than One Way...

One-step word problem

Sally used numbers to solve this problem.

Mr. Segundo sold 13 copies of his new book at the bookstore. He signed 8 of the books. How many books were not signed?

$$13 - 8 = 5$$

Show how Sally could use pictures to solve the same problem.

Then use words to explain another way Sally could solve it.

TEC43068 • (2.OA.A.1)

## They're Worth How Much?

Place value

A.  How many ten rods are shown?

B.  Can you make 100 with these rods?

C.  What is the value of all the rods?

D.  Show another way to make this value, but use only 6 base ten blocks.

TEC43068 • (2.NBT.A.1)

## Tell Me About Your Day

Time (AM and PM)

Make a list of five things you do each school day. Write the time of each event. Include AM or PM.

I wake up at 7:00 AM.

AM times start just after midnight and last until noon.

PM times start just after noon and last until midnight.

TEC43068 • (2.MD.C.7)

# Math Activity Cards

## A Ballpark Estimate

Round to the nearest 100

Brody and Cody each think they have about 200 sports games in their collections. Brody actually has 184, and Cody has 149. Who has the correct estimate? How do you know? Explain.

TEC43068 • (3.NBT.A.1)

## Fair and Square

Partitioning shapes

Copy the squares and their labels.
Show equal parts.
Below each square, write the name for one of its parts.

halves

$\frac{1}{2}$

thirds

fourths

sixths

eighths

TEC43068 • (3.G.A.2)

## Seating Chart

Word problems involving arrays

Ms. Wright has 20 students. She wants to arrange their desks in equal rows. Show two different ways she could arrange the desks.

Use pictures, numbers, and words to show your work.

TEC43068 • (3.OA.A.3)

## Show-and-Tell

Estimate mass

A dollar bill weighs about 1 gram.
Draw and label another object that weighs about 1 gram.
Then draw and label an object that weighs about 10 grams.

1 gram

TEC43068 • (3.MD.A.2)

---

Expanded form

# Spreading Out

Write 3 three-digit numbers.

▶ Use your age as the hundreds digit in the first number.

▶ Use your age as the tens digit in the second number.

▶ Use your age as the ones digit in the third number.

Write each number in expanded form.

TEC43070 · (2.NBT.A.3)

---

Shapes and attributes

# A Shape Parade

For each shape, write the number of angles.
Then draw another shape with the same number of angles.

A.

B.

C.

D.

E.

TEC43070 · (2.G.A.1)

---

Add or subtract within 100

# Super Solver

George solved these two problems.

A.
$$\begin{array}{r} 48 \\ + 36 \\ \hline 14 \\ + 7 \\ \hline 84 \end{array}$$

B.
$$\begin{array}{r} 94 = 80 + 14 \\ - 26 = 20 + 6 \\ \hline = 60 + 8 = 68 \end{array}$$

Explain the steps George took to find each answer.
Then use pictures, numbers, or words to solve each
problem a different way.

TEC43070 · (2.NBT.B.5)

---

Estimating lengths

# What's Bigger?

Copy and complete each sentence.

1. If a paper clip is about 1 inch long, then a
   might be 3 inches long.

2. If a paper clip is about 1 inch long, then a
   might be 6 inches long.

3. If a paper clip is about 1 inch long, then a
   might be 12 inches (1 foot) long.

TEC43070 · (2.MD.A.3)

---

# Math Activity Cards

**How to Use**  Copy this page; then cut apart the cards. Use them as center or free-time activities.

---

Commutative property of multiplication

## Busy Bakers

Sugar and Spice each have a pan of cookies.

Sugar's pan has 6 rows with 7 cookies in each row.

Spice's pan has 7 rows with 6 cookies in each row.

Who has more cookies? How do you know?

TEC43070 • (3.OA.B.5)

---

Perimeter

## All the Way Around

Draw and label three different polygons each with a perimeter of 12 units.

*Perimeter is the distance around a figure. Add the side lengths to find the perimeter.*

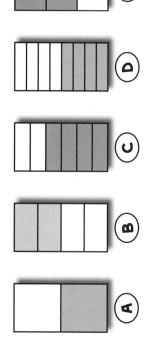

TEC43070 • (3.MD.D.8)

---

Multiplication

## Student Work Space

There are 8 groups of desks in Trey's class.

Each group has 4 desks.

How many desks are in Trey's class?

Solve.

Then write and solve another word problem where there are 8 groups of 4.

TEC43070 • (3.OA.A.1)

---

Equivalent fractions

## Proclaim the Same

Which fractions are equivalent? Write the letter sets. Then tell why the fractions are equivalent.

A    B    C    D    E

TEC43070 • (3.NF.A.3b)

---

How to Use  Copy this page; then cut apart the cards. Use them as center or free-time activities.

---

Partition and count

## Put in Parts

Reece partitioned this rectangle into 18 equal squares. Draw two more rectangles. Show two different ways to partition the rectangles into 18 squares.

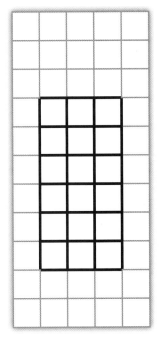

TEC43072 • (2.G.A.2)

---

Word problems: money

## Saving Up

Mac needs 95 cents to buy cheese. Write or draw three different ways he could make 95 cents.

A. Use only nickels and dimes.
B. Use pennies, nickels, and dimes.
C. Use nickels, dimes, and quarters.

TEC43072 • (2.MD.C.8)

---

Add within 1,000

## Show Your Strategy

Addie drew this picture to solve the problem.

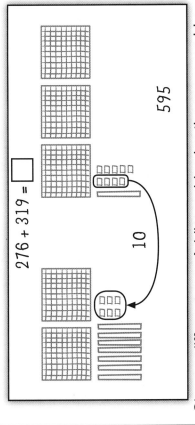

276 + 319 = ☐

595

10

Show a different way Addie could solve the same problem. Use words or numbers.

TEC43072 • (2.NBT.B.7)

---

Word problems: length

## Growing Up

To solve each problem, draw a picture. Then write a matching equation with a ☐ for the unknown number.

A. Sunny wants to grow as tall as her sister, Skye. Right now, Skye is 92 centimeters tall and Sunny is only 78 centimeters tall. How much more does Sunny need to grow to be as tall as her sister?

B. Bud has been busy growing. On Sunday, he was 35 centimeters tall. By the following Sunday, he was 52 centimeters tall. How much did Bud grow during the week?

TEC43072 • (2.MD.B.5)

---

# Math Activity Cards

**How to Use** Copy this page; then cut apart the cards. Use them as center or free-time activities.

---

## Card 1 (top-left)

Patterns (multiplication)

### What Makes a Dozen?

Find the product 12 on this portion of a multiplication table. Use the factors to complete the expression.

| ×  | 1 | 2  | 3  | 4  | 5  | 6  | 7  | 8  | 9  | 10 |
|----|---|----|----|----|----|----|----|----|----|----|
| 1  | 1 | 2  | 3  | 4  | 5  | 6  | 7  | 8  | 9  | 10 |
| 2  | 2 | 4  | 6  | 8  | 10 | 12 | 14 | 16 | 18 | 20 |
| 3  | 3 | 6  | 9  | 12 | 15 | 18 | 21 | 24 | 27 | 30 |
| 4  | 4 | 8  | 12 | 16 | 20 | 24 | 28 | 32 | 36 | 40 |
| 5  | 5 | 10 | 15 | 20 | 25 | 30 | 35 | 40 | 45 | 50 |
| 6  | 6 | 12 | 18 | 24 | 30 | 36 | 42 | 48 | 54 | 60 |

$12 = \underline{\quad} \times \underline{\quad}$

$\underline{\quad} = \underline{\quad} \times \underline{\quad}$

$\underline{\quad} = \underline{\quad} \times \underline{\quad}$

$\underline{\quad} = \underline{\quad} \times \underline{\quad}$

TEC43072 • (3.OA.D.9)

---

## Card 2 (top-right)

Area as additive

### It All Adds Up

José found the area of this shape. Look at his work and then explain what he did to get his answer.

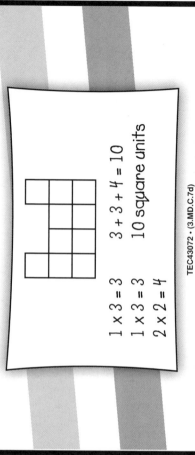

$1 \times 3 = 3$
$1 \times 3 = 3$
$2 \times 2 = 4$
$3 + 3 + 4 = 10$
10 square units

TEC43072 • (3.MD.C.7d)

---

## Card 3 (bottom-left)

Division as an unknown factor problem

### Involve the Inverse

For each problem, write a multiplication problem that can lead you to the answer. Then solve.

A. $56 \div 7 = \boxed{8}$,  $\boxed{8} \times 7 = 56$

B. $63 \div 9 = \square$

C. $45 \div 5 = \square$

D. $36 \div 4 = \square$

E. $40 \div 8 = \square$

TEC43072 • (3.OA.B.6)

---

## Card 4 (bottom-right)

Liquid volumes

### Too Much or Too Little?

If a liter holds about as much liquid as four cups, which of these containers hold more than a liter? Which containers hold less than a liter?

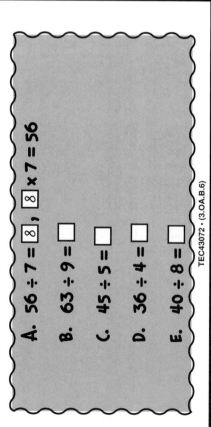

1 liter is about as much as

TEC43072 • (3.MD.A.2)

---

# CELEBRATE THE SEASON!

## 6 Fun Getting-Acquainted Ideas

### 1 Personal Info Prop

When students use this silly disguise, their getting-to-know-you jitters will be giggled away! First, tape a copy of the mustache pattern on page 208 to the end of an unsharpened pencil. Invite a student to hold the mustache to his face and say, "[Name], I 'mustache' you a question"; then have him ask a question to get to know you or a classmate better. Continue with other students. If desired, have each student create his own mustache prop to use during partner or small-group activities.

Colleen Dabney, Williamsburg, VA

> Ms. Dabney, I "mustache" you a question. How long have you been a teacher?

### 2 All Signs Point To...

Pria's Pier 1015 miles

The signs point to learning about student birthdays! To start, give each child a copy of a sign pattern on page 208 and have her write her name as part of a destination. Then guide her to use the digits of the month and day of her birthday to write the distance to the destination as a three- or four-digit number. For example, a September 1 birthday would be written "901" and a December 16 birthday would be written "1216." Provide time for the student to color and cut out her sign. Then have each child share her sign with the class. Order the signs by birthday to make a class signpost. Students get to share the dates of their special days, and you have a low-prep birthday display!

Amy Hart, Saint Sylvester School, Pittsburgh, PA

### 3 For One and All

With the help of a common game card, students are sure to have a good time learning about each other. Display a bingo card and review the numbers. Challenge each student to find numbers that represent himself, such as his house number, his age, the number of people in his family, or his bus number. In small groups, have each child share one of his number associations. If desired, have students write about their chosen numbers; then post the explanations and bingo card on a display titled "Numbers for One and All."

Nancy A. Franks, Indian Brook Elementary, Plymouth, MA

| B | I | N | G | O |
|---|---|---|---|---|
| 13 | 26 | 32 | 47 | 68 |
| 2 | 20 | 42 | 50 | 63 |
| 5 | 19 | Free  | 57 | 74 |
| 3 | 16 | 40 | 60 | 67 |
| 9 | 30 | 35 | 53 | 70 |

# 4

## At-a-Glance Preferences

These decorative index cards provide student information and more! To start, have each child use art supplies to decorate an index card with her name and her favorite things. Laminate the cards for durability and, if desired, attach a piece of yarn to each one. Have students wear their nametags until everyone is acquainted; then store the nametags in an accessible location. Later, have students wear their nametags so classroom visitors and substitutes can identify them, or remove nametags from the set to randomly call on students to answer questions and share ideas.

Heather Galindo, Harmony Science Academy, Brownsville, TX, and Jessyka Rafferty, Pittsburgh, PA

# 5

## Who's Just Like Them?

Instruct each student to stack three sheets of paper, fold them in half to make a booklet, and staple the papers along the fold. Next, give each child a copy of page 209 and have him color and complete the cover, cut it out, and glue it to the front of his booklet. Then have him complete each sentence, cut out the strips, and glue one to the top of each booklet page. Provide time for the student to compare his responses with his classmates and get the autographs of students whose answers match his.

Kelli L. Gowdy, High Point, NC

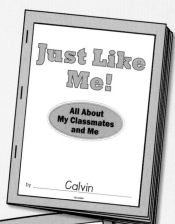

**tip** Make comparing responses a morning-work task. Each day, have students open their booklets to a designated sentence. Direct each child to sign the booklets that match his response.

This is a newspaper article about Taylor Quick. She is my favorite singer, and I love singing too!

My favorite animal is the ladybug, which is why I brought in this stuffed animal.

I chose this cookie cutter because I enjoy baking cookies.

# 6

## Me Times Three

To start these home-based projects, have each child decorate the outside of a paper lunch bag with her name. Then, at home, have her put inside the bag three small items that would help you and her classmates learn more about her. On an assigned day, have each child share her choices with the class and invite her classmates to ask questions as needed to clarify understanding. Not only will students be excited to share their personal items, but you can also start addressing your speaking and listening standards. (SL.2; SL.3)

Laura Jay, St. Stephen's School, Halifax, Nova Scotia, Canada

# Mustache Pattern
Use with "Personal Info Prop" on page 206.

# Sign Patterns
Use with "All Signs Point To…" on page 206.

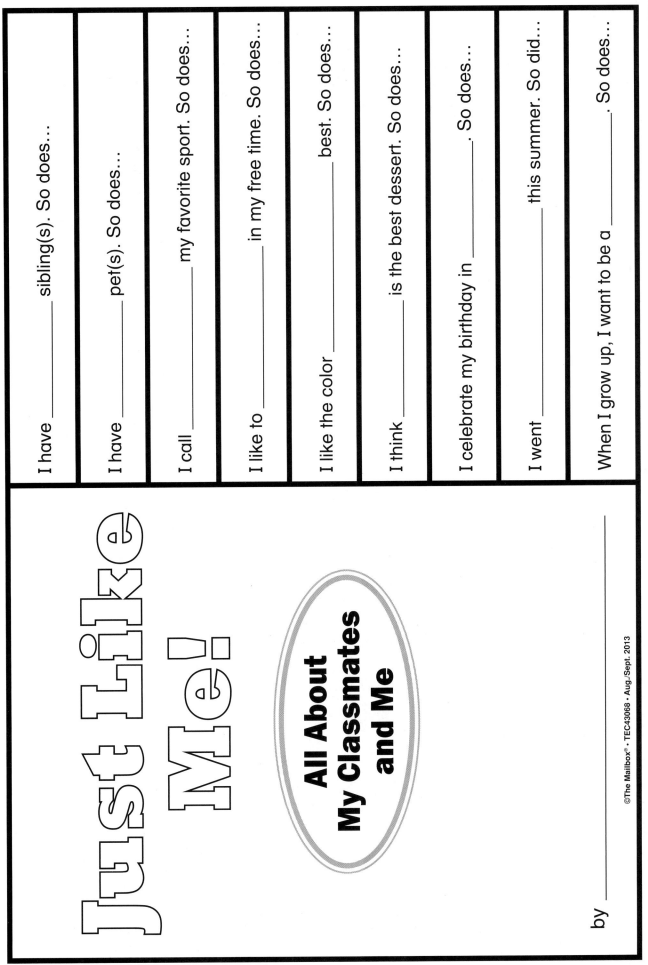

Just Like Me!

All About
My Classmates
and Me

by _____

I have _____ sibling(s). So does...

I have _____ pet(s). So does...

I call _____ my favorite sport. So does...

I like to _____ in my free time. So does...

I like the color _____ best. So does...

I think _____ is the best dessert. So does...

I celebrate my birthday in _____. So does...

I went _____ this summer. So did...

When I grow up, I want to be a _____. So does...

©The Mailbox® • TEC43068 • Aug./Sept. 2013

Note to the teacher: Use with "Who's Just Like Them?" on page 207.

# Celebrate the Season!

## Rake Them In
**Skill review (CCSS)**

**This teacher-led game is perfect for small-group review!**

**Set up:** Program a supply of leaf cutouts with review content, such as spelling words, math facts, or sight words. Place the leaves facedown in a pile in the center of the common workspace.

**Activity:** A student chooses a leaf and turns to the child on his right. He asks the child to spell the word or shows the child the fact to solve or the word to read. If she responds correctly, she rakes the leaf into her own pile. If her response is incorrect, the student on her right gets a chance to respond. Play continues in this manner as time allows; the player with the most leaves in his pile wins.

*Cheryl Rayl, Mayville Elementary, Mayville MI*

## In the Lab
**Interpret products or quotients (3.OA.A.1, 2)**

**Turn your classroom into a hands-on learning lab and give your young mad scientists a chance to experiment with numbers.**

**Set up:** Gather a variety of Halloween party favors—such as plastic bugs, rubber eyeballs, and spider rings—and place each set at a different location (station) in your room. Also place at each station a multiplication and division flash card. (Make sure you have enough party supplies to create the product and dividend.)

**Activity:** Student pairs visit each station. The students use the party supplies to model each problem, draw a matching picture on a sheet of paper, and write the resulting equation. **To provide practice with odd and even (2.OA.C.3),** write a different number from 1–20 on a supply of cards. Place one card at a station with a set of supplies. The students use the supplies to determine whether the number is odd or even, draw a matching picture, and label the picture with the correct term.

*adapted from an idea by Barbara Duran, Dorris Jones Elementary, Rockwall, TX*

## A Sweet Tooth
**Writing a narrative (W.2.3; W.3.3)**

You're sure to see students "goblin" up this fun activity, which is perfect for the Halloween season.

**Set up:** Give each child a candy corn and lead him to imagine that it is really a goblin's tooth.

**Activity:** The student writes a story about a goblin that includes events related to this tooth. Then he draws a corresponding picture that incorporates the candy corn.

*Heather Aulisio, Tobyhanna Elementary Center, Pocono Pines, PA*

 Turn to pages 213–216 to find activities just for Thanksgiving.

# Fire Prevention Week

Name _____

1. Fire experts say you should plan two ways out of every room. Why is this important?

2. In case of a fire, families should have a meeting place in front of their homes. What would be a good meeting place for your family? Give directions that tell how to get from your bedroom to this meeting place.

3. Pretend it's just a few days after your birthday. You smell smoke in your house. Before you safely exit your house, you grab your new birthday presents to take with you. Is this a good idea? Why or why not?

4. How can you and your family stay safe from fire while cooking in the kitchen?

5. What is "stop, drop, and roll"? When should you use it?

**How to Use** Give each child a copy of this page and have him write responses in his journal during Fire Prevention Week (the week in which October 9 falls). Provide time for students to share their writing aloud and use their ideas to lead a discussion of fire safety.

# Valuable Loot

**30¢**

**35¢**

**50¢**

**10¢**

**26¢**

**15¢**

**6¢**

**20¢**

**50¢**

**15¢**

**35¢**

**11¢**

**26¢**

**2¢**

## Directions for two players:

1. Cut off the key below. Choose a crayon.
2. When it's your turn, use the pencil and paper clip to spin the spinner two times.
3. Find the total value of the two spins.
4. Point to a candy with the matching value.
5. Have your partner check the key.

    If your answer is correct, color the candy.

    If it is incorrect or any matching candies are already colored, your turn ends.

6. The player with more colored candies wins.

©The Mailbox® • TEC43069 • Oct./Nov. 2013 • (2.MD.C.8)

## Valuable Loot

### Answer Key

2¢ = penny, penny

6¢ = penny, nickel

10¢ = nickel, nickel

11¢ = penny, dime

15¢ = nickel, dime

20¢ = dime, dime

26¢ = penny, quarter

30¢ = nickel, quarter

35¢ = dime, quarter

50¢ = quarter, quarter

TEC43069

**Partner Game** Give each pair of students a copy of this page, scissors, two different-color crayons, a paper clip, and a pencil.

Name _____  Date _____

# Turkey Dinners

Use the data to make a line plot.
Then answer the questions.

**Tom Turkey measured the lengths of 16 friends' dinner tables.**

**Table Lengths**

| | | | |
|---|---|---|---|
| 8 feet | 6 feet | 10 feet | 4 feet |
| 8 feet | 12 feet | 6 feet | 8 feet |
| 7 feet | 10 feet | 8 feet | 6 feet |
| 5 feet | 9 feet | 8 feet | 10 feet |

**Table Lengths**

0  1  2  3  4  5  6  7  8  9  10  11  12
(feet)

1. What is the longest table length measured? _____

2. What is the shortest table length measured? _____

3. Which table length is measured most? _____

4. How many tables are longer than 8 feet? _____

5. How many tables are less than 8 feet? _____

6. Which table lengths are not measured? _____

**Bonus:** Would the line plot look different if you measured and plotted each of your classmates' dinner table lengths instead? Explain.

# Gobble! Gobble! It's Turkey Time!

## Dig in!

Your students are sure to gobble up these Thanksgiving Day–themed activities!

## A Full Belly
**Key details in informational text (RI.3.2)**

Whether students are reading about turkeys or learning more about the Thanksgiving celebration of 1621, this decorative organizer makes identifying key points much more fun! Using a copy of page 216, a student defines key terms or describes key people on each of the feathers. Then he writes the title of the text on the turkey's belly and colors the turkey. **To extend the activity,** the child cuts out his turkey, glues it to a sheet of paper, and lists below it a summary of each key point found in the reading.

adapted from an idea by Renee Marie Plant, Liberty Elementary, Broken Arrow, OK

Thanksgiving with my family is quite an event. We have a lot of people in my family, so squeezing into my grandma's house is a challenge. The grown-ups sit at the dining room table while the kids eat on a card table in the kitchen. I often sit on a step stool instead of a chair, but I don't mind! We eat tons of yummy food! There's always turkey, gravy, and potatoes. We also have stuffing, green beans, and yams. It's a lot of work for my grandma to pull together, so I always remember to thank her at the end of our meal.

## My Family Feast
**Language skills (L.2; L.3)**

Take a peek into students' holiday traditions while reinforcing language skills. Invite each student to draw a picture of what a typical Thanksgiving Day with his family looks like. Encourage the child to use plenty of details. Next, have the student write a description of the picture. Then name a language skill—such as identifying reflexive pronouns, regular and irregular plural nouns, or conjunctions—and have each child highlight the examples of that skill that he used in his writing. If desired, bind the drawings and descriptions in a class book titled "Our Family Feasts."

adapted from an idea by Kelly Lu, Berlyn School, Ontario, CA

# "Tic-Tac-Turkey"
## Knowledge of language

To help students utilize seasonal vocabulary in their writing, draw a tic-tac-toe grid on the board. In each grid space, write a different seasonal word. When students write, instruct them to choose three words from a row, column, or along a diagonal and challenge them to use all three in their work.

Heather Aulisio, Tobyhanna Elementary Center, Pocono Pines, PA

| Pilgrim | thankful | feast |
|---|---|---|
| November | turkey | family |
| Native Americans | autumn | harvest |

# Preparing Plates
## Multiplication word problems (3.OA.A.3)

Serve each student a personalized helping of math practice. To start, each child draws on a paper plate a Thanksgiving Day meal that includes three different foods. Next, the student draws a table for each food, showing how many items would be needed to fill ten plates. Then she refers to each table to write and solve one word problem for each food.

Elizabeth Gaglio, Chamberlayne Elementary, Richmond, VA

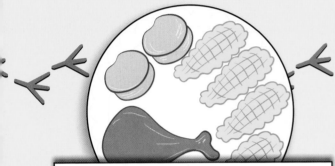

Audrey

| Plates | 1 | 2 | 3 | 4 | 5 | 6 | 7 | 8 | 9 | 10 |
|---|---|---|---|---|---|---|---|---|---|---|
| Rolls | 2 | 4 | 6 | 8 | 10 | 12 | 14 | 16 | 18 | 20 |

Each of Audrey's family members gets 2 rolls to eat during Thanksgiving Day dinner. If there are 7 people in Audrey's family, how many rolls will be needed? 2 x 7 = 14

tip → Have students cut images from store circulars and glue the cutouts on their plates instead of drawing.

# The Table Is Set!
## Measurement tools (2.MD.A.1)

Students will be thankful for this hands-on center! In advance, set a table with rectangular placemats, paper plates, candles, and a variety of fall foods, such as a squash, a pumpkin, and an ear of corn. For each item on the table, prepare a task card like the ones shown. Place the task cards on the table with a ruler, a measuring tape, and a yardstick. A child visiting the center reads each task card and writes his answer on a sheet of paper. If needed, the child can test each tool on the corresponding item.

1. What is the best tool to measure the length of the table?

2. What is the best tool to measure the length around the pumpkin?

3. What is the best tool to measure the length of the candle?

# Turkey Pattern

Use with "A Full Belly" on page 214 and "Welcome to Our Room!" on page 272.

TEC43069

# Celebrate the Season!

## Wrapped in Warm Feelings
### Perimeter and area (3.MD.C.7b; 3.MD.D.8)

**This dual-purpose activity has students thinking about math and the positive qualities of their classmates.**

**Setup:** Instruct each child to bring in a lidded shoebox. Gather gift tags and gift wrap. Copy 218 and put it in a plastic page protector. Set out the activity card with the materials listed on it.

**Activity:** A child follows the directions on the activity card. When he has completed the task, cut an opening in the top of his box. Direct the child to write his name on a gift tag and stick it on the top of his box. Set out the box where his classmates can easily access it. Invite each of his classmates to write a short note to the student, telling what she likes about him; then have her put it in the box. Later, have each child unwrap his box and read his notes.

Maureen Beyt, Countryside School, Champaign, IL

*tip* → The classroom community-building part of this idea works great for both 2nd and 3rd graders!

## Action on Every Page
### Simple verb tenses (L.3.1e)

| Past | Present | Future |
|---|---|---|
| signed | | |
| painted | | |
| called | | |
| answered | | |
| nipped | | |

**Use a holiday classic to familiarize students with verbs!**

**Setup:** Get a picture book version of *A Christmas Carol* by Charles Dickens.

**Activity:** Familiarize students with the story by reading *A Christmas Carol* aloud. Encourage students to listen for the verbs in the story. Next, place the book at a center. When a child visits the center, he draws a three-column chart like the one shown on a sheet of paper. As he reviews the book, he lists the simple verbs in the corresponding columns.

Tricia Davis, Mulberry Creek Elementary, Cataula, GA

## "Waddle" You Know?
### Shared research (W.2.7)

**Dive in and send students on a fact-finding mission!**

**Setup:** Post a list of penguin-related topics like the ones shown. Make copies of page 219.

**Activity:** Discuss what students know about penguins. Then instruct each student to choose a topic to research and sign her name below it. After research groups have formed, direct students to use reference materials to learn more about their chosen topic. Give each group a copy of page 219 and have them write their topic on the top line. Next, instruct students to write three facts in the numbered sections of their organizer and draw a picture, diagram, or map in the final section. Provide time for students to share their findings with the class; then bind the pages to make a class book.

Pat Twohey, Smithfield, RI

**Topics**
Kinds of Penguins
Body of a Penguin
Penguin Habitats
Penguins as Swimmers
Life Cycle of a Penguin

# It's a Wrap

**What You Need**
- lidded shoebox
- gift wrap
- index card
- tape
- ruler
- scissors

① Turn the box over so you are looking at the bottom face.

② On the index card, draw a picture of the shape you see.

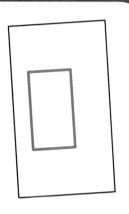

③ Measure the side lengths of the bottom face to the nearest inch.

④ Label the picture with the matching numbers.

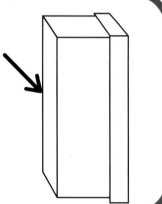

13    7    7    13

⑤ Write an equation to show the perimeter of the face.

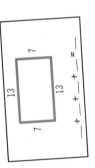

13    7    7    13

_ + _ + _ + _ = _

**Perimeter** is the distance around a figure.

⑥ Write an equation to show the area of the face. Use a calculator to solve.

13    7    7    13

_ x _ = _

**Area** is the number of square units needed to cover a figure.

⑦ Wrap the box. Tape the index card to the bottom of the box.

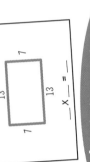

©The Mailbox® • TEC43070 • Dec./Jan. 2013–14 • (3.MD.C.7b; 3.MD.D.8)

**Note to the teacher:** Use with "Wrapped in Warm Feelings" on page 217.

# "Waddle" you know about

_____ ?

topic

① ② ③

by _____

**Note to the teacher:** Use with "'Waddle' You Know?" on page 217.

# Look at That Tree!

Write each addend in expanded form.
Add. Then color the ornament with the matching sum.

**A.** 25 → 20 + 5
32 → 30 + 2
+ 52 → 50 + 2
_____
100 + 9 = 109

**B.** 41 →
33 →
+ 45 →
_____

**C.** 31 →
45 →
+ 12 →
_____

**D.** 81 →
82 →
+ 23 →
_____

**E.** 50 →
33 →
+ 17 →
_____

**F.** 24 →
15 →
+ 41 →
_____

**G.** 64 →
20 →
+ 26 →
_____

**H.** 11 →
34 →
20 →
+ 24 →
_____

**I.** 25 →
32 →
32 →
+ 23 →
_____

**J.** 40 →
38 →
21 →
+ 19 →
_____

Tree ornaments: 80, 88, 89, 100, 118, 109, 112, 110, 119, 186

**Bonus:** Choose a problem.
Show another way to solve it.

©The Mailbox® · TEC43070 · Dec./Jan. 2013–14 · Key p. 312 · (2.NBT.B.6)

# Chinese New Year

_____
name

©The Mailbox® • TEC43070 • Dec./Jan. 2013–14

**3**

To get ready for Chinese New Year, many families clean their homes. Many members of a family get together to share a Chinese New Year dinner. The dinner might include foods like rice cakes, chicken dishes, and fruit.

---

Glue.

**2**

Chinese New Year can start between January 21 and February 20. This year, it starts on January 31. It marks the start of the year of the horse.

**1**

**A tradition** is a custom or belief that is passed along through a family. One tradition for many families from China is to celebrate Chinese New Year.

---

**5**

Some cities have parades for families to go to. Dancers perform. They wear brightly colored costumes. The costumes look like lions and dragons.

**4**

Children get money in red packets (envelopes). The money is to bring the children good luck.

---

**How to Use** Direct each child to cut out a copy of this page and glue the strips together. After reading the text and discussing the holiday, have the student accordion-fold the strip to make a booklet. Then he colors the cover and outlines the dragon's body on the other pages.

Player 1 _____  Player 2 _____

# Tearin' It Up
## Multiply within 100

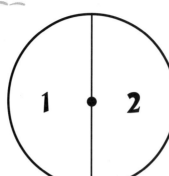

Start

Start

2 x 5 =

7 x 3 =

7 x 7 =

5 x 9 =

9 x 2 =

3 x 5 =

5 x 5 =

9
x 3

4
x 9

6
x 3

2
x 7

4
x 2

8 x 8 =

6 x 8 =

1
x 6

6 x 6 =

7
x 9

3 x 3 =

3
x 8

7 x 6 =

**Directions for two players:**

5 x 4 =

1. Choose a snowboarder. Put your marker on the first space of the path.

1 x 9 =

8 x 7 =

2. When it's your turn, solve the problem. Have your partner check your product with the calculator.

8 x 4 =

4 x 6 =

- If it is correct, write the product on the space. Use a paper clip and a pencil to spin the spinner. Move forward that number of spaces.

5 x 7 =

6 x 5 =

- If it is incorrect, keep your game marker in place.

2 x 6 =

8 x 5 =

3. Take turns until one player reaches "Finish" and wins!

4 x 7 =

**Finish**

**Finish**

**Partner Game** Make a copy of this page for each pair of students. Give the players two game markers, a paper clip, and a calculator.

# A Flurry of Writing Fun

With these winter-themed ideas, you're sure to inspire "brrrr-illiant" imagined narratives! (W.2.3; W.3.3)

*Heather Aulisio, Tobyhanna Elementary Center, Pocono Pines, PA*

 ## Shake Things Up

This idea is "snow" much fun! First, gather a variety of snow globes. (Plastic ones are often available at dollar stores.) Label each snow globe with a different number and put them at a center with student copies of page 225. A student chooses a snow globe. Then he imagines what life inside that snow globe would be like, naming a possible character who lives there and potential problems the character might face. Next, the child completes page 225. Then he uses his organizer to write a story.

 ## Dressed for Success

Use a simple Santa Claus prop to help students deliver some festive stories! First, cut three holes in a large sheet of poster paper, making one for a head and two for arms, as shown. Draw details around the holes so the prop resembles Santa. Next, snap a photo of each child wearing the prop. Print the photos and have each child attach her photo to the top of a sheet of paper. Lead the student to imagine she is Santa as she writes a story based on one of these prompts:

- Describe a problem that happened in the workshop just days before Christmas and how you solved it.
- Tell about the time you got stuck going down a chimney.
- Share your favorite tale of driving the sleigh on Christmas Eve.

Bind the completed stories in a class book titled "Tales From the North Pole." Then invite each child to slip into the Santa prop, hold the book, and read her story aloud. Ho! Ho! Ho!

*tip* Prepare a prop for Mrs. Claus, Baby New Year, or Father Time. Lead students to write a story from the character's point of view.

# From an Elf's Eyes and Ears

It'll be a busy day in Santa's writing workshop when you use this clever idea! First, have each child roll a sheet of red or green paper into a cone to make a hat. While you help students staple their hats, have each child color a copy of the elf ear patterns from page 226. The child cuts out the ears and glues them to the sides of his hat. Then he wears the hat as he writes a story from an elf's point of view. (If desired, he uses a prompt from page the bottom of 226 as inspiration.)

Eric the Eager Elf

Do you love your job? I do! Each day when I wake up, I can't wait to get to work! I throw on my clothes, grab a quick breakfast, and then take off for the workshop. You see, I am lucky. I work in Santa's workshop!

# Snowflakes and Such

To set the scene for a magical story, give each child two sheets of white paper. On one, have the student use a black crayon to draw a wintry scene of her choice. Then have her lay the other paper atop it and use a white colored pencil to trace the image. Instruct the child to store her original drawing in a safe place. After she lightly writes her name or student number on the back of the traced drawing, collect these papers and redistribute them so no student has her own paper. Direct each child to reveal the hidden picture by painting her paper with blue watercolors. After the paint dries, lead the student to refer to the picture's setting as she writes a winter-themed story. Invite students to share their stories and reveal whose pictures inspired them.

Have you heard the story of the State Street snow fort? It's awesome! It all started with the blizzard of 2013. All the kids were tired of playing indoors. That's when Marissa got an idea.

Name _____ Date _____

# Stuck in a Snow Globe

I chose globe _____.

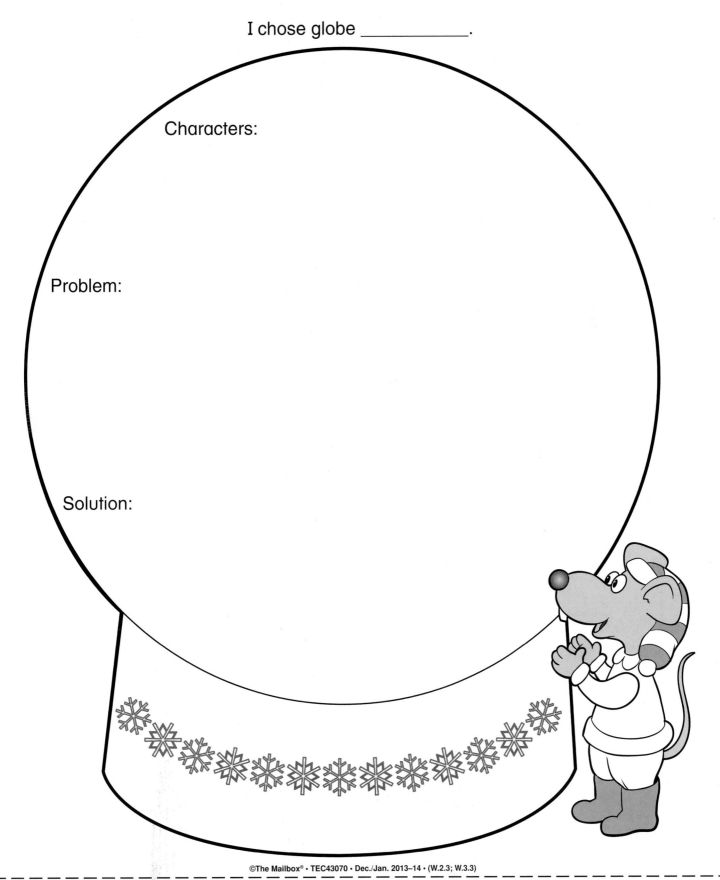

Characters:

Problem:

Solution:

# Elf Ear Patterns and Writing Prompts

Use with "From an Elf's Eyes and Ears" on page 224.

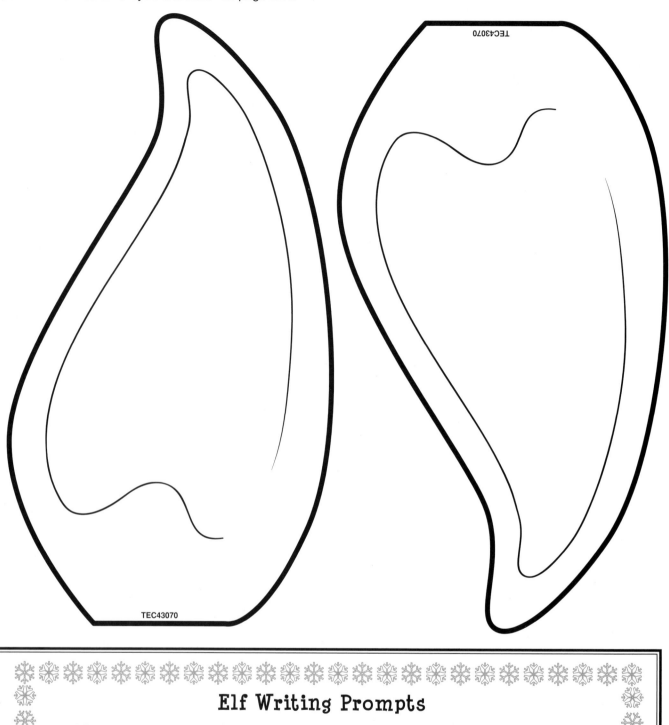

TEC43070

TEC43070

## Elf Writing Prompts

• You are an elf working in Santa's workshop. Tell your story.

• Write a story about an adventure you—one of Santa's elves—had with Santa.

• How do you—one of Santa's elves—feel about Santa's reindeer? Tell a story that explains why you feel this way.

©The Mailbox® • TEC43070 • Dec./Jan. 2013–14

# Celebrate the Season!

## "Heart-y" Goals
**Writing: informational (W.2.2; W.3.2)**

**This lovely display not only features your favorite February historic figures, but it also leads students to plan goals for the rest of the school year!**

**Setup:** Post along the top of a bulletin board pictures of historic figures who achieved important goals and, for each photo, write on an index card a brief description of what the person accomplished. Display the index cards under the corresponding photos.

**Activity:** Each child writes on a paper heart a goal she hopes to accomplish by the end of the year and posts it on the board.

Judy Wetzel, Bull Run School, Centreville, VA

I would love to know my multiplication facts from memory. My goal is to know them in a snap by summer.

---

## Love to Learn
**Skill review (CCSS)**

**Offer your learners a sweet way to practice any number of skills with this matching activity.**

**Setup:** Trace a large heart on card stock and cut it out. Label each of a supply of muffin liners with a different image or definition; then glue the muffin liners to the heart (candy box). Label a supply of brown paper circles (candies) with a matching word for each muffin liner. If desired, prepare a key and set it out with the candies and the candy box.

**Activity:** A child puts each candy on a matching section of the candy box. Then he checks his work.

Kathryn Davenport, Partin Elementary, Oviedo, FL

---

## A "Bear-y" Special Valentine
**Writing: narratives (W.2.3; W.3.3)**

**Valentine's Day is the perfect opportunity to practice letter-writing skills!**

**Activity:** Each student cuts out a copy of the bear patterns from page 229 and adds facial details. Next, the student plans a letter to a special friend, teacher, or family member. He copies the letter onto the bear. Then he cuts a heart from a 6" x 7" red paper rectangle, writes the recipient's name on it, and glues the hands to the heart. Finally, the child staples the heart atop the bear's midsection, as shown.

Janette E. Anderson, Fremont, CA

To: Memaw

Love,
Vance

# Take Heart!
## Cardholders

**Looking for a quick and easy cardholder? Here's one!**

**Activity:** Each child writes his name along the bottom of a handled paper gift bag. He traces a heart shape above his name. Then he uses a cotton swab to dot pink or red paint inside the tracing. After the paint dries, the child sets up the bag on his desk in preparation for valentine deliveries.

Heather Aulisio, Tobyhanna Elementary Center, Pocono Pines, PA

# Heads Up!
**Writing: informational (W.2.2; W.3.2)**

Follow up a president-based reading, video, or web presentation with these activities that are perfectly suited for Presidents' Day. Then display the completed projects around the room for students to read and enjoy.

## George Washington
**Setup:** For each small group, cut a supply of 1" x 11" paper strips. Also make copies of the George Washington profile on page 230.

**Activity:** The group members color the profile as desired; then they list on another sheet of paper facts they learned about George Washington. Next, each child writes on a strip a different fact from the list. Then she tightly wraps the strip around her pencil to curl the paper. She glues the curled strip to the head section of the group's profile paper.

George Washington

## Abraham Lincoln
**Setup:** Share with students that Mr. Lincoln carried important papers in his hat.

**Activity:** A student cuts a large circle from a sheet of black construction paper. Then he folds another sheet of black paper into a cylinder. He tapes the ends of the cylinder together; then he tapes the cylinder to the circle. The student writes on a sheet of notebook paper other facts he learned about Abraham Lincoln and tucks the paper into the top of the hat.

April Parker, St. Pius X School, Greensboro, NC

The luck of the Irish is with you! Find **practice sheets** on pages 231–233. Then turn to pages 238–241 for **St. Patrick's Day activities**.

**Bear Patterns**
Use with "A 'Bear-y' Special
Valentine" on page 227.

TEC43071

# George Washington

**Note to the teacher:** Use with "Heads Up!" on page 228.

Name_____  Date_____

# Share the News

Use addition to solve each subtraction problem.
Explain your thinking.

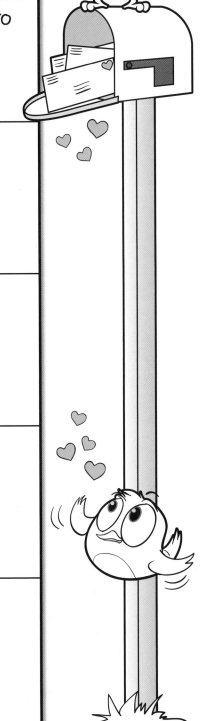

| A. | 53<br>− 17<br>36 | I thought, "17 and what makes 53?" I counted up 3 from 17 to 20. Then I added 30 more to make 50. I counted on 3 more from there to 53.<br><br>$3 + 30 + 3 = 36$ |
|---|---|---|
| B. | 81<br>− 24 | |
| C. | 32<br>− 16 | |
| D. | 48<br>− 29 | |
| E. | 65<br>− 37 | |

**Bonus:** Why can you use addition to solve a subtraction problem?

# Did You Know?

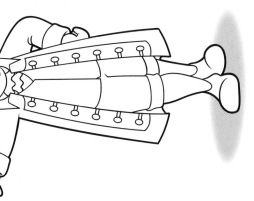

Use words like *and*, *but*, *for*, or *so* to combine the sentences.

Underline the president's name in each sentence.
Label each star with the president's initials.
Combine the two sentences about each president into one sentence on the matching line.

**GW** George Washington ate few desserts.

☆ One of George Washington's favorite foods was ice cream.

☆ Andrew Johnson was a tailor before he became president.

☆ William Henry Harrison was president for only 31 days.

☆ Ronald Reagan was once an actor.

☆ Abraham Lincoln had a job chopping wood for fences before he took office.

☆ Abraham Lincoln knew how to swing an ax.

☆ Andrew Johnson knew how to sew.

☆ William Henry Harrison died of pneumonia.

☆ Ronald Reagan was in many movies.

**GW** _____

**WHH** _____

**AL** _____

**AJ** _____

**RR** _____

**Bonus:** Write two sentences about the current president. Then use *and*, *but*, *for*, or *so* to combine the sentences into one.

©The Mailbox® • TEC43071 • Feb./Mar. 2014 • Key p. 312 • (L.2.1f; L.3.1i)

# Springing Ahead

Solve.
Use the number line to help you.

6:45 | 7:00 | 7:15 | 7:30 | 7:45 | 8:00 | 8:15 | 8:30 | 8:45 | 9:00 | 9:15

**A** Frankie starts catching flies at 7:15 AM. He catches big flies in the first 10 minutes. Then he catches small flies in the next 15 minutes. What time does he finish catching flies? _____

**B** Frankie leaves his lily pad at 7:45 AM. He arrives at Francine's pad at 8:20 AM. How long did it take Frankie to get to Francine's pad? _____

**C** Francine needs to go to her cooking lesson. It takes her 20 minutes to get there. If her lesson begins at 8:25 AM, what time does she need to leave her pad? _____

**D** Francine's cooking lesson begins at 8:25 AM. It ends at 9:10 AM. How long does the lesson last? _____

**E** Fraser starts his chores at 7:05 AM. He cleans the top of his lily pad for 10 minutes. Then he cleans the underside of his lily pad for 20 minutes. What time does Fraser finish his chores? _____

**F** Frieda leaves to run errands at 7:50 AM. She returns to her pad at 9:00 AM. How long is she gone? _____

**G** Fritz wakes up at 9:15 AM. His brother Franz woke up 50 minutes earlier. What time did Franz wake up? _____

**H** Francine wants to make fly soup. The soup takes 35 minutes to cook. What time does she need to start cooking the soup if she wants it ready at 9:15 AM? _____

**Bonus:** Francine and Frankie start eating dinner at 5:45 PM. They finish 20 minutes later. Draw a number line and solve.

# Honoring History Makers

Ideas for Black History Month (February), National Women's History Month (March), or anytime you study influential people

## Connecting to the Past

This art-based idea focuses on the work of Langston Hughes, a well-known African American author who wrote poetry and plays. Tell students he wrote the poems for the book *The Sweet and Sour Animal Book* in 1936, but the collection wasn't published until 1994. At that time, students created the illustrations. Share *The Sweet and Sour Animal Book* and then assign each child a poem to copy (with credit to the author) and illustrate. Bind the pages into a class book. *Marianne Cerra, St. Ignatius R. C. School, Sinking Spring, PA*

## Fact or Fiction?

After studying history makers, have students apply what they've learned to a class game. Direct each child to list on an index card one factual statement and one fictional statement about a history maker she has studied. Then have her underline the factual statement. Collect the cards and verify the facts. To play the game, divide the class into teams. Read a card aloud and guide Team 1 to separate the factual statement from the fictional. If correct, award the team two points and move the card to a discard pile. If incorrect, move the card to the bottom of the stack and read the next card to Team 2. Continue as time allows or until all cards have been played. The team with the most points wins. *Colleen Dabney, Williamsburg, VA*

> Harriet Tubman taught herself how to drive a train.
>
> Harriet Tubman helped slaves escape to freedom by way of the Underground Railroad.

## Survey Says!

Get students talking about women in history. First, prepare a simple survey with questions like the ones shown. Send a copy of the survey home and have each child interview his mother or another significant adult female in his life. After students return the surveys to school, take time each day to discuss a question. Chart the answers and use the information to inspire research or ignite discussion. *Mary Ann Gildroy, Roundup, MT*

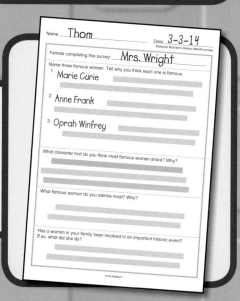

Turn to **pages 235 and 236** for **step-by-step projects** you can use with the whole class or that can be set out in centers for independent practice. Use one for Black History Month and the other for National Women's History Month. There's also **a practice sheet** about **Mae Jemison** on **page 237**.

# A Tucked-Away Timeline

**What You Need**
- reference books
- sheet of skin-color paper
- sheet of construction paper
- notebook paper
- paper scraps
- scissors
- glue
- markers

① Choose a history maker. Use the reference books to help you list five or more of his or her important life events. Write them in order. Have your teacher check your list (timeline).

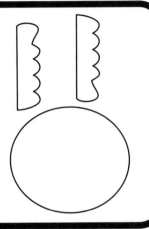

② Cut an oval from the skin-color paper. Then cut two hands.

③ Use the paper scraps, markers, and glue to add details that make the oval look like the face of the history maker.

④ Glue the face.

⑤ Copy the timeline.

⑥ Fold the paper in half, bringing the bottom end to the top.

⑦ Write the name of the history maker. Glue the hands.

George Washington Carver

**Step-by-Step Activity** Copy this page. Project it onto your whiteboard, or place the activity card in a plastic page protector and put it at a center with the materials.

# Cause-and-Effect Camera

## History Makers

**What You Need**

- 3" x 5" index card
- 5" x 11" paper strip
- crayons
- glue

① Glue the card to the paper strip.

② Fold the rest of the strip in half. Then unfold it.

③ Draw the viewfinder of a camera.

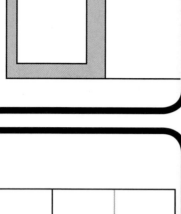

④ Draw the face of a history maker in the viewfinder. Write his or her name below the picture.

Elizabeth Cady Stanton

⑤ Write to tell what the history maker did in his or her life that was so important. Draw a matching picture.

Elizabeth Cady Stanton

She was an early leader in the women's rights movement. She wanted women to be treated the same way as men.

Ballot

⑥ Write a sentence telling how his or her actions changed the lives of other people or how it affected your life. Draw a matching picture.

Elizabeth Cady Stanton

She was an early leader in the women's rights movement. She wanted women to be treated the same way as men.

Ballot

As a result of her actions, women were given the right to vote in 1920.

⑦ If time allows, turn the project over. Write a different fact about the history maker in each section. Then fold the bottom sections behind the top so the viewfinder is visible.

©**The Mailbox**® • TEC43071 • Feb./Mar. 2014

**Step-by-Step Activity** Copy this page. Project it onto your whiteboard, or place the activity card in a plastic page protector and put it at a center with the materials.

# On Her Way to Space

Use the passage to complete the timeline.

Mae Jemison always loved science. In fact, when Mae was just five years old, she knew she wanted to be an astronaut.

Mae worked hard to reach her goal. She read lots of books. She studied hard. Mae even finished high school at age 16. Then she went to Stanford University. After four years there, she went to Cornell University to study to be a doctor.

Mae wanted to help people. Soon after she became a doctor, she joined the Peace Corps. Mae cared for sick people in Africa for two years.

Mae still wanted to visit space. When she was 29 years old, she applied to the space program. Two years later, she was finally chosen.

Mae trained for two years. Finally, in 1992, she went to space. Mae was the first African American woman to travel to space. There, she did experiments. She studied how space affects human bones. Dr. Jemison reached her lifelong goal.

**1961** When Mae was five years old,

**1973** Mae worked hard. When she was 16 years old,

**1983** Mae wanted to help people. After she became a doctor,

**1985** When Mae was 29,

**1992** When Mae was 35,

**Bonus:** Look at the completed timeline. How are the events in Mae's life connected?

# Leapin' Leprechauns!
## Golden Ideas for St. Patrick's Day

## Lucky to Teach You
### Skill review (CCSS)

Kick off St. Patrick's Day with a sweet treat. Fill a resealable plastic bag with Lucky Charms cereal, for each student. Attach a mailing label with the message shown and give one to each child. Then have students complete one or more of the activities below before munching on their holiday snacks.

- Write in your journal a list of ten reasons why you are lucky.
- Graph the number of each kind of marshmallow.
- Identify the fractional amounts each marshmallow represents.

*Heather Aulisio, Tobyhanna Elementary Center, Pocono Pines, PA, and A. J. Ryan, Duxbury, MA*

## Four-Leaf Practice
### Basic facts (2.OA.B.2; 3.OA.C.7)

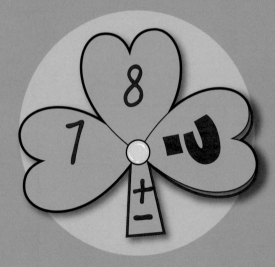

To put a spin on fact review, give each child a green copy of the clover patterns on page 240. A student chooses a fact family and writes each number of the fact family on a separate clover section. Next, she writes the corresponding symbols on the stem and cuts out the patterns. She uses a brass fastener to attach the section labeled "?" atop the clover; then she finds a partner. The child spins the top section so it covers one of the clover sections and challenges her partner to think about basic facts and name the covered number. Then the students switch roles before finding a new partner. *April LoTempio, Ben Franklin Elementary, Kenmore, NY*

**tip** Collect the clovers and place them at a center for individual or partner review.

## Go Green
### Conserving resources

There's more than one way to incorporate green into your St. Patrick's Day activities! Check out this easy science idea. First, guide students to name steps they can take to protect the environment. List their ideas on the board. Next, instruct each child to write on each leaf of a shamrock pattern a different way he can help the environment. Provide time for the child to outline the shamrock with a green crayon or cut out the shamrock and glue it to a sheet of recycled green paper. Then post the shamrocks on a display titled "We're Going Green for St. Patrick's Day." *Cheryl Rayl, Mayville Elementary, Mayville, MI*

# Leprechauns With Loot
## Money (2.MD.C.8)

Students hunt for leprechauns' treasures at this fun center and build their money skills in the process. In advance, label each of ten paper lunch bags with a different leprechaun name. Place inside each bag a handful of plastic coins; then make a key with each leprechaun's name and coin value. A student writes the name of a leprechaun, finds the value of the coins, and writes the value on her paper. She returns the coins to the bag before repeating the process with the other bags. After the child finds all the values, she orders them from least to greatest to find the name of the leprechaun who had the most money. If desired, reward each child who determines the correct name with a chocolate gold coin or piece of butterscotch. *Cheryl Rayl, Mayville Elementary, Mayville, MI*

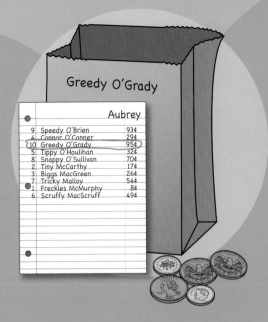

Greedy O'Grady

Aubrey

| | | |
|---|---|---|
| 9 | Speedy O'Brien | 93¢ |
| 4 | Connor O'Conner | 29¢ |
| 10 | Greedy O'Grady | 95¢ |
| 5 | Tippy O'Houlihan | 32¢ |
| 8 | Snappy O'Sullivan | 70¢ |
| 2 | Tiny McCarthy | 17¢ |
| 3 | Biggs MacGreen | 26¢ |
| 7 | Tricky Malloy | 54¢ |
| 1 | Freckles McMurphy | 8¢ |
| 6 | Scruffy MacScruff | 49¢ |

Name Carter     Date 3-17-14
Prefixes and root words

lucky

un-

unlucky   unpack
unkind    uninvited
unliked   uncap
unpeeled  unhurt

# Follow the Rainbow
## Prefixes and root words (L.2.4b, c; L.3.4b, c)

Lead students to a better understanding of words and word parts and their meanings. In advance, cut eight 1" x 3" paper strips for each child. To begin, instruct each child to color and outline a copy of the rainbow on page 240 as shown. Direct the student to write a prefix on the cloud and, if desired, have him include the prefix's meaning below it. Then have the child write on each paper strip a different root word that makes a real word when it's combined with the prefix. Help the student staple the stack of strips to the rainbow; then have him list the resulting words on the pot of gold. Provide time for students to share their words and their meanings in small groups. *adapted from an idea by Julie Laney, Acworth, GA*

# Hands-On Portrait
## Writing narratives: imagined (W.2.3; W.3.3)

Use this quick art project to inspire trickster tales of leprechauns and their gold! To make a leprechaun, each child paints one palm orange and then presses it onto a sheet of paper as shown. After the paint dries, the student cuts an oval from skin-toned paper and decorates it with facial details. She also cuts ears from the same paper. Then she glues the oval and ears atop the painted print. Finally, she cuts a leprechaun's hat from paper scraps, glues it to her paper, and adds details to the perimeter of the paper. Now that her leprechaun has appeared, she's ready to write his tale! *Heather Aulisio, Tobyhanna Elementary Center, Pocono Pines, PA*

 Challenge students to complete copies of **page 241** in their free time!

# Clover Patterns

Use with "Four-Leaf Practice" on page 238.

TEC43071

---

Name _____    Date _____

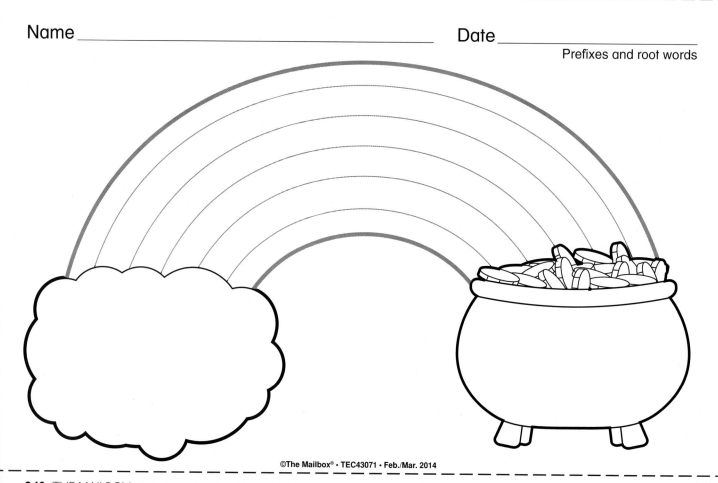

**Note to the teacher:** Use with "Follow the Rainbow" on page 239.

Name _____

Date _____

# Leprechaun Challenge

Answer each question correctly to earn the leprechaun's gold!

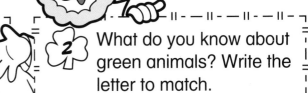

**1** Can you find five green salad foods? Circle them.

allettucentopepperocucumber
salaceleryespinachafooledyou

**2** What do you know about green animals? Write the letter to match.

reptile ____          A. parakeet

insect ____          B. alligator

amphibian ____          C. frog

bird ____          D. grasshopper

**3** What words do you know that start like *green*? Write letters to finish each word. (Don't repeat words!)

gra_____          gra_____

gre_____          gre_____

gri_____          gri_____

gro_____          gro_____

gru_____          gru_____

**4** Can these things be green? Write yes or no.

paper money          _____

real giraffes          _____

tea          _____

eyes          _____

tomatoes          _____

fingernails          _____

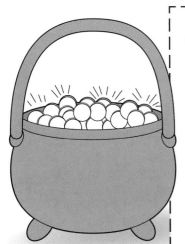

**5** What do the underlined expressions mean? Write the letter to match.

She is a <u>green-eyed monster</u>. ____          A. luck growing plants

He is <u>green behind the gills</u>. ____          B. jealous

You have a <u>green thumb</u>. ____          C. sick

It is a <u>green</u> product. ____          D. OK to start

They have the <u>green light</u> for the job. ____          E. earth friendly

---

**Note to the teacher:** Give each child a copy of this page to complete in his free time. If desired, provide each child who answers all questions correctly a small prize, such as chocolate candy coins or a seasonal pencil.

# Celebrate the Season!

## A Shower of Ideas
### Writing opinions (W.2.1; W.3.1)

Rain or shine, this activity helps students identify reasons that support opinion statements.

**Set up:** Draw on the board a large umbrella outline. Below the umbrella, draw a puddle outline.

**Activity:** Just above the umbrella, write an opinion about a recent event. Lead students to provide reasons that support the opinion and write them in the umbrella outline. Write any statements that do not support the opinion in the puddle. When you have three solid reasons to support the opinion, clear all the sentences from the board except for one from the puddle. Write that statement in the umbrella and challenge students to name a corresponding opinion and two more reasons that support the opinion. Continue as time allows.

adapted from an idea by Cheryl Rayl, Mayville Elementary, Mayville, MI

The recorder recital was the best one in years!

All students were prepared.
Everyone played together.
The songs were fun to listen to.

My dad sat in the back.

## A Brand-New Ball Game
### Spelling review

Are your students ready for a big-league game? Give this outdoor activity a try!

**Set up:** Program each of a supply of index cards with a different spelling word. Depending on the word's difficulty, also write on each card "single," "double," "triple," or "home run."

**Activity:** Divide students into two teams and head outside to the ball field. Instruct players from Team 1 to take a position on the field. Give the pitcher the cards. Instruct a player (batter) from Team 2 to come to the batter's box and have the pitcher call out the top word from the stack. Direct all students to spell the word silently while the batter spells it aloud. If the batter correctly spells the word, he runs the number of bases written on the card. If he misspells the word, the player earns an out for his team. After the batter's turn, the pitcher moves the card to the bottom of the stack and calls out the next word to the next player. When a team has three outs, direct the teams to change places. The team that scores more runs wins.

Margaret E. Albertson, Rancho Cucamonga, CA

community

triple

**tip** Have students rotate positions while playing defense so everyone gets a chance to be the pitcher.

 Find a **step-by-step activity** for Mother's Day on page 243 plus seasonal skill sheets on pages 245 and 246.

# A Little Love Note

**What You Need**

- copy of page 9
- scissors
- crayons

① Cut out the pop-up card.

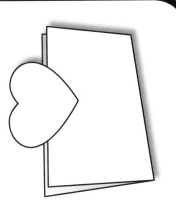

② Fold the card in half.

③ Write a poem or message to your mom, your grandmother, or another special lady in your life.

④ Color the heart.

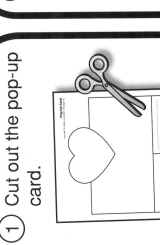

⑤ Fold the heart down and close the card.

⑥ Decorate the front cover.

⑦ Write your name and the year on the back cover.

Made with love by _Olivia_ in _2014_

**Step-by-step craft:** Copy this activity card and put it in a plastic page protector for durability. Then put the activity card and needed materials at a center.

# Pop-Up Card

Use with "A Little Love Note" on page 243.

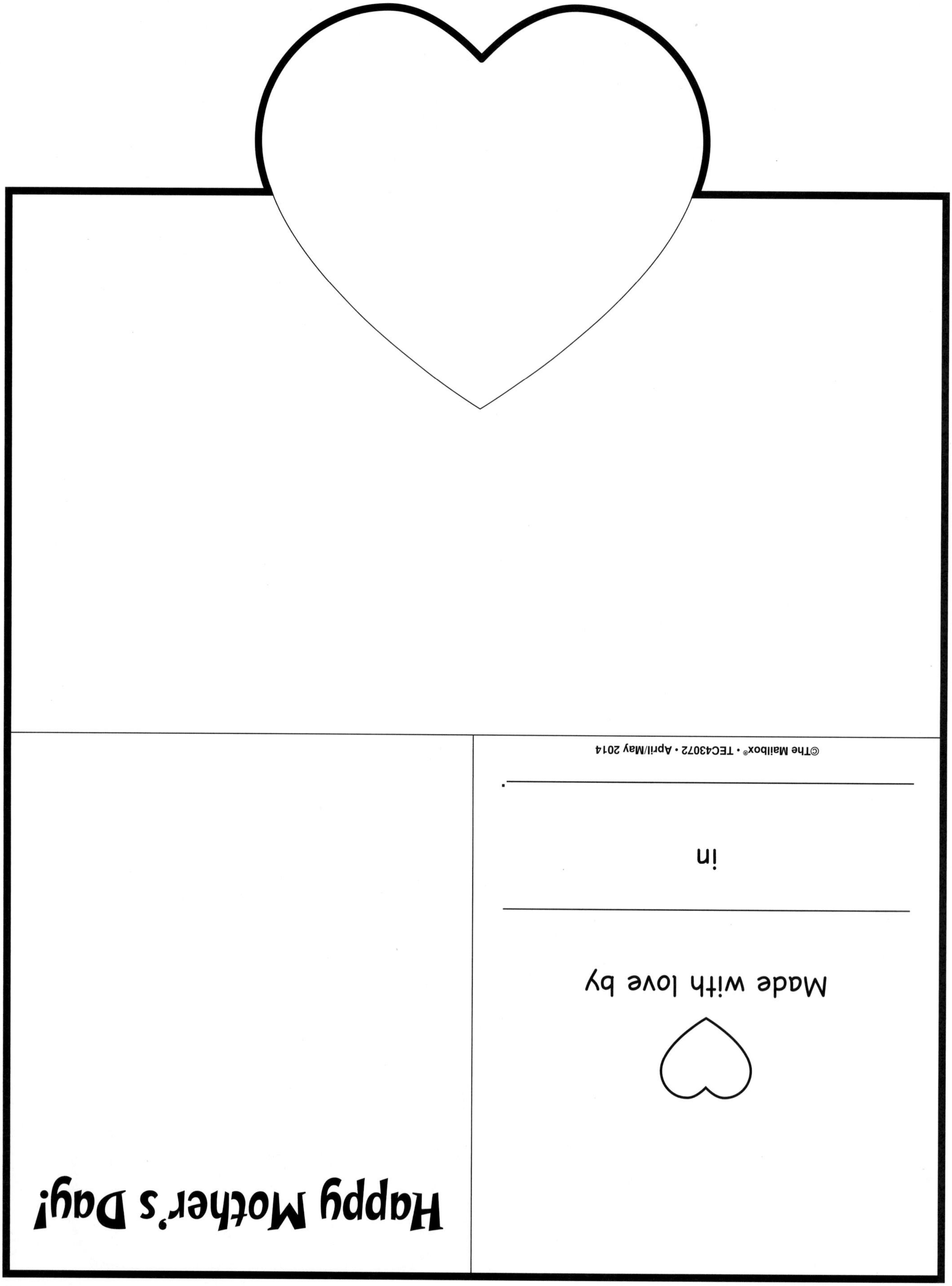

Happy Mother's Day!

Made with love by

in

Name _____

Date _____

Word problems: add and subtract within 100

# Colorful Eggs

Use the number line to solve each problem.
Write the answer and circle the operation you used.
Find the matching answer on an egg. Color it to match the color in the problem.

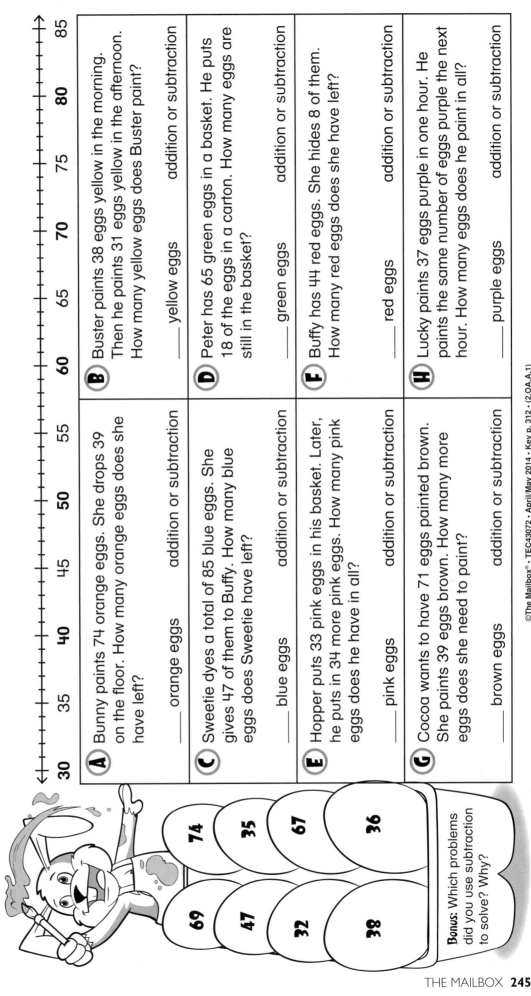

30  35  40  45  50  55  60  65  70  75  80  85

**A** Bunny paints 74 orange eggs. She drops 39 on the floor. How many orange eggs does she have left?

_____ orange eggs    addition or subtraction

**B** Buster paints 38 eggs yellow in the morning. Then he paints 31 eggs yellow in the afternoon. How many yellow eggs does Buster paint?

_____ yellow eggs    addition or subtraction

**C** Sweetie dyes a total of 85 blue eggs. She gives 47 of them to Buffy. How many blue eggs does Sweetie have left?

_____ blue eggs    addition or subtraction

**D** Peter has 65 green eggs in a basket. He puts 18 of the eggs in a carton. How many eggs are still in the basket?

_____ green eggs    addition or subtraction

**E** Hopper puts 33 pink eggs in his basket. Later, he puts in 34 more pink eggs. How many pink eggs does he have in all?

_____ pink eggs    addition or subtraction

**F** Buffy has 44 red eggs. She hides 8 of them. How many red eggs does she have left?

_____ red eggs    addition or subtraction

**G** Cocoa wants to have 71 eggs painted brown. She paints 39 eggs brown. How many more eggs does she need to paint?

_____ brown eggs    addition or subtraction

**H** Lucky paints 37 eggs purple in one hour. He paints the same number of eggs purple the next hour. How many eggs does he paint in all?

_____ purple eggs    addition or subtraction

69   74
47   35
32   67
38   36

**Bonus:** Which problems did you use subtraction to solve? Why?

©The Mailbox® • TEC43072 • April/May 2014 • Key p. 312 • (2.OA.A.1)

# Trash Dash
## Division

### Earth Day Cleanup

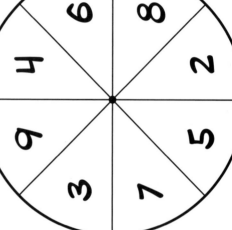

**Player 1**

| | | | |
|---|---|---|---|
| 54 ÷ 9 = | 24 ÷ 6 = | 15 ÷ 3 = | 48 ÷ 6 = |
| 35 ÷ 7 = | 81 ÷ 9 = | 32 ÷ 8 = | 21 ÷ 3 = |
| 16 ÷ 2 = | 36 ÷ 9 = | 21 ÷ 7 = | 24 ÷ 6 = |
| 20 ÷ 4 = | 12 ÷ 4 = | 6 ÷ 2 = | 36 ÷ 6 = |
| 16 ÷ 4 = | 28 ÷ 4 = | 12 ÷ 6 = | 63 ÷ 7 = |
| 27 ÷ 3 = | 16 ÷ 8 = | 49 ÷ 7 = | 12 ÷ 2 = |

**Player 2**

| | | | |
|---|---|---|---|
| 24 ÷ 3 = | 20 ÷ 5 = | 14 ÷ 2 = | 54 ÷ 6 = |
| 35 ÷ 5 = | 48 ÷ 8 = | 28 ÷ 7 = | 14 ÷ 7 = |
| 36 ÷ 4 = | 12 ÷ 4 = | 45 ÷ 9 = | 18 ÷ 3 = |
| 9 ÷ 3 = | 32 ÷ 8 = | 72 ÷ 8 = | 30 ÷ 6 = |
| 24 ÷ 4 = | 28 ÷ 7 = | 40 ÷ 5 = | 8 ÷ 4 = |
| 72 ÷ 9 = | 24 ÷ 8 = | 15 ÷ 5 = | 42 ÷ 6 = |

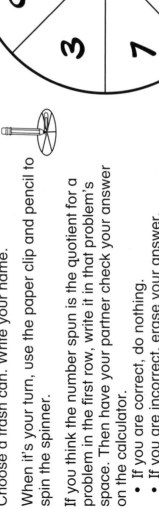

Spinner numbers: 9, 4, 6, 8, 2, 5, 1, 3

**Directions for two players:**

1. Choose a trash can. Write your name.

2. When it's your turn, use the paper clip and pencil to spin the spinner.

3. If you think the number spun is the quotient for a problem in the first row, write it in that problem's space. Then have your partner check your answer on the calculator.
   - If you are correct, do nothing.
   - If you are incorrect, erase your answer.

4. Take turns until one player correctly solves all four problems in the first row. Then move to the second row to begin a new round.

5. The player who wins more rounds wins the game.

**Partner Game** Make a copy of this page for each pair of students. Give the players a paper clip and a calculator.

©The Mailbox® • TEC43072 • April/May 2014 • (3.OA.C.7)

# LOL!

## Fun English Language Arts activities for National Humor Month (April)

### It Was So Funny...

*Students' sidesplitting stories take center stage with this three-part idea.*

**Writing (W.3.3; W.3.6):** Direct each student to write a personal narrative about a humorous event. Then have him choose three of the funniest moments, digitally illustrate them, and incorporate them in a digital slide show program. Provide time for the child to practice reading his story while sharing his slide show. Or invite the student to choose a classmate to operate the slide show. Have them work together to get the timing right before presenting the story to the class.

### Then

**Speaking (SL.3.4, 5):** Have the student share his story with the class, reinforcing the funniest moments by sharing the slides as he reads.

### Then

**Listening (SL.3.1.c):** Invite students to ask the presenter questions to gather more information or to clarify any misinformation.

Q: Why was everyone so tired on April 1?
A: They had just finished a March of 31 days!

Q: Why shouldn't you tell an egg a joke?
A: Because it might crack up!

### Riddle of the Day

*This amusing activity makes every child a comedian!*

**Fluency (RF.2.4a, b):** To start, lead students to understand the importance of timing and emphasis on key words when telling a joke or riddle. Next, cut apart a copy of the riddle cards from page 248. Give a card to each student and assign her a date in April to share it with the class. Provide time for her to practice.

### Then

**Listening (SL.2.2):** After the student has shared her riddle, direct another student to apply his background knowledge to explain the humor behind the riddle.

# Riddle Cards

Use with "Riddle of the Day" on page 247.

Q: Why was everyone so tired on April 1?
A: They had just finished a March of 31 days!

Q: What do you call a dog on the beach in the summer?
A: A hot dog!

Q: Why did the leopard wear a striped shirt?
A: So it wouldn't be spotted!

Q: What do you get if you cross a parrot with a shark?
A: A bird that will talk your ear off!

Q: What's the king of the classroom?
A: The ruler!

Q: What do you get when you cross a caterpillar and a parrot?
A: A walkie-talkie!

Q: Why did the policeman go to the baseball game?
A: He heard someone had stolen a base!

Q: What do frogs wear on their feet?
A: Open "toad" shoes!

Q: What do you give to a sick lemon?
A: "Lemon-aid"!

Q: Why did the clown go to the doctor?
A: Because he was feeling a little funny!

Q: What did the spider do on the computer?
A: It made a website!

Q: Why did the golfer wear two pairs of pants?
A: In case he got a hole in one!

Q: How do baseball players stay cool?
A: They sit next to the fans.

Q: What do hockey players and magicians have in common?
A: They both do hat tricks!

Q: Why did the chicken cross the playground?
A: To get to the other slide!

Q: What type of markets do dogs avoid?
A: Flea markets!

Q: What was the detective duck's goal?
A: To "quack" the case!

Q: What do you call a sleeping dinosaur?
A: A "dino-snore"!

Q: Why was the math book sad?
A: Because it had too many problems!

Q: Why shouldn't you tell an egg a joke?
A: Because it might crack up!

Q: What do you call a peanut in a spacesuit?
A: An "astro-nut"!

Q: What goes tick, tick, woof, woof?
A: A watchdog!

Q: What did the tornado say to the car?
A: Do you want to go for a spin?

Q: Why wouldn't they let the butterfly into the dance?
A: Because it was a "moth ball"!

TEC43072

# Get CRACKIN'!

## Easy ideas for incorporating *plastic eggs* and *skill review*

## "Eggs-tra" Review

Students practice identifying **main idea and details (RI.3.2)** with this small-group activity. First, cut the sentence strips from a copy of page 250. Place each strip in a separate egg. Read the paragraph aloud; then give each child an egg. Guide students to open their eggs and determine who has the main idea and who has the details. Then lead students to discuss how the details support the main idea. **As an alternative independent activity**, cut apart a story or a technical procedure and place each piece in a separate egg. A child opens each egg and sequences the sentences from beginning to end.

Kim Manning, Schultz Elementary, Irving, TX

Most butterflies lay very small eggs on leaves.

## Topics Over Easy

This idea, which increases students' interest in responding to **writing prompts (W.2.1–3; W.3.1–3)**, needs little "eggs-planation." Place inside each of 12 eggs a different writing prompt. Put the eggs in a basket or a clean egg carton. Each day, invite a child to open an egg and reveal the day's writing prompt, or put the carton at a center for independent writing tasks.

Heather Aulisio, Tobyhanna Elementary Center, Pocono Pines, PA

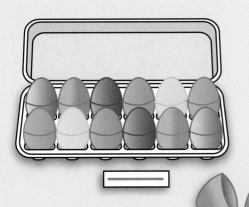

## Shell Out Some Change

Use an egg hunt to build **money skills (2.MD.C.8)**. Here's how. First, place different plastic coins in each egg in a supply of eggs. Set the eggs out around the room. Next, post a list of egg decorations on the board and list a price for each item. Direct student pairs to collect a predetermined number of eggs. After they have opened the eggs, instruct students to write a number sentence to show the value of the coins collected. Then have the students list the items they could purchase with the coins they have. If desired, set out the decorations for students to "purchase" with their plastic coins and then glue to a copy of an egg pattern.

adapted from an idea by Heather Aulisio

pair of wiggle eyes = 25¢
strip of wavy ribbon = 40¢
strip of straight ribbon = 35¢
glitter glue = 15¢
sticker = 10¢

# Sentence Strips and Paragraph

Use with "'Eggs-tra' Review" on page 249.

**main idea**

You may think only birds lay eggs in nests, but many different animals hatch from eggs. | TEC43072

**details**

Most butterflies lay very small eggs on leaves. | TEC43072

When the eggs hatch, the leaves become an instant food source for the caterpillars. | TEC43072

Some snakes lay eggs in shallow holes. | TEC43072

Other snakes use rotten logs or tree stumps to lay their eggs. | TEC43072

One kind of mammal called a platypus even lays eggs. | TEC43072

Its eggs are laid in a burrow of leaves and grass. | TEC43072

# Eggs!

You may think only birds lay eggs in nests, but many different animals hatch from eggs. Most butterflies lay very small eggs on leaves. When the eggs hatch, the leaves become an instant food source for the caterpillars. Some snakes lay eggs in shallow holes. Other snakes use rotten logs or tree stumps to lay their eggs. One kind of mammal called a platypus even lays eggs. Its eggs are laid in a burrow of leaves and grass. These are just a few animals that lay eggs. Can you name others?

## The "Write" Stuff
**Writing: explanatory (W.2.2; W.3.2)**

**A batch of sidewalk chalk provides practice with writing directions and makes a fun year-end gift.**

**Set up:** Gather a class supply of paper bathroom cups, plaster of paris, powdered tempera paint, a large bucket, and craft sticks. Make student copies of page 252. Before you prepare the chalk, tell students to pay careful attention because they will be writing directions to match the steps. Instruct them to jot notes on their copies of the organizer.

**Activity:** To make the chalk, mix in the bucket one cup of plaster of paris with three-fourths cup of water. Then add powdered tempera paint and stir. Pour the contents into the bathroom cups. Repeat as needed to make one cup of chalk for each child. (Repeating the steps should help students catch every detail.) After the mixture dries (about 24 hours), squeeze the chalk from the cups and put each piece in a resealable bag. Have each student use his notes to write directions; then send a piece of chalk home with his directions.

Colleen Dabney, Williamsburg, VA

Happy Father's Day to a dad who always saves the day and is powerful enough to handle anything that comes his way!
Love,
Mia

Super Dad to the Rescue

Super Dad does 6 loads of laundry each week. If there are 4 weeks in a month, how many loads of laundry does Super Dad do in one month?

Super Dad to the Rescue

Super Dad lifts 3 buses off the highway. If each bus weighs 12 tons, how much weight does Super Dad lift?

## Super Dad
**Word problems (2.OA.A.1; 3.OA.A.3)**

**This superhero saves the day with his fun word problems!**

**Set up:** Make student copies of the word problem cards on page 253.

**Activity:** Give each child a copy of the cards. Instruct each student to draw facial details on her superhero outlines to match a dad she knows well. Then have her color the outlines. Next, direct the student to write on the top card a word problem to reflect what the dad does in real life. Have her write on the bottom card a word problem that reflects what the dad might do if he were a superhero. Copy each child's cards, cut them apart, and bind them to make a class book. Set the book at a center for free-time problem-solving practice. Then invite each child to use her original word problem cards as part of a Father's Day card like the one shown.

adapted from an idea by Heather Aulisio, Tobyhanna Elementary Center, Pocono Pines, PA

Turn to pages 254–262 for more *seasonal activities*.

# How to Make Sidewalk Chalk

**Materials**
List what your teacher used to make the chalk.


**Steps**
Tell what your teacher did to make the chalk.

First,



Next,



Then



How long did it take for the mixture to dry?


What did your teacher do after the chalk was dry?


©The Mailbox® • TEC43073 • June/July 2014

**252** THE MAILBOX **Note to the teacher:** Use with "The 'Write' Stuff" on page 251.

Super Dad to the Rescue

©The Mailbox® • TEC43073 • June/July 2014

Super Dad to the Rescue

©The Mailbox® • TEC43073 • June/July 2014

# Love the Lake!

Write the word that best completes each sentence.
Decide if the word is an adverb or an adjective.
Color the number by the code.

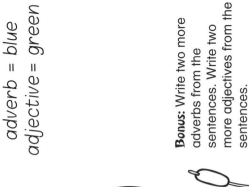

**Color Code**
*adverb = blue*
*adjective = green*

**Bonus:** Write two more adverbs from the sentences. Write two more adjectives from the sentences.

1. It is a ——— hot summer.
   terrible, terribly

2. Sharon Heron and her friends like to spend time at the ——— lake.
   local, locally

3. Sharon is glad this ——— lake is nearby.
   beautiful, beautifully

4. Today, many ——— friends are waiting for her to join them.
   eager, eagerly

5. She ——— runs toward the water.
   quick, quickly

6. Sharon ——— dips her toe in the lake.
   careful, carefully

7. She squeals ——— when she feels the cool water.
   loud, loudly

8. Sharon tells her buddies, "I would jump in, but I'm not very ———."
   brave, bravely

9. She ——— perches herself on a rock.
   quick, quickly

10. Sharon enjoys the splashes of water her ——— friends make.
    playful, playfully

It's all she needs to keep cool.

©The Mailbox® • TEC43073 • June/July 2014 • Key p. 312 • (L.2.1e)

# Big Blue

Read.

It is lunchtime in the ocean. A great blue whale sees some **krill** nearby. These shrimplike creatures live close to the water's surface. All of a sudden, the whale **lunges** at them with a wide-open mouth. It quickly closes its mouth over the krill. The whale's throat skin **expands**. A pouch, created by **throat pleats**, allows the whale to hold a large amount of food and water in its mouth. **Baleen** is also found in its mouth. When the whale pushes its heavy tongue against the baleen, the fringed plates help strain out water while trapping the krill.

After eating, the whale goes to the water's surface to breathe. Air and water spurt out of its **blowhole**. This spray can go up to 30 feet into the air! The force of air causes a **thunderous** noise. The whale is still hungry. It slaps its **flukes** on the water's surface. The two lobes of its tail are the last part seen before the whale dives down in search of more food.

blowhole

fluke

throat pleats

baleen

Write the bold word that matches each clue.
Underline clues from the passage or diagram that help you.

1. to become bigger _____

2. a loud sound, like thunder _____

3. part of the whale's tail _____

4. small sea creatures _____

5. skin folds in a whale's throat _____

6. nostril-like hole for breathing _____

7. move forward quickly _____

8. fringed plates in a whale's jaw _____

**Bonus:** Look at the first paragraph. Which bold word might you also find in a passage about ice? Why?

# Time to Reflect
## Easy Ideas to Wrap Up the Year

Use your free time to read a good book.

### Tips for Next Year's Class

Now that your students are classroom experts, invite them to give advice for next year's class.

- **Back-to-school display:** Have each child use a permanent marker to program a small strip of bulletin board border with words of wisdom for your incoming students. (Have the student use the back of the strip for a white surface.) Hang the border atop brightly colored paper and you have a welcoming display started for next year. *Maureen Clements, Richard L. Rice Elementary, Marlton, NJ*

- **Personalized bookmarks:** Have each child write his words of wisdom on a paper rectangle. Then have him draw a picture on the opposite side and sign his name. Guide him to punch a hole in the top of the bookmark, insert a colorful strip of ribbon, and tie it off. *Kathleen Scavone, Coyote Valley Elementary, Middletown, CA*

What is the answer to a division problem called?

quotient

### Review Relay

Give students a chance to show what they've learned this year with a fun class game. In advance, have each child write on separate index cards three questions based on content covered during the school year and their answers. Collect the cards. Then fill three buckets with colored chalk. Take the class outside to a blacktop area, divide students into three teams, and have each team line up on one side of the surface. Place a bucket directly across the blacktop from each team. To play, read a question aloud. The first player from each team runs to her team's bucket, takes a piece of chalk, and writes the answer on the blacktop. Each player with the correct answer earns a point for her team. Continue reading cards. The first team to earn ten points wins. *Heather Aulisio, Tobyhanna Elementary Center, Pocono Pines, PA*

Jamie,
I had so much fun doing spelling reviews with you.
Reid

## Memory Box

Collect happy memories in this handy carryall. To make a memory box, have a child bring a shoe box from home and help him cut an opening in the lid. Then instruct the student to use construction paper scraps to label the box with his name, grade, year, and class and decorate it with images that remind him of the school year. Next, provide time for each child to use a paper strip to write a short message to each of his classmates, sharing a memory of a fun time together or sharing positive qualities he saw in the student during the year. Have each student deliver his messages to his classmates' boxes. *Karen Luba, Racine, WI*

tip → Sign the back of a class photo and put one in each child's box.

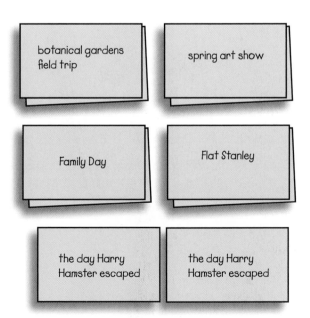

botanical gardens field trip

spring art show

Family Day

Flat Stanley

the day Harry Hamster escaped

the day Harry Hamster escaped

## Remember When...?

Encourage students to reflect on favorite memories with a simple game of Concentration. In advance, label each of ten pairs of cards with a different activity or event from the school year. Scramble the cards and place them facedown in a pocket chart. Guide students to take turns revealing two cards at a time. Each time a match is made, invite class members to share what they remember about the corresponding experience.

# Get Wind of This Idea

**These windsocks are a breeze to make, and they provide time for students to reminisce about the school year. Here's how!**

1. Divide students into small groups, assigning each group a different month in which you have been in school.

2. Project a copy of the instructions from page 259 on the board and give each group the needed materials.

3. Direct students to complete Step 1; then have them write their assigned month on their papers and the name of a memorable class or school event. Instruct the groups to continue to Step 2, drawing pictures or images related to their event.

4. Have students in each group follow the remaining steps to complete their windsock.

5. Order the projects from the beginning of the year to the end. Then hang a length of clothesline near the ceiling, attach clothespins, and clip each windsock to a clothespin.

The resulting timeline will serve as a happy reminder of the year's events and, if kept hanging until next year, will also make an attractive way to introduce incoming students to what's ahead.

*adapted from an idea by Barbara Duran*
*Dorris Jones Elementary*
*Rockwall, TX*

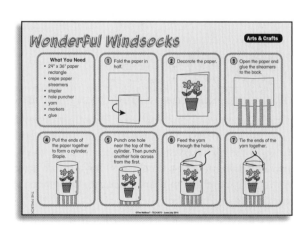

May
flower study

# Wonderful Windsocks

### What You Need

- 24" x 36" paper rectangle
- crepe paper streamers
- stapler
- hole puncher
- yarn
- markers
- glue

**1** Fold the paper in half.

**2** Decorate the paper.

**3** Open the paper and glue the streamers to the back.

**4** Pull the ends of the paper together to form a cylinder. Staple.

**5** Punch one hole near the top of the cylinder. Then punch another hole across from the first.

**6** Feed the yarn through the holes.

**7** Tie the ends of the yarn together.

**Note to the teacher:** Use with "Get Wind of This Idea". Later, put a copy of this card in a plastic page protector and put it out as an easy arts-and-crafts center that works for any season!

# Sweet Memories

End of the year

Complete each sentence with a memory from this school year.

| | | |
|---|---|---|
| **1** I really liked it when | **2** The most surprising thing that happened was | **3** The greatest book I read was |
| **4** The best story I wrote was | **5** The funniest moment was | **6** The most interesting thing I learned was |
| **7** The hardest thing for me to learn was | **8** The easiest thing for me to learn was | **9** My favorite special class was |
| **10** At recess, I loved to | **11** I am most proud of myself for | **12** I will never forget |

**How to Use** Make student copies of this page. Have each child complete a copy as a free-time activity or as a prewriting activity for a year-end report.

# A Bang-Up Job

Use these sparkling activities to set the stage for Flag Day, Independence Day, or any other time of year you focus on **patriotism**.

## Celebrating Freedom

After discussing what students love about their country, use this simple acrostic project to let them reflect on what freedom means to them. Direct each child to complete a copy of the poem organizer from page 262, building on prior knowledge and past experiences to write words and phrases related to freedom. Next, instruct the student to color her paper and, if desired, have her add red, blue, or silver glitter glue for a festive touch. Mount student papers on alternating red, white, and blue construction paper; then bind the pages in a class book titled "Freedom Is Fun!"

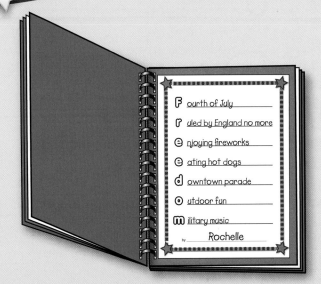

F ourth of July
R uled by England no more
E njoying fireworks
E ating hot dogs
d owntown parade
O utdoor fun
m ilitary music

by Rochelle

Sam

### Memorial Day
by Mario

This past May, my town had a parade and picnic in honor of Memorial Day. I got to help! I had to wake up very early on the day of the parade. First,

## Stars, No Stripes

This decorative desk clip doubles as a stellar work holder. To make one, provide access to a card stock star and red, blue, or white construction paper. Have a child trace a star, cut it out, and write his name on it. Then provide glitter glue or foil star stickers in the same colors and have the student add embellishments to his star. Next, hot-glue a clothespin to the back of each star and put a piece of magnetic tape on the back of the clothespin. Post a prompt like one provided; then direct each student to write his response on a separate sheet of paper. Have the child clip his final draft to his clothespin and hang it from his desk or other magnetic surface.

**Opinion:** What makes our country great?

**Informative/Explanatory:** What does someone who lives in another country need to know about the one you live in? Use facts.

**Narrative:** Write a story about a time when you took part in a patriotic celebration.

F
r
e
e
d
o
m

by _____

# Arts & Crafts

# Arts & Crafts

## Start With Art

Kick off the new school year with this simple apple project; then display students' projects in a window.

Laura Johnson, South Decatur Elementary, Greensburg, IN

**Materials for each student:**

mixture of equal parts water and liquid glue
red, green, or yellow tissue paper squares
foam plate
brown and green paper scraps

paintbrush
scissors
liquid glue

**Steps:**

1. Turn the plate upside down. Use the paintbrush to cover a small section of the plate with a thin layer of the water and glue mixture.
2. Place tissue paper squares atop the plate. Add more mixture and tissue paper until the plate is covered.
3. Cover the tissue paper with another layer of the water and glue mixture.
4. Cut a stem shape from brown paper and a leaf shape from green paper. Write your name on the leaf. Glue the stem and leaf to the tissue paper.
5. Allow the project to dry overnight. Peel the apple off the plate.

## Vacation Visor

Capture summer memories and learn about your new students with this personalized craft. If desired, have each student refer to his illustrations to write an informative piece (W.2.2; W.3.2) that tells how he spent his summer.

Dee Dee Cooper, Monterey Elementary, Monterey, LA

**Materials for each student:**

tagboard copy of page 267
paper plate
stapler

scissors
crayons

**Steps:**

1. Draw a picture on the visor to show how you spent your summer.
2. Cut out the visor.
3. Cut out a circle from the middle of the paper plate. Place the plate on your head.
   If it fits like a hat, stop cutting.
   If it does not fit, take the plate off your head. Cut the circle until it fits.
4. Staple the visor to the paper plate.

# Arts & Crafts

## Designer Web

Capture students' imaginations with this simple craft. Then have each child use his completed web to inspire an imagined story about a spider (W.2.3; W.3.3) or to jump-start an informational piece that compares web spinners and spiders that don't spin webs (W.2.2; W.3.2).

Susie Kapaun, Orchard Park, NY

**Materials for each student:**
sheet of black construction paper          salt
liquid glue          food coloring

**Steps:**
1. Squeeze glue onto your paper to make a web shape. Use intersecting lines.
2. Coat the glue with a thick layer of salt.
3. Shake off any extra salt.
4. Squeeze drops of food coloring onto the salt.
5. Allow the glue to dry.

## Give Thanks

After each child makes this turkey pouch, have her hang it in her cubby or on a low display. Invite each student to complete one copy of a note strip from page 268 for each classmate, telling why he is thankful to have her in class. Provide time for students to distribute the notes to their classmates' pouches.

**Materials for each student:**
2 paper plates          hole puncher
24" length of yarn          stapler
construction paper—brown, red, orange, yellow          glue
scissors          crayons

**Steps:**
1. Turn a plate (plate 1) over. Cut two inches from the top as shown. Write your name on the plate and then color it brown. Color the top half of the other plate (plate 2) brown.
2. Trace your shoe onto a sheet of brown paper. Cut it out. Add details to make a turkey face.
3. Cut several feather shapes from red, orange, and yellow paper.
4. Glue the shoe cutout atop the colored half of plate 2. Glue the feathers to the back of the plate.
5. Place plate 1 atop plate 2. Staple the edges together.
6. Use the hole puncher to make two holes in plate 2. Feed the ends of the yarn through each hole and tie the ends together.

 Use the feather patterns on page 275 to make tracers.

## Holiday Gift Caddy

This snowpal is the perfect container for a small student-made gift. Or fill it with edible treats, and it makes an adorable gift all on its own!

Kelly A. Lu, Berlyn Elementary, Ontario, CA

**Materials for each student:**

clean Chinese-takeout box
2 large pom-poms
pink ink pad
cotton ball

paper scraps: orange, black, white
hole puncher
scissors
glue

**Steps:**

1. Cut two circles from black paper (eyes). Glue them to a flat face of the box.
2. Cut two smaller circles from white paper. Glue them to the eyes.
3. Cut a triangle from orange paper (nose). Glue it below the eyes.
4. Use the hole puncher to make black paper circles for the mouth. Glue them below the nose.
5. Dip the cotton ball on the ink pad. Dab the ink on the box near the mouth.
6. Glue the pom-poms to each side of the box (earmuffs).

## Scratch-Off Fun

Turn your students' gift coupons into something special in just a few simple steps!

April LoTempio, Ben Franklin Elementary, Kenmore, NY

**Materials for one coupon:**
2¾" x 8½" card stock rectangle
solution of 2 parts silver acrylic paint and 1 part dishwashing liquid
clear packing tape or clear Con-Tact covering
paintbrush
markers

To: Dad
Scratch off one circle to reveal your special gift.
Love, Riley

My help shoveling snow

**Steps:**

1. Use markers to decorate the card stock as a gift coupon for a loved one. List three gifts.
2. Cover the rectangle with tape or Con-Tact covering.
3. Paint a circle of solution atop each gift.
4. After the solution dries, deliver the coupon to your loved one. Invite him or her to scratch off one circle to reveal the gift.

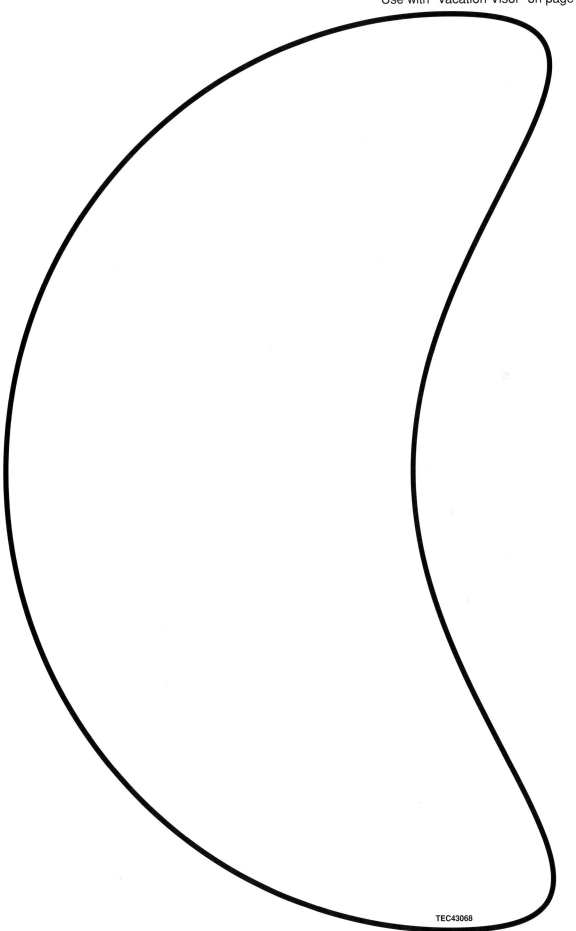

TEC43068

# Note Strips

Use with "Give Thanks" on page 265.

To:
I am **thankful** for you because
_____
_____.
From:

To:
I am **thankful** for you because
_____
_____.
From:

To:
I am **thankful** for you because
_____
_____.
From:

To:
I am **thankful** for you because
_____
_____.
From:

To:
I am **thankful** for you because
_____
_____.
From:

To:
I am **thankful** for you because
_____
_____.
From:

To:
I am **thankful** for you because
_____
_____.
From:

To:
I am **thankful** for you because
_____
_____.
From:

To:
I am **thankful** for you because
_____
_____.
From:

To:
I am **thankful** for you because
_____
_____.
From:

To:
I am **thankful** for you because
_____
_____.
From:

To:
I am **thankful** for you because
_____
_____.
From:

# Displays That Do More
# Than Decorate

# DISPLAYS
## That Do More Than Decorate

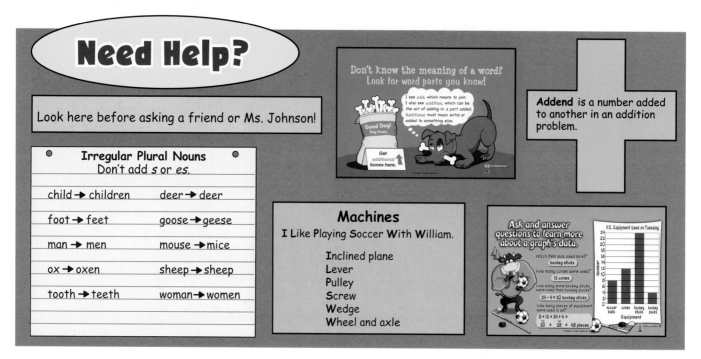

### Need Help?

Look here before asking a friend or Ms. Johnson!

**Irregular Plural Nouns**
Don't add *s* or *es*.

| | |
|---|---|
| child ➔ children | deer ➔ deer |
| foot ➔ feet | goose ➔ geese |
| man ➔ men | mouse ➔ mice |
| ox ➔ oxen | sheep ➔ sheep |
| tooth ➔ teeth | woman ➔ women |

**Machines**
I Like Playing Soccer With William.

Inclined plane
Lever
Pulley
Screw
Wedge
Wheel and axle

Don't know the meaning of a word?
Look for word parts you know!

**Addend** is a number added to another in an addition problem.

Ask and answer questions to learn more about a graph's data.

Designate one area of your room as the help wall. Display posters, chart paper lists, and examples of newly learned skills. Teach students to refer to the wall before asking for assistance. Update the wall as new information is learned, removing old content as needed.

Laura Johnson, South Decatur Elementary, Greensburg, IN

Repurpose jeans that no longer fit to make a motivating good-work display. Hang the pants below the title shown. When a child earns an exemplary score on a test, writes a fascinating story, or gives an insightful answer during a discussion, direct her to write her name on a slip of paper and put it in one of the pockets. Periodically select a pocket and draw the names from it. Award those students a small prize, such as a homework pass, a seasonal pencil, or a roll of Smarties candies. Empty the other pocket, praise those students, and then begin the process again.

Heather Aulisio, Tobyhanna Elementary Center
Pocono Pines, PA

Smarty Pants!

To promote good citizenship, cut out several copies of a star pattern from page 274. Also post on a board the title shown. Each time a child exhibits a positive behavior, write his name on a star and tell what he did to earn it. Or label a small star from page 274 for each child and post the stars on the board so the names aren't showing. Then display a copy of the large star below the title. Each week, turn over a star to reveal the next star student of the week and place it on the large star. When the student's week is over, place her star name-side up with the other stars on the display.

Stacie Holzinger, Millington Elementary, Millington, NJ

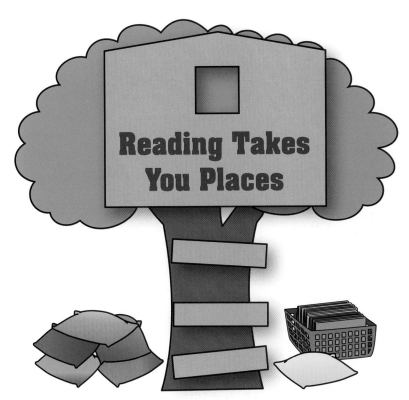

Plant a cozy spot for reading and students will want to visit it all year long! First, use a flattened cardboard box to make a tree house shape and label it as shown. Post the tree house atop a butcher paper tree. At the base of the tree, add fluffy cushions, pillows, and a basket of books (including your favorite Magic Tree House titles). Invite students to settle in the area during independent reading time.

Diane Bell, Pulaski Elementary, Pulaski, PA

tip → To assign students to the area, write each child's name on a paper strip and tape a strip on each ladder rung. Periodically update the names.

## "Fang-tastic"!

To prepare this motivational display, post a simple night scene and label it as shown. Next, instruct each child to trace a copy of the bat pattern on page 275 onto black paper and cut it out. Direct the child to use a white crayon to add facial details that include fangs; then have him write his name on his bat. Post the bats on the display. Each time a child achieves a desired goal, give him a sticker to place on his bat. At the end of the month, reward students who earned a predetermined number of stickers. As an alternative, label a supply of bats with different goals for your whole class, such as "100 Percent Homework," "Hallway Compliments," and "Quiet Transitions." Each time the class achieves a goal, add a sticker.

Traci Mayfield, O'Fallon, IL

*tip* → Have students use metallic markers on the bats to make their names pop.

This inviting door display is just right for fall. On brown paper, make an enlarged copy of the turkey from page 216 (body only) and cut it out. Next, have each child trace a copy of a feather template (patterns on page 275) onto colorful paper, cut it out, and then write her name on it. Post the feathers around the turkey and add the title shown.

adapted from an idea by Regina Clapper, S. S. Dixon Intermediate, Pace, FL

# DISPLAYS That Do More Than Decorate

## It's "SNOW" SECRET... These Books Are Cool!

Encourage students to share their favorite winter reads. Set out three different-size circle tracers, white paper, paper scraps, scissors, glue, and a stapler. To share a book, a student makes three circle cutouts and glues them together to make a snowman shape. On the top circle, the child writes the title of the reading. On the middle circle, he writes why he likes the book; and on the bottom circle, he writes a brief summary. Then the student uses the paper scraps to add other details to the snowman, such as a hat or scarf, before adding his snowman to a display with the title shown.

Brooke Shaw, Columbia, SC

Celebrate the New Year with this easy-to-prepare display. Copy the bell pattern on page 276 onto colored paper. Direct each child to write the year and a school-related resolution on the bell and then cut it out. Next, have the child glue the clapper to the bottom of the bell. Post the completed bells on a display titled as shown. For a personal touch, have each child glue a small school photo to the clapper.

Karen Slattery
Dunrankin Drive Public School
Mississauga, Ontario, Canada

# Star Patterns

Use with "Star Students" on page 271.

TEC43068

TEC43068

## Bat Pattern
Use with "'Fang-tastic'!" on page 272.

TEC43069

## Feather Patterns
Use with "Welcome to Our Room!" on page 272.

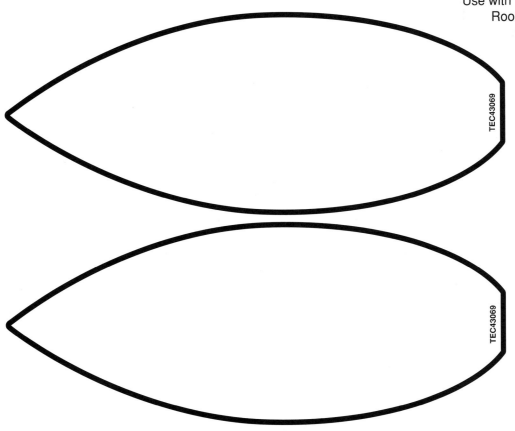

TEC43069

TEC43069

# Bell Pattern

Use with "Give a Cheer! We're Ringing in the New Year" on page 273.

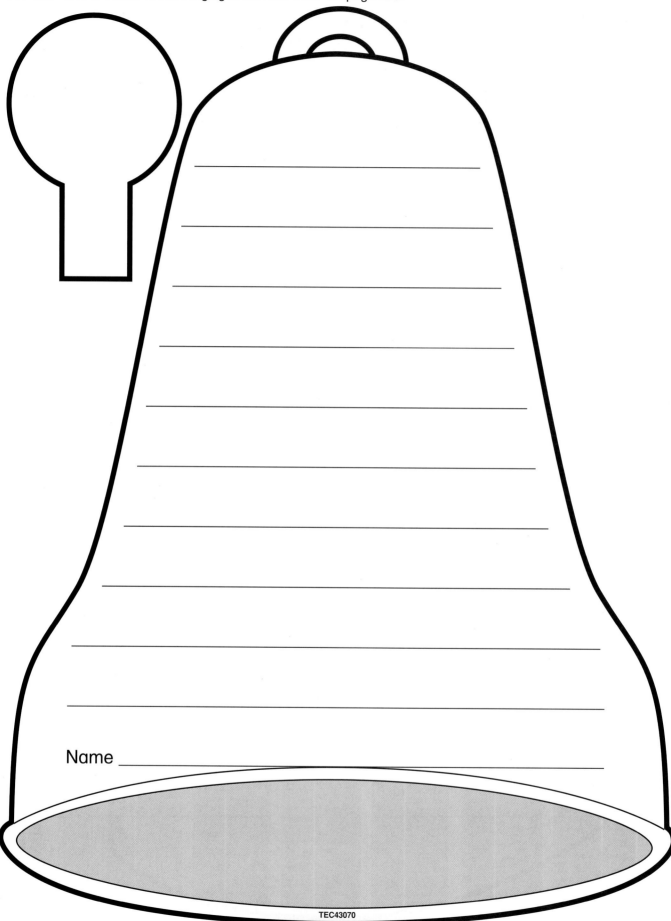

Name _____

TEC43070

# Management Tips and Timesavers

## Planning Ahead

Here's an easy way to **get ready for students who join your class midyear.** As you prepare desk nametags, welcome packets, homework folders, and other supplies, set aside a few extra sets. Place each set in a separate mailing envelope and label it as shown. File the envelopes in a safe place and, if a new student enrolls midyear, all you need to do is take out an envelope to find everything your new student needs.

Linda Meister, Beech Grove Elementary, Massillon, OH

# MANAGEMENT TIPS AND TIMESAVERS

## Join the Club!

Use this simple incentive to **encourage students to complete their homework.** Before you pass out the first assignment, tell students that anyone who completes every assignment for the month will be invited to join the 100% Homework Club. Also tell students that members of the club will enjoy a lunch in the classroom with you. Track students' progress; then schedule the lunch on the first school day of the following month. While they're eating, tell the club members how proud you are of them. Then give each child a prepackaged dessert or a certificate honoring his hard work. Works like a charm!

Heather Aulisio, Tobyhanna Elementary Center, Pocono Pines, PA

## Wild About Partners

To **help students manage their partner work,** display cutouts or pictures of two different animals. Instruct each student of a duo to choose a different animal; then tell students which animal goes first or which student completes each part of a task. As a variation, post two seasonal images instead.

Kelly Lu, Berlyn School, Ontario, CA

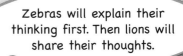

Zebras will explain their thinking first. Then lions will share their thoughts.

Owls will measure. Bats will write.

Give this to Ms. Mitchell-Hamilton. Thanks!

## Take Note

Here's an easy way to **keep track of master copies** of forms and lists students access on their own. Place a sticky note on the original copy and label it like the one shown. Put the copy on the bottom of the corresponding stack of reproducibles. When a student comes to this paper, direct him to bring it to you; then make plans to copy it as soon as possible. After the copy is made, return the original with the sticky note to the bottom of the corresponding stack. Since students bring you the originals, you don't have to dig through your files to find them for copying, saving you time and energy!

Lugene Mitchell-Hamilton, Arkport Central School, Arkport, NY

# MANAGEMENT TIPS and TIMESAVERS

## It's in the Bag

Your **guided reading materials** will be organized and ready to use with this simple tip. Label a two-gallon resealable plastic bag with a leveled reader title. Then place in the bag the books, reproducibles, center materials, and any other instructional supplies directly related to it. Place the bag in a large crate, organized alphabetically by title or when it's used. Not only are all the materials you need in one place, but they will be easy to find next year too!

Tara Kicklighter, Bunnell Elementary, Bunnell, FL

The Life of a Pumpkin

The Life of a Pumpkin

Words to Know
need
stem
vine

Riley

Caleb

## Team Captains

Manage **student helpers** with ease. For each small group of students, assign a captain and direct the captains to collect papers, pass out supplies, lead group discussions—whatever jobs you need completed. To track the captains, post a display of megaphones and pom-poms in your school colors. Each time you assign new captains, write each student's name on a cutout related to the current sports season—such as footballs in the fall, basketballs in winter, and baseballs in spring—and post it on the display.

Wendy Wilcoxen, North Elementary, Breckenridge, TX

## Star Behavior

To **encourage best efforts among table group members**, place copies of the bucket patterns (page 282) in the center of the group. Each time table members demonstrate good listening or direction following, place a star on the bucket. At the end of the week, give each student at the table that earns the most stars a reward, such as a homework pass or a seasonal pencil. **As an alternative,** reward individual students by having each one who exhibits positive behavior write her name on a paper star. Direct each child to place her star in a real bucket. At the end of the week, draw names and give those students a reward.

Jami Brabson, Cedar Bluff Intermediate, Knoxville, TN

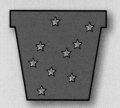

## Passing Inspection

**Get students involved in classroom cleanup** by assigning one student in each small group to act as inspector. Each time the class prepares to leave the room, each group's inspector checks the status of his group members' desktops and floor spaces. Each group member fixes any problems—such as trash on the floor or materials that need to be returned—and once he gets the inspector's okay, lines up to leave.

Jessica Hines
Rivercrest Elementary
Bogata, TX

# MANAGEMENT TIPS AND TIMESAVERS

## Convenient Class List

This quick tip will not only help you **manage homework and other student papers** with ease, you'll also have a reusable class list! First, type your class list in rows and columns; then print several copies. Use packing tape to affix a list to your whiteboard, on folders you take home, near your homework tray, or even at each center. Simply mark each child's name with a dry-erase marker as you correct her paper, or have her mark off her name when she turns in an assignment or completes a center. Then wipe it off and reuse it later. Easy, right?

Dan Sturlaugson, Muller Elementary, Tampa, FL

## Cut Back on Congestion

**Keep student traffic at the classroom library to a minimum** and ensure that each child has a book ready to read. First, give each child a fabric shopping bag to place on the back of his chair. Direct the student to keep his library books as well as a few books from your classroom library in the bag. When it is silent reading time or when a child has free time, he takes one of the books from his bag to read.

Brooke Loafman
Castleberry Elementary
Fort Worth, TX

*tip* → Have students replace books from the class library during noninstructional time, such as after unpacking in the morning.

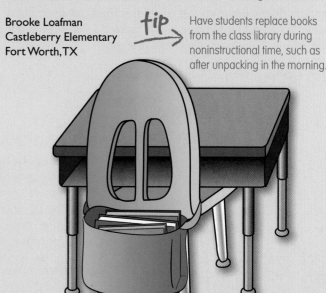

## A Year-End Boost

As the year winds down, **keep class behaviors positive** with this simple reward system. Write on each of a supply of cards a fun but uncommon activity, such as those shown. Secure the cards facedown on a bulletin board or on your whiteboard. When the class meets a common goal for good behavior, select a card, turn it over, and reveal the activity. Students will love the chance to participate in the out-of-the-ordinary reward.

Heather Malin, Stanley M. Koziol Elementary, Ware, MA

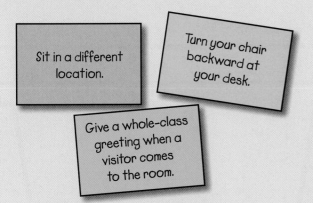

Sit in a different location.

Turn your chair backward at your desk.

Give a whole-class greeting when a visitor comes to the room.

## Grab-and-Go Games

To make **managing classroom games** easier for students, gather a clean, lidded container (such as an icing container) for each game. Put the materials needed to play the game inside the container. On the outside of the container, tape a paper strip with the game's title and, if the directions are not included on the gameboard, tape a copy of them to the container as well. Set out the gameboards with the matching containers. A student who wants to play a game has everything he needs in one place!

Sarah Eaton, Elizabeth Scott Elementary, Chester, VA

# MANAGEMENT TIPS AND TIMESAVERS

## Luck of the Draw

A single deck of playing cards provides several **management shortcuts.** Each day, give each child a card. If desired, secure to each child's desk a clear adhesive pocket in which to store the card. Then have the child refer to the card throughout the day for the following tasks:

- Responding to a question ("Please share your answer for problem three, jack of diamonds.")
- Lining up ("If you are an ace, you may line up…")
- Forming groups ("Clubs work together to research mammals; hearts work together to research reptiles…")
- Finding partners ("Find your color and number match, such as four of hearts and four of diamonds.")

April LoTempio, Williamsville, NY

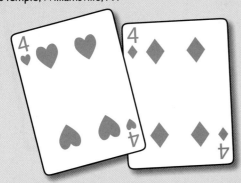

## To the Top

Motivate students to **complete work on time.** First, cut paper strips and hang them on a wall so they resemble a ladder. If desired, add a motivating message on each rung, like the ones shown. Then, for each child, cut a paper circle and label it with her name. Put all the circles at the bottom of the ladder. Each time a student successfully completes an assignment on time, have her move her circle up to the next rung. When she reaches the top of the ladder, award a prize such as a pencil topper or bookmark. Then have her move her circle back to the bottom of the ladder. **For a more individualized approach** to tracking daily homework or completing class work, prepare a ladder outline on paper and date each rung after a child completes a task.

Sharon Chriscoe, Pinnacle, NC

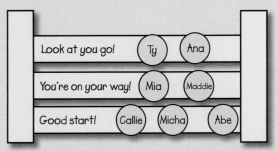

Look at you go! Ty Ana

You're on your way! Mia Maddie

Good start! Callie Micha Abe

# Bucket Patterns
Use with "Star Behavior" on page 280.

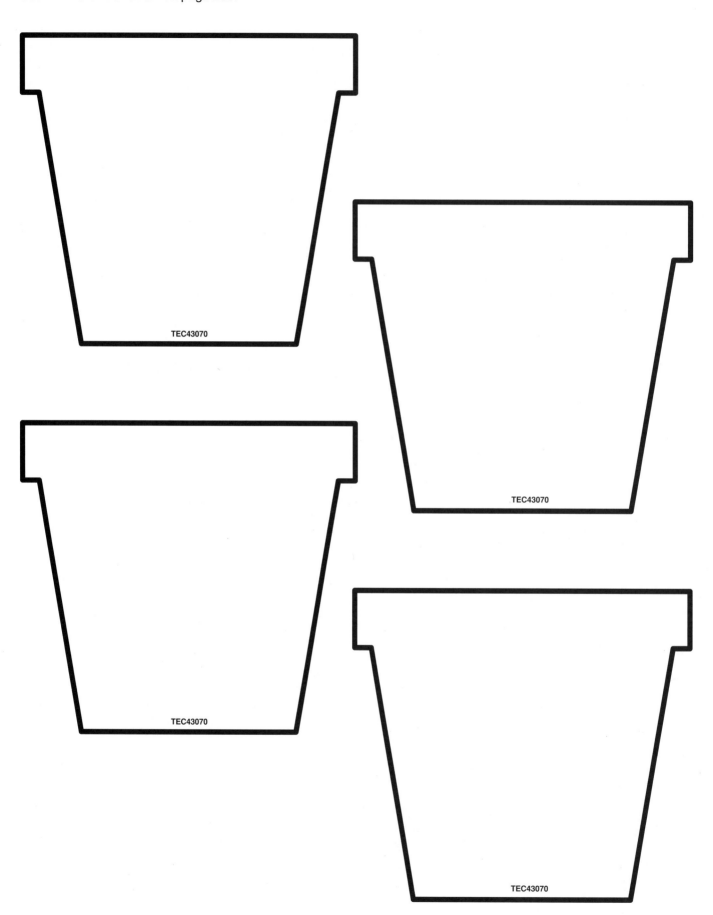

TEC43070

TEC43070

TEC43070

TEC43070

# Using Pocket Charts

## Student Experts

To **limit distractions while you work with small groups**, enlist the help of your student experts. Write on separate sentence strips expert titles like the ones shown and a brief description of each expert's skills. Then program paper cutouts with each child's name. Place the strips in a pocket chart and place a cutout next to each strip. Periodically update the chart with different students' names.

Lienna Dickens, Mark Twain Elementary, Houston, TX

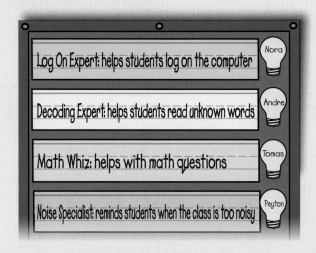

## Stop and Go Signals

This **student work indicator** helps you and your students know who needs to revisit an assignment and who is ready to proceed to the next activity. First, cut a class supply of green paper strips and red paper strips. Personalize each pocket of a deep-pocket pocket chart for each child and slide a green strip into each pocket. When a student has work to complete or correct, place the assignment in his pocket and replace the green strip with a red one. (Set the green strip nearby.) After the child completes or corrects the paper, he returns it and a green strip to his pocket. In one glance, both you and your students know the status of their work.

Courtney Barfield, New Hope Elementary, Locust Grove, GA

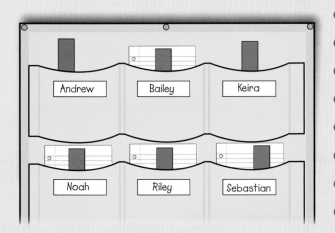

## Ticket, Please

Here's an idea that serves as a multipurpose timesaver! To **store exit ticket responses**, label each pocket of a calendar-size pocket chart with a child's name or student number; then hang it near your classroom door. Before a lesson ends, direct students to place their tickets in their pockets before lining up, leaving, or moving to the next task. Not only does it provide a personalized place for each child's response, this organizer will help students wrap up the activity and help you plan for the next one.

**To get extra mileage from this organizer**, use it to take attendance! Place an index card in each pocket. When students arrive each day, direct each child to remove the index card from her pocket and place it in a stack nearby. What an easy way to gauge who's absent!

Heather Aulisio, Tobyhanna Elementary Center, Pocono Pines, PA

# Partnering With Parents

## Get all your students' caregivers on the same team with these fun ideas!

An apple for the teacher
Is really nothing new
Except when you remember
Parents are teachers too!

## A Team Approach

To show parents you're working toward a common goal—helping their children grow and succeed as learners—label a supply of colorful paper apples as shown. If desired, add a piece of magnetic tape to the back of each apple. Then place one apple atop each stack of paperwork you plan to distribute at Parent Night. They're sure to appreciate this simple gesture.

Suzanne Kurasz
Veterans Memorial Elementary, Brick, NJ

| Name | How I Can Help | Contact Information (phone, email, text) |
| --- | --- | --- |
| ~~~ | ~~~ | ~~~ |
| | | |
| | | |

I'd love to reel in some parent helpers! Tell me about your "o-fish-al" talents and how you can help our class!

## Fishing for Help

At Parent Night, set out snack-size bags of gummy fish or fish-shaped crackers. Label each bag as shown and put the bags in a fishbowl. Place a pen and sign-up sheet near the bowl.

If you already know the dates of events that will require parent help (field trips, class projects, picture day), place copies of calendar pages with your volunteer sign-up materials. Direct parents to sign the calendars to indicate the events they can help with. At the beginning of each month, make copies of the volunteer calendar. Send home a copy to each parent listed as a reminder of the date and to confirm availability.

Colleen Dabney, Williamsburg, VA, and Lisa Mountcasel, Elizabeth Scott Elementary, Chester, VA

## A Simple Survey

Everybody wins with this quick "Q and A" activity! To prepare, make a class supply of the survey on page 285. Before Parent Night, have each child complete the left side of the survey. Instruct the student to write his name on the right side before folding back his answers. Before parents arrive, take a peek at each student's answers when you place students' papers on their desks. As parents arrive, direct them to jot down what they think their children's answers are. Then have parents unfold the paper to compare answers. Not only can each parent use the survey as a way to connect school and home with her child, you will learn a little more about your students.

Carolyn Hart, Hiddenite Elementary, Hiddenite, NC

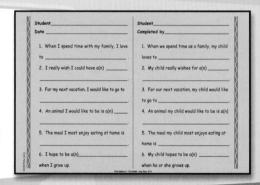

## Building Your Team

Before inviting parents to help in the classroom, host a short meeting or send home information to address your school's volunteer policies, sign-in procedures, and safety plans (such as exiting for a fire drill). After parent volunteers have been oriented, take a snapshot of each one. Write the volunteers' names on separate paper strips; then post each photo and matching strip together on a display titled "Meet the Rest of Room [number]'s Team!" Parents will surely feel like a part of your team, while students, school staff, and substitutes will all know who's helping on the sidelines!

Mary Ann Gildroy, Roundup, MT

**Student** _____

**Date** _____

1. When I spend time with my family, I love _____ to _____.

2. I really wish I could have a(n) _____.

3. For my next vacation, I would like to go to _____.

4. An animal I would like to be is a(n) _____.

5. The meal I most enjoy eating at home is _____.

6. I hope to be a(n) _____ when I grow up.

---

**Student** _____

**Completed by** _____

1. When we spend time as a family, my child loves to _____.

2. My child really wishes for a(n) _____.

3. For our next vacation, my child would like to go to _____.

4. An animal my child would like to be is a(n) _____.

5. The meal my child most enjoys eating at home is _____.

6. My child hopes to be a(n) _____ when he or she grows up.

©The Mailbox® • TEC43068 • Aug./Sept. 2013

**Note to the teacher:** Use with "A Simple Survey" on page 284.

# Manipulatives in Motion

Roll and spin your way to more engaged students!

## Lucky Numbers

Use dice to **manage student participation and classroom helpers!** In advance, cut a hundred chart to match the number of students in your room and place it in a plastic page protector. Assign each child a number on the chart and then gather dice: three for a class of up to 18 students, four for a class of 19 to 24 students, and five for a class of 25 to 30 students. When you need a student helper or volunteer, roll all or some of your dice. Then announce the sum, use a dry-erase marker to mark the corresponding number on the chart, and instruct the child to contribute to the lesson or complete the job. *Leanne Baur, Hall's Cross Roads Elementary, Aberdeen, MD*

| 1 | 2 | 3 | 4 | 5 | 6 | 7 | 8 | 9 | 10 |
|----|----|----|----|----|----|----|----|----|----|
| 11 | 12 | 13 | 14 | 15 | 16 | 17 | 18 | 19 | 20 |

## Vocabulary Builder

Here's a spin on **vocabulary review** that works with any subject. To prepare, label a spinner with some of the tasks shown. Also post a list of words. When reviewing words, invite a student to spin the spinner and choose a word from the list. Then have him complete the task. *Janeen Beresh, Ritzman Community Learning Center, Akron, OH*

Act it out.
Name a word that means the opposite.
Name a word that means almost the same.
Give the meaning.
Ask a classmate to give the meaning.
Use it in a sentence.
Tell why it is important to the reading.
Give an example for it.
Tell a category this word would fit in.

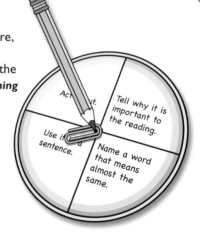

Tell why it is important to the reading.
Act it out.
Use it in a sentence.
Name a word that means almost the same.

 **tip** Use a paper clip and pencil to spin the spinner.

## Twice as Nice

Get students' language skills rolling with these two ideas that use cubes.

**Fact and opinion:** Copy the cube pattern from page 287 onto card stock. Cut out and assemble the cube; then place it at a center with a current reading. After reading, the child rolls the cube and writes a matching statement based on what she read. *Beth Vanaman, Wilmington Manor Elementary, New Castle, DE*

**Adjectives and nouns:** Label a supply of blank cubes with adjectives and another supply with nouns. Invite a child to roll a cube from each supply and then act out what she rolled. Direct the class to guess which nouns and adjectives are being pantomimed. *Heather Aulisio, Tobyhanna Elementary Center, Pocono Pines, PA*

## 6. Opinion

I'm not sure whether I agree or disagree with this opinion.

## 5. Opinion

This is an opinion I disagree with.

## 4. Opinion

This is an opinion I agree with.

TEC43070

## 3. Fact

I can prove it by finding the information online.

## 2. Fact

I can prove it by rereading a text.

## 1. Fact

I can prove it because I can see it in my life.

# It's a Makeover!

**Breathe new life into classroom materials with a few simple changes.**

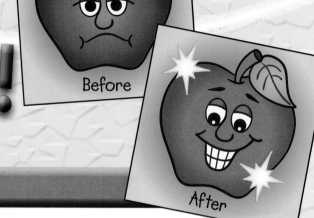

Before

After

## Books and Magazines

Remove and laminate covers of worn-out paperback books. Place the covers at a center for students to sort by genre or to kick-start a writing assignment. Or use the covers to decorate literature-based bulletin boards. *Cheryl Rayl, Mayville Elementary, Mayville, MI*

Take pages from a book you plan to retire from your classroom library and glue them to construction paper. Have the child sequence the events and, since some of the text pages may be glued to construction paper, guide the student to identify any important events that are missing from the story. *Madeline Spurck, Neil A. Armstrong Elementary, Richton Park, IL*

Snip pictures from old magazines and store them by topic, such as animals, places, and people. Whenever students need images for collages or posters, direct them to the pictures. The pictures also work well for writing inspiration. *Sandra Taylor, Asbury Elementary, Hampton, VA*

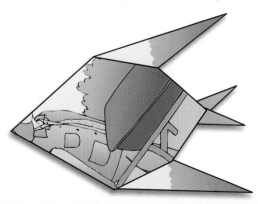

For year-end practice with reading directions, use old magazine or book pages for origami art. Cut the pages into large squares and put the squares with directions for origami art projects. (To find directions online, search for "origami instructions.") *April Parker, St. Pius X School, Greensboro, NC*

# Playing Cards

Turn worn or incomplete sets of cards into manipulative flash cards, perfect for beginning-of-the-year review. Simply remove the face cards and then glue pairs of cards together as shown. Set them out for students to practice addition. A child reads the numbers on both sides of a card and, if he needs help finding the sum, counts the images. As an alternative, use the cards to teach students the commutative property.
*Hope Taylor Spencer, McLeansville, NC*

If you have a deck that is short a few cards, don't fret! The cards are perfect for building a house of cards. Tell students that kids in colonial times used cards to build towers. Then show them how to start a tower (see image). Once they have the basics, students can use the cards during free time or for a fun indoor recess activity!
*Heather Malin, Stanley M. Koziol Elementary, Ware, MA*

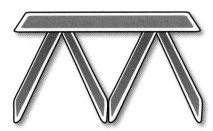

# Other Teaching Supplies

Set aside items that are no longer of use in your classroom, such as old curriculum posters, outdated textbooks, or sets of unused stickers. At the end of the year, place the items in your class treasure chest or use them in a year-end auction. Students will love the chance to get their hands on the materials and—if they play school—will treasure having "real" teaching supplies to use at home.
*Cheryl Rayl, Mayville Elementary, Mayville, MI, and Madeline Spurck, Neil A. Armstrong Elementary, Richton Park, IL*

# Check These Out!
## Quick Tech Tips

 ### Organized Ideas
**Using digital tools to produce writing (W.2.6; W.3.6)**

Did you know there are free websites that will help students plan their writing? To find these tools, search for "free mind mapping tools for teachers." Then have students use the concept maps and picture tools to help guide their writing. By inserting clip art and words, or even drawing their own pictures, students can gather their thoughts during the prewriting stage. Some sites include a tool that allows students to then organize their ideas in an outline.

Donald Barringer, Glenn Elementary, Durham, NC

 ### Set Up for Success
**Using digital tools to produce writing (W.2.6; W.3.6)**

To give students choices when producing their writing, set up simple templates on your classroom computers. Make templates for brochures, slide shows, and reports; then save them. When a child is ready to publish his work, have him choose a template and type in his text. If desired, encourage him to add pictures and use decorative fonts. When he is ready to save his project, help the student use his name to rename the file or move it to a personal folder.

Barbara Duran, Dorris Jones Elementary, Rockwall, TX

 ### Easy as 1, 2, 3
**Managing technology**

Keep track of your classroom tablets by assigning each one a number. Simply set each tablet's wallpaper with a different number. If desired, add your name and school name under the number as well, just in case the tablet should be taken from your room and need to be returned. When you distribute the tablets to students, keep a list of which tablet each child receives.

Julie Brady, Fairfax, VA

# Our Readers Share

# Our Readers SHARE

## Guess What?

I've got a great idea that allows students (and teachers) to share personal news. I place a large sheet of paper in an easily accessible area of my room named our "Guess What?" corner. When students have free time, I invite them to visit the corner to write their news or to read what has been written. I post a new sheet of paper when the current one is filled with news. *Melissa R. Ashbaugh, Almont Community School, Almont, MI*

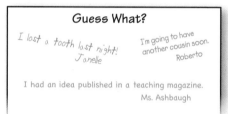

### Guess What?

I lost a tooth last night!
Janelle

I'm going to have another cousin soon.
Roberto

I had an idea published in a teaching magazine.
Ms. Ashbaugh

## TOP-NOTCH IDEA

To motivate my students to do their best, I give them personalized pencil toppers. In advance, I cut ovals from decorative paper, punch two holes, and add a motivating message to each one. Whenever I see a child who needs extra encouragement, I add her name to a message and slip a pencil topper on her pencil. *Cynthia Holcomb, San Angelo, TX*

Zoe,
Keep working hard! I'm proud of you!

## I Spy

Here's a way to introduce students to your classroom and save your voice! First, I take pictures of items I want students to locate in my room, such as tissues, reference books, and the pencil sharpener. I organize the photos on a grid and then make student copies of the grid. As an opening-day activity, I direct student pairs to explore our classroom and have each child circle on his paper the items found. Students love the challenge, and I've even created a version for parents to complete at open house. *April LoTempio, Ben Franklin Elementary, Kenmore, NY*

Name Tyson

I Spy in Room 224...

| | | | |
|---|---|---|---|
| 1 | 2 | 3 | 4 |
| 5 | 6 | 7 | 8 |
| 9 | 10 | 11 | 12 |

## Happy Memories

At the start of the school year, I show an empty jar to my students. I explain that it is our class memory jar and invite them to add memories to it. I tell them that each time something memorable happens during the year, they should write about it on a piece of paper and place the paper inside the jar. Then, on the last day of school, I read the contents of the jar so we can reflect on a memorable year! It's a fun way to capture the year's events. *Heather Aulisio, Tobyhanna Elementary Center, Pocono Pines, PA*

### The MAILBOX BLOG

 I love to play That's Me on our first day. I say a statement and, if the statement is true for a student, he stands up and says, "That's me!" It's a great way for students to get to know each other and learn what they have in common. *Kim Frantzen, Evelyn Hamlow Elementary, Waverly, NE, via The Mailbox® Blog*

# Our Readers SHARE

## SPREAD THE WORD

I use my restroom pass to remind students to wash their hands. To make the pass, I trace a handprint onto construction paper and cut it out. I label the thumb as our restroom pass and include my name. Next, I write on each palm a reminder for hand washing. Then I laminate the pass. *Colleen Dabney, Williamsburg, VA*

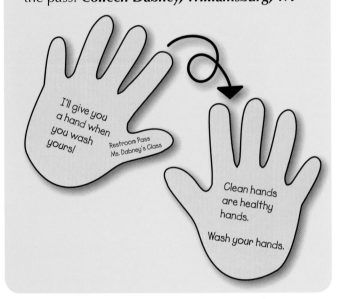

I'll give you a hand when you wash yours!

Restroom Pass
Ms. Dabney's Class

Clean hands are healthy hands.

Wash your hands.

## Glad You're Here

With help from my students, I'll be ready to welcome a substitute if the need arises. After students are familiar with our rules and routines, I enlist their help in writing an acrostic poem. I write the letters of the word "welcome" down the left side of a sheet of chart paper. Then students and I name an important piece of information about our class for each letter. When we have a final draft produced, I have each child sign the welcome poster and store it with my other substitute supplies until needed. *Heather Aulisio, Tobyhanna Elementary Center, Pocono Pines*

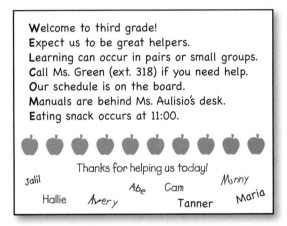

Welcome to third grade!
Expect us to be great helpers.
Learning can occur in pairs or small groups.
Call Ms. Green (ext. 318) if you need help.
Our schedule is on the board.
Manuals are behind Ms. Aulisio's desk.
Eating snack occurs at 11:00.

Thanks for helping us today!

Jalil       Abe    Cam       Manny
  Hallie  Avery       Tanner  Maria

## The MAILBOX BLOG

I like to make what I call "Rotten Banana Fruit Salad" on the first day of school. As I assemble a salad of fresh fruit, I have students compare the fruit to the qualities of a good classmate. Then I pull out a rotten banana and try to add it to the salad (much to students' dismay). A discussion of how one rotten banana can spoil the salad (or a class activity) follows; then students enjoy a sample of the salad. *Melissa A. Campbell, Willis Valley Elementary, Fort Payne, AL, via The Mailbox® Blog*

## Lunchtime Celebration

For a special birthday surprise, I send a letter home to each child just before her birthday inviting her to eat lunch with me. (Boys and girls who celebrate summer birthdays receive their letters during the last month of school.) Students are excited to accept their invitations, and I look forward to spending one-on-one time with each child. *Mandy Herring, Gardner Magnet School, Hot Springs, AR*

You're Invited!

Dear Ella,

How exciting! Your birthday is right around the corner! I hope you can join me for lunch on your special day, September 27. We'll eat in the classroom and talk about whatever you'd like. I hope you can join me then.

Sincerely,
Ms. Herring

## MUMS FOR A LUCKY "MUM" OR DAD

To make my classroom extra inviting during conferences, I prepare a simple centerpiece. First, I cut a hole in the top of a pumpkin and then scoop out the flesh. Next, I place a potted mum in the hole. I set the resulting centerpiece on my conference table. At the end of each conference, I invite parents to complete a ticket to enter a drawing for the centerpiece. After conferences are completed, I select a name and send the centerpiece home with the student whose "mum" or dad won it. *Heather Aulisio, Tobyhanna Elementary Center, Pocono Pines, PA*

## Lend a Hand

Last year, broken bones caused two of my students to wear slings. Since they couldn't hold their papers still, completing their work was a challenge. To make things easier for them, I lent each child a decorative paperweight. It held papers in place while the student worked! *Kasey Kervin, Starline Elementary, Lake Havasu City, AZ*

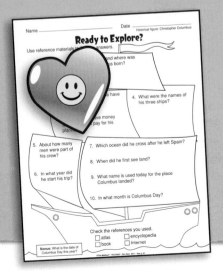

## Tattle Tamer

Some of my students love to tattle. Whenever a child tries to tattle on another, I stop her and ask her to say something nice about the other student. Usually, by the time she thinks of something nice to say, she forgets to tattle. *Michelle Lanham, Will Rogers Elementary, Shawnee, OK*

The MAILBOX BLOG

I use page protectors to keep my originals neat. I also slip each of my single-page gameboards inside one too. This way, I don't have to worry about laminating the gameboard and, when students are done practicing a gameboard's skill, I can easily store it in a binder too! *Nichole Dirks via The Mailbox® Blog*

## Supportive Statements

During math instruction, I encourage students to support their answers. Since such explanations often require transition words, I integrate the terms from our writing standards (*because, as a result, due to, therefore*) into our math instruction. To help students use them, I display the words and model scenarios in which my students might use each one. Then I reward students who include these terms in their answers. Students quickly begin to use these words on a daily basis, both in writing and math lessons. **Sandy Koerner, Fox Hollow Elementary, Port Richey, FL**

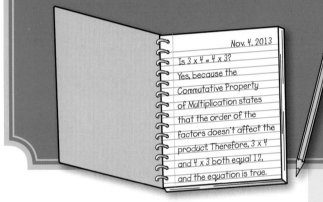

Nov. 4, 2013
Is 3 x 4 = 4 x 3?
Yes, because the Commutative Property of Multiplication states that the order of the factors doesn't affect the product. Therefore, 3 x 4 and 4 x 3 both equal 12, and the equation is true.

The **MAILBOX** BLOG

I keep my classroom stocked with baby wipes at all times. I use them to clean student whiteboards, remove ink from transparencies, wipe down dirty desks, and even clean sticky hands. They are a real timesaver! *Jessica Blaha via The Mailbox® Blog*

## Say No to Spills

I was looking for a way to eliminate paint spills and found an answer—plastic cups with domed lids. I simply put paint in the cups and attach the lids. When my students use the paint cups, they place a small paintbrush through the hole in the lid. The lid keeps the paint from spilling, plus students can wipe off excess paint before pulling the brush out of the cup. What a simple solution! *Heather Aulisio, Tobyhanna Elementary Center, Pocono Pines, PA*

## FALL IN LINE

To manage my students when they are in line, I prepare an assigned order and post it near my classroom door. First, I take a picture of each child and have her glue her picture to a paper circle (frame). I also direct her to write her name on the frame. Then I use Sticky-Tac adhesive to post the frames in order next to the door. This way, everyone knows the order, and if I'm absent, a substitute can easily identify who goes where. Plus the Sticky-Tac adhesive allows me to reposition the frames as needed. **Lois Stuart, Texas Preparatory School, San Marcos, TX**

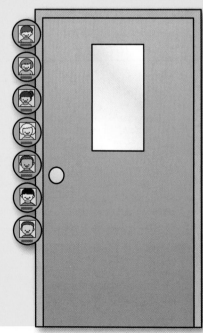

# *Our Readers* SHARE

## STOCK UP FOR STAFF

By taking advantage of holiday sales and hanging on to hotel toiletries when I go on vacation, I can share items that make work feel a little more like home. I simply place these items, like scented soaps and lotions, in a basket. Then I place the basket in the staff restroom. Sometimes I also set out a container of breath mints, which are perfect for conference days. It's an easy gift everyone can enjoy! ***Sue Kreibich, Washington-Kosciusko Elementary, Winona, MN***

## Common Interests

When a new student joins my class, I ask him to write a list of his hobbies and interests. Then, each day for a week, I share a different item from the list with the class and find out who has similar interests. I provide time for the students to sit together and chat. After a few days, my new student has made friends and everyone knows a little more about him! ***Humaira Saeed, Children's Manor Montessori School, Ellicott City, MD***

Welcome to our class, <u>Ashton!</u>
What is your favorite food? <u>Tacos</u>
Do you have a favorite sport? If so, what is it? <u>I don't really</u>
<u>like to play sports, but I watch basketball with my dad.</u>
Do you have a favorite animal? If so, what is it? <u>Ligers are</u>
<u>cool. They are part lion and part tiger.</u>
What do you like to do after school? <u>I go to afterschool</u>
<u>care. After I do my homework, I like to play checkers</u>
What do you like to do over the weekend? <u>I am learning</u>
<u>how to paint. I like to paint pictures of my friends and places</u>
<u>I remember from Colorado.</u>

**tip** If you're worried about finding classroom time for the common-interest conversation, reveal the information before lunch and encourage students to talk while they eat.

## A Handy Helper

I've found a way to make glitter more manageable for my students and me. I pour each of my colors of glitter into a separate, clean coffee creamer container. Then I label the container with the color. With the cap twisted on, students can easily pour a workable amount of glitter onto their projects. With the cap twisted off, I can pour students' excess glitter back into the container. Not only is there less waste, but there's less mess too! *Heather Aulisio, Tobyhanna Elementary Center, Pocono Pines, PA*

Green

The MAILBOX BLOG

When communicating with parents, keep an open door as well as an open mind. Involve them as much as possible in every aspect of their child's journey. Every parent wants to feel that his or her child is special to you in some way. *Natasha Balfour, Dixie Elementary, Tyler, TX, via The Mailbox® Blog*

# Our Readers SHARE

## In Clear View

In addition to knowing the essential question of a lesson or unit, it is important for my students to also know how they will be expected to demonstrate this knowledge. To do this, I laminate a simple poster like the one shown for each subject and display it in clear view of students. I use a dry-erase marker to write on each section and refer to the corresponding poster at the beginning of each lesson. It's an easy way to keep students posted on their expectations! *April LoTempio, Ben Franklin Elementary, Kenmore, NY*

| Essential Question(s)  | Sharing Answers  |
|---|---|
| How do you keep to the topic when writing? | Group report |

## Brain Sprinkles

When my students need a confidence boost before presenting a report or sharing with the class, I offer them some brain sprinkles. Here's how I make them. First, I put a cup of rice into an empty coffee container. I secure the lid to the container with hot glue or clear packing tape; then I cover the container with Con-Tact covering. Before a student begins her presentation, I remind her of the qualities I hope to see and hear. Then I shake the container over the child's head. The sprinkling action alleviates stress and helps the child focus to do her best! *Karen Slattery, Dunrankin Drive Public School, Mississauga, Ontario, Canada*

Before a student teacher arrives, I put together a notebook of important information that includes a letter of introduction from me, a copy of our crisis plan and a building diagram, a labeled photo of our staff, plus resources and websites I find useful. Not only can she find information she needs in one place, but my student teacher can use the notebook to record notes of her own during her time with us. *Vicki O'Neal, Lincoln School, Baxter Springs, KS, via The Mailbox® Blog*

## A DECORATIVE TOUCH

Instead of purchasing a designated pocket chart to store my behavior system in, I simply bought a jewelry bag from a local discount store. I still have plenty of storage pockets for my color-coded cards and, despite the low cost, it's sturdy enough to reuse year after year! *Julia Guerrero, Palmcroft Elementary, Yuma, AZ*

# Our Readers Share

## Hands-Free Helper

My students love to play card games but often struggle with holding several cards at once. To solve this problem, I make hands-free holders. First, I cut an empty egg carton in half, turn each half upside down, and slice a slit across the top of each egg holder. I set out the holders with my card games. When students play, they take a holder and place one card in each slit. This way, their cards are hidden from their opponents, so they can focus their attention on strategizing and having fun! *Heather Aulisio, Tobyhanna Elementary Center, Pocono Pines, PA*

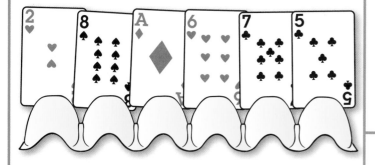

## Red Display

I designate one bulletin board in my classroom as the red board. I cover the board with a red background and leave it that way all year long. Not only does the red work well as a backdrop for Valentine's Day, but it coordinates with displays featuring the Olympic Games, influential people, patriotic themes, and even apples in September and Christmas in December! Whether I use the board to display student work or to showcase a unit of study, the red background is always up and ready to use! *Cheryl Rayl, Mayville Elementary, Mayville, MI*

## Transferring Student

To honor a student who must transfer midyear, I do my best to make his last day a special one. Here are just a few ways I treat him:

- I name the day in honor of the student, such as "Pat Day." I write the name of the celebration on a sheet of chart paper, hang it on the classroom door, and invite his classmates to sign a message to him.
- I suspend regular helper duties for the day and allow the transferring student to complete them all.
- I invite the student to choose which book I read during our read-aloud time. I also invite him to do the reading!
- I provide time at the end of the day for the student to say good-bye to the class as a whole. Then I give the child the signed chart paper.

*Tina Bilger Vaughn, Christiansburg, VA*

**BRAG** Not only did I volunteer to read aloud, but I also spoke loudly and clearly!

## BRAG Tags

The teachers at my school team-teach, so to improve communications with my coteaching colleague, I create BRAG tags. I label brightly colored squares of card stock "BRAG," which stands for "Being Really Awesome and Great," and attach metallic ribbon to each one. When I see a student who I want to brag about, I write a description of her efforts or actions on a square. Then I invite the child to wear her BRAG tag for the rest of the day. Students love the attention, and the tags serve as a great visual reminder of the positive things that students on our team are doing. *Melissa A. Campbell, Wills Valley Elementary, Fort Payne, AL*

# Our Readers Share

## Having a Ball

A five-minute fun jar motivates my students to complete classroom tasks. To make the jar, I label each of a supply of brightly colored superballs with brief—but highly desired—activities. Then I place the balls in a small container. When the class finishes an assignment early with at least five minutes left before the next one, I draw a ball from the jar. Students are rewarded with the activity written on it. Talk about fun and motivating!

*Melissa A. Campbell*
*Wills Valley Elementary*
*Fort Payne, AL*

## Varied Colors

When I have an activity that calls for brown paint, I like to set out coffee as well. When students dip their brushes in the coffee, it allows them to vary their earth tones on their project. Plus it's a great way to use stale leftovers! *Catherine Fontana, Bloomfield Elementary, Bloomfield, NJ*

## On Top of It

Transferring information from a textbook to paper can be a tricky task for students. To make completing such assignments easier, I direct my students to paper-clip a transparency sheet atop the textbook page. I have them use overhead pens to complete the activity on the transparency sheet. Not only does this method help the students, it also conserves paper! *Anita Dodell, Oceanside, NY*

## Time to Shine

Rather than sharing warm fuzzies, I have my students send a sparkle as a way to recognize their classmates' positive behaviors. All I do is place a bowl of glitter pom-poms (sparkles) near a pocket chart labeled with each child's name. Whenever a student has something nice done for her, such as helping her pack up or giving her a compliment, she places a sparkle in the child's pocket. I like to get in on the act too! Then, at the end of day, I invite students to check their pockets and return their sparkles to the bowl. Students' smiles always sparkle from the recognition! *Heather Aulisio, Tobyhanna Elementary Center, Pocono Pines, PA*

 Short on pocket charts? Label a cup for each child with her name or number.

# Our Readers Share

## Ouch Pouch

Transporting bandages, tissues, and other necessities to the playground has never been easier. I simply repurpose an old wristlet purse into an ouch pouch. I stuff the wristlet with first aid items and hang it by my classroom door. When my class goes to recess, I put the ouch pouch on my wrist, and everything we need for minor mishaps is easily accessible.
*Heather Aulisio, Tobyhanna Elementary Center, Pocono Pines, PA*

## Can You Dig It?

Here's a cute way to show appreciation for classroom volunteers. For each helper, I purchase a small plastic sand shovel. I put the shovel in a clear plastic bag; then I add a treat to the bag, such as popcorn or candy. I tie the top of the bag with colorful ribbon and include a short note like the one shown. My classroom helpers love this creative gesture.
*Heather Aulisio*

**Glad we could scoop you up!**
Thanks for all your help this year.

Ms. Aulisio's class

## A Cozy Reward

To celebrate students reaching a class goal, I have a slipper day. Students change into their favorite slippers when they arrive at school and enjoy the casual footwear while in the classroom. Later in the day, I raffle off a pair of one-size-fits-all novelty slippers. Fun! *Heather Aulisio*

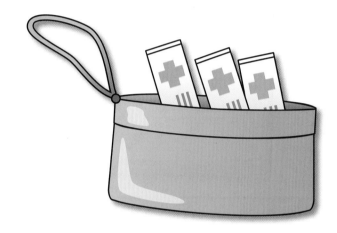

## Summertime Review

When I prepare summer packets for my students, I include a silly joke, riddle, or poem at the end of each week of activities. I also include a sheet of stickers for parents to use when their children's assignments are successfully completed. These added touches keep students motivated to complete the work. *Cheryl Rayl, Mayville Elementary, Mayville, MI*

# Problem Solved!

# Problem Solved!

## How do you help students get *back in the swing of things*?

## Your Solutions to Classroom Challenges

Before the first day of school, I make each child an apple bag. In a red bag, I place supplies the student will need, such as erasers, bookmarks, and a snack. I twist the top of the bag and wrap brown packaging tape around it to make a stem. Then I tape a green felt leaf to each stem. When students arrive, each one has on his desk an apple bag filled with the things he needs to get through the day!

*Lori Yowler, Northwestern Elementary*
*Springfield, OH*

To make sure my students get home safely, I prepare a list of students' bus numbers and drop-off locations (home, afterschool care, etc.). As students come into the classroom, I give each child a friendly greeting and then ask for her bus information. If she can tell me without hesitation, I put a check next to her name. If she needs a moment to tell me or can't remember at all, I give her a sticker with her bus information and direct her to place it on her backpack. If there is a discrepancy between the child's response and my information, I circle the child's name and check with the office at lunch to make sure everyone has the correct information before dismissal.

*Heather Aulisio*
*Tobyhanna Elementary Center*
*Pocono Pines, PA*

 **tip** Use this basic technique to make sure students know their lunch numbers, library codes, and computer passwords.

In 2009, 70 percent of six- to 17-year-olds reported being highly engaged in school (liking school, being interested in school, and working hard in school).

*US Census Bureau,*
*A Child's Day, 2009*

I get my students' creative juices flowing and introduce various classroom expectations by showing them a rock. I tell them that the rock is a reminder that they will be expected to work hard this year. Then I give each small group of students one of the objects shown. I challenge them to make a connection between the object and being successful this year. Before student groups share their ideas, I remind the class to be good listeners and to be open minded to other people's ideas.

*Kim Minafo*
*Apex, NC*

> rubber band: stay flexible
> sticker or glue stick: stick together
> erasers: everyone makes mistakes
> Life Savers candy: be helpful
> joke book: have fun
> puzzle piece: work together

# Problem Solved!

## How do you *display student work with ease?*

## Your Solutions to Classroom Challenges

 I don't take down the displays I use year after year. I simply disguise them. By covering these displays with a new layer of bulletin board paper, I can still use the board space while keeping my reusable display intact. It's less work in the long run!

*Randie Faulkner, Coyote Ridge Elementary, Carrollton, TX*

Clothespins make quick work of displaying my students' assignments. First, I label a set of clothespins with students' names or numbers. Then I use adhesive hooks to hang a clothesline along a wall or under the board's chalk ledge. I hang the clothespins in alphabetical or numerical order; then I clip each child's work to his clothespin. There are no staples to remove, which makes changing out the displayed work a breeze!

*Evelyn Council, Selwyn Elementary, Charlotte, NC*

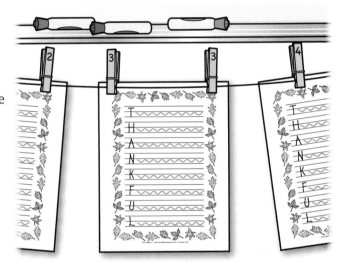

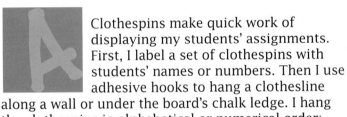

I make a reusable display with decorative desktags. To start, I label a supply of desktags each with a different student's name; then I hot-glue two clothespins to each tag. Next, I use packing tape to secure each tag to a wall, or I staple the tags to a cork strip. When I have student artwork or assignments to display, I simply hang the paper with the matching clothespins. The clothespins make updating student work a snap, and as an added bonus, each child can easily locate her sample!

*Amber Stout, Jefferson Elementary, Pierre, SD*

 In 2010, 299 second- and third-grade teachers responded to an online poll by The Mailbox® telling how often they change the displays in their classrooms. Of them, 41 percent change their displays once a month, 32 percent do not follow a predetermined schedule, and 13 percent rarely change their displays.

# Problem Solved!

## Your Solutions to Classroom Challenges

**How do you manage students who work with support staff?**

*"It takes a whole village to raise a child."*

—Igbo and Yoruba Proverb

To make the transition back into the classroom a bit easier, **I keep a missed-work clothesline** near my classroom door. While a child is out of the room, I clip any paperwork he missed to the clothesline, keeping the most recent paper on top. When the student returns to the classroom, he removes his papers and takes them to his seat. He works on what he can until I can assist him individually.

*Heather Aulisio, Tobyhanna Elementary Center*
*Pocono Pines, PA*

Keeping track of student work can be a challenge as it moves from classroom to classroom, so I **created a worksheet receipt form** to help the classroom teachers I work with. I staple the form to an assignment and write the date I give it to the student. I also have the student sign the form to verify this is the date it was assigned. Then, when the activity is completed and turned in, the form is signed and dated by her classroom teacher. It's an easy way to track how long students take to complete an assignment, and it ensures that everyone is working together to stay on top of student work.

*Pat Mills, Union, KY*

**I set up tag teams** to help students get back on track when they return to my room. I make simple tag shapes from construction paper and yarn and give them to students who visit other teachers. Before a child heads out, he hands his tag to a classmate who has already been designated as one of his tag team members. The classmate is responsible for gathering paperwork and explaining what was missed when the child returns.

*Rolanda Mackey, Brownsfield Elementary, Baton Rouge, LA*

# How do you *manage students who have a lot to say?*

## Your Solutions to Classroom Challenges

**I place a small supply of sticky notes on my students' desks.** When a child has something to share but has already had the floor or doesn't get a chance because other students were chosen, I encourage her to write her thoughts on a sticky note. Students place their notes on a specially designated area on my desk, and I review them. If a student has an especially thoughtful idea to share, I post it on a display for everyone to see.

*Rebecca Landreth*
*Erdenheim Elementary*
*Flourtown, PA*

I like to use a hundred chart to add. It's easy to add all the tens by moving down the rows. Then I count on to add the ones.

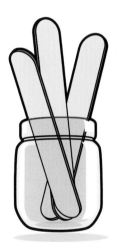

To curb "outburst-itis," **I designate an empty baby food jar or other clear container for each repeat offender.** Every time a student blurts out a response, I drop a craft stick in his jar. If he earns three sticks during one lesson, he is put in a talking time-out for three minutes. Having the privilege to participate taken away reminds students of the need to raise their hands and share the floor.

*Cyndy Johnson, Prairie Elementary, Yelm, WA*

**I set up a "blurt box"** on my whiteboard. Each time a student blurts out an answer or a comment, I quietly put a tally mark in the box. At the end of the day, I have the students count aloud with me as I total the tally marks. I then write the number in the box, circle it, and erase the tallies. I challenge students to reduce the number of tallies the next day.

*Renea Magnani, Dunbar Elementary, Glen Ellen, CA*

# How do you *prepare for a substitute teacher?*

## Your Solutions to Classroom Challenges

 One way I make sure my sub is prepared for an emergency is by **preparing a special badge holder**. I gather a badge holder with a neck strap. In it, I place a mini version of our class list and leave directions for the substitute to wear the holder. If a fire drill or another emergency pops up, she can easily refer to the list to do a quick check of the roll. She can also use it when she picks students up from special classes or lunch.

*Heather Aulisio, Tobyhanna Elementary Center, Pocono Pines, PA*

 Include the number of students at the bottom of the list for an easy head count. Instruct the sub to mark with a pencil any student who is absent and then adjust the count.

Ms. Aulisio's Class

 To keep the day flowing smoothly, I **ask my more challenging students to help the sub** with certain tasks. I write a note to the student, requesting that he assist with a job, such as monitoring our classroom technology or keeping the classroom tidy during the day. Not only will this student be engaged in this helpful behavior, but the substitute will have one less chore to worry about during the day!

*Barbara Duran, Dorris Jones Elementary, Rockwall, TX*

 I always include a **backup plan**. When preparing for a substitute, I make two copies of my class schedule and plans. I leave one set on my desk for the substitute and pass another set to a fellow teacher. That way, my colleague can answer questions if needed or, if she's asked to step in until a substitute arrives, my colleague knows what needs to be done in my classroom.

*Kim Manning, Schulze Elementary, Irving, TX*

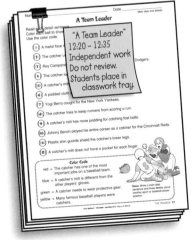

"A Team Leader"
12:20 – 12:35
Independent work
Do not review.
Students place in classwork tray.

 Rather than leaving lengthy lesson plans, **I use sticky notes to keep things simple** for my substitute. I place a sticky note atop each activity students should complete. On each sticky note, I name the activity and tell when it should be completed. I also indicate how it should be completed (independently, as a whole group, or as partners), if it should be reviewed or not, and where the completed activity should be placed.

*Melissa Renae Ashbaugh, Almont Community School, Almont, MI*

# Answer Keys

**Page 25**
1. Bud E. Bear and his mom
2. Bud's house on a Saturday; the store on the same day; back at Bud's house (kitchen) later that day
3. He offers to go shopping for his mom.
4. It is raining, and he doesn't want the groceries to get wet. He hurries home.
5. no; His mom calls him a "drizzly bear," and he starts to apologize for getting the groceries wet.
6. She uses the groceries he bought to make him sugar cookies.

**Page 33**
1. She put it in her pail.
2. happy; In the poem, she bounced down the trail. When characters bounce, they are often happy.
3. upset; In the poem, everyone heard her holler. When characters holler, they may yell or cry out as if in pain.
4. It fell out through a hole in the pail.

Bonus: Drawings will vary but should show that Penny is upset.

**Page 34**
1. mammal
2. It might roll itself into a tight ball, run away, or dig a new tunnel.
3. Its parents have hard shells. A pup's shell is soft and feels like leather. It takes a few days to harden.
4. Its snout may be pointy or shaped like a shovel. It has strong front feet and curved claws.
5. It has hair. It gives birth to live young.
6. It digs up insects using its snout and claws. It uses its sticky tongue to pull termites from tight spaces.
7, 8. Answers will vary.

Bonus: Answers will vary.

**Page 35**
1. He is running late.
2. He cares for him. He asks if he is okay and offers his hand to help him up.
3. impatient; Crash taps his foot and checks his watch.
4. thoughtful; Explanations will vary.
5. Crash lets Flip go down the stairs first, he guides Mrs. Dinky across the street, and he doesn't explain why he is late to his coach.

**Page 36**
1. happ(ly), nois(y), trust(y), d(isembark), faith(ul)
2. -y, -ly, -ful
3. C, A, B
4. to get out of a vehicle
5. Answers will vary but the subtitles should indicate a succession of events, such as "The Bus Arrives," "Boarding the Bus," "At School."

Bonus: Answers will vary but should indicate that it's a positive experience. Words that support the answer may include *Without complaint, without a fuss, happily,* and *wave and smile.*

**Page 37**
Answers for 2 and 5 will vary.
1. It shows how hail forms.
3. paragraphs 3 and 4
4. Answers will vary but may include what hailstones look like and what kind of damage they cause.

Bonus: Answers will vary but should indicate that much of the text was about how hailstones are formed, which is what is also shown in the diagram.

**Page 38**
1. remembered
2. baffled, confused; Possible answers include *shocked, startled,* or *stunned.*
3. The shop was having a massive sale
4. inside the store; Two of the three stanzas tell what is in it.
5. Answers will vary.

Bonus: yes; Answers will vary.

**Page 39**
Clues will vary.
1. loses
2. worried
3. find
4. not willingly
5. take
6. floats
7. hidden
8. dives
9. leaves
10. tired

Bonus: A; Answers will vary.

**Page 40**
1. The head of the bright yellow flower is made of many flowers put together.
2. The leaves have notches in them. They look like teeth. In French, the words *dent de lion* mean lion's teeth.
3. a white, milky liquid; It can be used to treat bee stings.
4. The leaves from young plants can be tossed in salads or cooked like spinach. The roots can be roasted or used as tea.
5. roots

Bonus: Answers will vary.

**Page 41**
1. He needs braces.
2. a young goat
3. sorry, regrets
4. boxes, old sneakers, shoelaces, garden tools, tin cans
5. no; He is still chewing things he shouldn't be chewing!

Bonus: A star should be drawn next to the last line of the second stanza. The child might color the exam chair or the poster of teeth.

**Page 48**
Answers for 1–3, 6, and 7 will vary.
4. A. It will ama(ze ro)deo fans.
   B. My teacher put a pe(n in e)ach desk.
   C. We walked (on e)ggshells around her.
   D. We will get extra recess i(f our) class is good.
   E. Is the number of students in our clas(s even )or odd?
5. A. kid    B. shed    C. ruler    D. screen
8. '; It is used to make nouns possessive and in contractions.

**Page 49**
Answers for 1, 3, and 5 will vary.
2. nice, mice; neat, feet; ten, men; keep, sheep; hear, deer; steeple, people
4. I will spend Thanksgiving Day at Big Bear Lake in California.
6. A. sang
   B. thought
   Sentences will vary.
7. the later years of a person's life, especially after he has stopped working
8. A. noun, subject of the sentence   B. verb

**Page 50**
Answers for 3, 4, and 8 will vary.
1. bow, go, glow, know, low, no, blow
2. □ = is, ▽ = not, ◇ = she, ○ = will
5. where/wear, do/due/dew, bears/bares, poll/pole; Answers will vary.
6. he, it, we, she; They're pronouns.
7. brace, brick, clack, trace, track, trick

**Page 51**
Answers for 1, 2, 5, 7, and 8 will vary.
3. CUPID
4. Why do most frogs like St. Patrick's Day?
   Because frogs always wear green
6. Possible answers include the following:

| p | l | a | y |
|---|---|---|---|
| b | a | n | k |
| b | u | r | n |
| b | o | o | t |

| p | l | a | y |
|---|---|---|---|
| b | u | r | n |
| b | a | n | k |
| b | o | o | t |

| b | a | n | k |
|---|---|---|---|
| b | u | r | n |
| b | o | o | t |
| p | l | a | y |

**Page 52**
Answers for 2, 5, 6, and 8 will vary.
1. They are all reflexive pronouns. *Myself, himself,* and *itself* are singular. *Ourselves* and *themselves* are plural.
3. precut, prefilled; Explanations will vary.
4. d(ai)sy and swe(ee)t p(ea)
7. no; The exclamation point should be placed within the quotation marks.

Answers for 1, 2, 4, 5, and 7 will vary.
3. A. hot spot
   B. thin grin
   C. wise prize
   D. old cold
6. theater
8. A. Go to bed.
   B. Eat your lunch.
   C. Love you!
   D. We will see.

**Page 81**

| | | | |
|---|---|---|---|
| april Fools' day | christmas | easter | father's day |
| groundhog day | halloween | hanukkah | Independence day |
| mother's day | new year's eve | st. patrick's Day | thanksgiving Day |
| | valentine's day | Veterans day | |

1. St. Patrick's Day
2. Easter
3. Hanukkah
4. New Year's Eve
5. Mother's Day
6. April Fools' Day
7. Halloween
8. Independence Day
9. Thanksgiving Day
10. Valentine's Day
11. Veterans Day
12. Groundhog Day

Bonus: Answers will vary but should use *Christmas* and *Father's Day*.

**Page 82**
1. hikes
2. lunches
3. hats, teeth
4. maps, bottles
5. men, women, children
6. families, dogs
7. Leaves, feet
8. turkeys, deer
9. snakes, bushes
10. Geese, birds
11. benches
12. jokes

Bonus: lunches—add -es to words that end in *ch, sh, s, x,* or *z*; hats—add -s to most nouns; teeth—change the spelling of some words

**Page 84**
1. so
2. but
3. for
4. so
5. or
6. for
7. nor
8. but
9. yet
10. and
11. but
12. and

Bonus: To link two parts of a sentence.

**Page 85**

| | Yes | No |
|---|---|---|
| 1. Ima Robber (rides) into town. | B | N |
| 2. She (tie) up her horse, Lightning. | O | L |
| 3. They (makes) a good team. | H | G |
| 4. She (spots) the town bank. | U | E |
| 5. Ima (cover) her face. | W | D |
| 6. She (grabs) her empty money sack. | M | C |
| 7. Lightning (neighs) loudly. | F | K |
| 8. Ima (walk) into the bank. | T | L |
| 9. She (take) all the money. | A | I |
| 10. The bankers (chases) after her. | Y | R |
| 11. Ima (jumps) on Lightning. | K | M |
| 12. Swiftly, they (ride) out of town. | W | D |
| 13. The bankers (tells) the sheriff where Ima goes. | G | Y |
| 14. The sheriff quickly (catches) up to Ima. | N | S |
| 15. Ima (give) all the money to the sheriff. | L | A |

SHE WANTED TO MAKE A CLEAN GETAWAY.

Bonus: 2. ties  3. make  5. covers  8. walks  9. takes  10. chase  13. tell  15. gives

**Page 86**
Order will vary.
1. Whenever Kat sings, people always listen.
2. Since Kat wants to be a rock star, she tries out for *Talent Stars*.
3. Kat sends in a tape of her singing before she gets on the show.
4. If the judges like Kat, they will invite her to perform on the show.
5. Although Kat sings at home, she never performs for lots of people.
6. Kat checks the mailbox every day even though she just sent in her tape.
7. Kat is nervous when her letter arrives.
8. As long as Kat sings, she will be a star in her parents' eyes.

Bonus: independent, dependent

**Page 113**
1. Answers will vary but should include four of the following:
   0 + 16, 1 + 15, 2 + 12, 3 + 13, 4 + 12, 5 + 11, 6 + 10, 7 + 9, 8 + 8,
   9 + 7, 10 + 6, 11 + 5, 12 + 4, 13 + 3, 14 + 2 , 15 + 1, 16 + 0.
2. Answers will vary but may include the following:
   A. making a ten and adding 6, using doubles fact 7 + 7 and adding 2, using doubles fact 9 + 9 and subtracting 2, counting on from 9;
   B. using the related addition fact 5 + 8, counting back from 13.
3. A. 120  B. 167  C. 200  D. 205  E. 1, 5
4.

| Students' Favorite Lunches | |
|---|---|
| Pizza | ☺☺☺☺☺ |
| Chicken Strips | ☺☺ |
| Cheeseburger | ☺☺☺ |

☺ = 1 student

5. 18 boys, 12 girls
6.

7. 25; Explanations will vary.
8. yes; There are 1,000 milliliters in one liter. Since the tank holds 10 liters, he can pour more water into it.

**Page 114**
Answers for 2 and 8 will vary.
1. 6; Explanations will vary.
3. 178, 207, 187
4. yes; Explanations will vary.
5. 4:00 PM, 4:40 PM
6. 50 pounds
7. 6  000 000 000 000 000 000

**Page 115**
1. $25
2. 3 boxes; Explanations will vary.
3. 11 inches; Explanations will vary.
4. Al, January 20; Keira, January 5; Todd, January 3
5. 740 lights
6. Answers will vary.
7. They have equal perimeters.
8. 4; Explanations will vary.

**Page 116**
1. Answers will vary.
2. A. 7; It's the only odd number. B. 3 + 5; It's not a near double fact, its sum is a single digit, and it's sum is even. C. ▷; It's not a quadrilateral.
3. 8 tens 5 ones, one hundred 12 ones, 12 tens; 85, 112, 120
4. Drawings will vary; 20 leaves
5. 10 hours
6. 960, 159
7. 3 ÷ 15 = 5 should be written 15 ÷ 5 = 3.
8. 800 coins

**Page 117**
Answers for 1 and 3 will vary.
2.

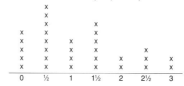

4. 5 + 5 = 10
   ○ ○ ○
   ○ ○ ○
   ○ ○ ○
5. cardinals; Explanations will vary.
6.

Rainfall in April (inches)

```
        x
        x
        x                   x
        x                   x
   x    x         x         x
   x    x    x    x         x
   x    x    x    x    x    x    x
   x    x    x    x    x    x    x
 ──────────────────────────────────
   0    ½    1    1½   2    2½   3
```

7. 50 grams, less than a kilogram; A kilogram equals 1,000 grams, and 50 is less than 1,000.
8. Possible answers are 2 x 20, 4 x 10, 5 x 8, 8 x 5, 10 x 4, 20 x 2, and 40 x 1.

1. 3 feet; There are 12 inches in one foot and 36 inches in three feet.
2. 11, 22, 33, 44, 55, 66, 77, 88, 99; The sum is 495, which is less than 500.
3. They both show numbers in equally spaced increments. They both go from least to greatest from left to right.
4. C; The parts in A are not equal. The parts in B show halves, not fourths.
5. 44, 46; Add 2; multiply by 2
6. A. 3 (6 × 1 = 6) 8
   B. 4 (5 × 3 = 1 5)
   C. 9 (7 × 2 = 1 4)
   D. 4 2 (3 × 2 = 6)
   E. (6 × 0 = 0) 6 9
   F. (3 × 8 = 2 4) 7
7. Seth won the race.

|       | 1st | 2nd | 3rd | 4th |
|-------|-----|-----|-----|-----|
| Jamie | x   | ✓   | x   | x   |
| Myra  | x   | x   | ✓   | x   |
| Seth  | ✓   | x   | x   | x   |
| Bo    | x   | x   | x   | ✓   |

8. no; She will only have 300 freezer pops. Principal Stern will need to buy two more boxes to have enough for each student.

Drawings will vary.
A. even   B. odd   C. even   D. odd
E. odd    F. even  G. even   H. odd

Bonus: Answers will vary.

Favorite Juice Flavors (bar graph)

1. 55 people
2. 5 people
3. 5 people
4. grape, apple
5. 15 people
6. lemon-lime and orange
7. lemon-lime and cherry
8. apple and lemon-lime; Answers will vary.

Bonus:

| Favorite Juice Flavors | |
|------------------------|---|
| apple      | ☐☐☐☐ |
| berry      | ☐ |
| lemon-lime | ☐☐☐ |
| orange     | ☐☐ |
| grape      | |
| cherry     | ☐ |

☐ = 5 people

| | | Yes | No |
|---|---|---|---|
| 1. | 2 hundreds + 5 tens + 3 ones > 235 | B | O |
| 2. | 649 = 6 tens + 4 hundreds + 9 ones | M | K |
| 3. | 3 tens + 7 hundreds + 2 ones = 732 | C | R |
| 4. | 1 hundred + 8 ones < 180 | I | A |
| 5. | 289 > 2 hundreds + 9 tens + 8 ones | E | R |
| 6. | 4 tens + 3 hundreds + 1 one > 314 | N | E |
| 7. | 9 hundreds + 5 tens < 905 | T | A |
| 8. | 468 = 8 ones + 4 hundreds + 6 tens | H | S |
| 9. | 712 < 2 hundreds + 7 tens + 1 one | R | D |
| 10. | 2 ones + 6 hundreds + 3 tens > 263 | W | K |
| 11. | 4 tens + 7 ones + 5 hundreds = 547 | E | T |
| 12. | 9 tens + 8 ones + 1 hundred = 981 | W | G |
| 13. | 153 < 5 hundreds + 1 ten + 3 ones | M | O |
| 14. | 6 tens + 7 hundreds + 8 ones < 768 | H | L |
| 15. | 431 > 5 tens + 4 hundreds + 3 ones | E | S |

He will TAKE A METEOR SHOWER.

Bonus: 2. >; 5. <; 7. >; 9. >; 12. <; 14. =; 15. <

A. 6:03   B. 12:14   C. 3:25   D. 8:49   E. 1:45
F. 11:50  G. 2:08    H. 4:51   I. 3:31   J. 7:57
K. 12:01  L. 9:23    M. 4:36   N. 10:10  O. 5:47

Bonus: Clocks should show 1:38, 6:21, and 11:05.

1. 12 inches, 18 − 6 = 12 or 6 + 12 = 18
2. 4 inches, 9 − 5 = 4 or 5 + 4 = 9
3. 10 inches, 18 − 8 = 10 or 8 + 10 = 18
4. 15 inches, 7 + 8 = 15
5. 15 inches, 6 + 9 = 15

Bonus: Gretta, Grammy, and Gunter; 6 + 5 + 7 = 18

A. 12:40   B. 11:40   C. 12:55   D. 12:45   E. 12:25
F. 1:00    I. 11:20   K. 1:05    N. 12:05   O. 1:10
R. 12:20   S. 11:35   T. 11:55   U. 11:15   W. 12:30

IT WENT BACK "FOUR" SECONDS.

Bonus: 11:15 AM, 11:20 AM, 11:35 AM, 11:40 AM, 11:55 AM, 12:05 PM, 12:20 PM, 12:25 PM, 12:30 PM, 12:40 PM, 12:45 PM, 12:55 PM, 1:00 PM, 1:05 PM, 1:10 PM

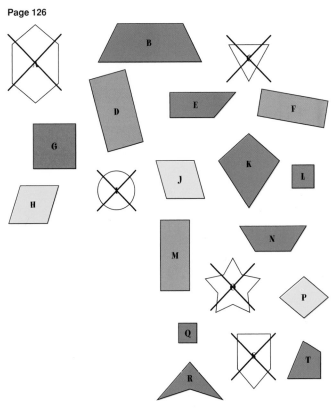

Bonus: Answers will vary but should include that they are closed shapes with four straight sides.

1. 10, 20, 30, 40; 40 snowballs
2. 5, 10, 15, 20, 25; 25 snowballs
3. 0 10 20 30 40 50 60 70 80 90; 9 buckets
   1 2 3 4 5 6 7 8 9
4. 10, 20, 30, 40, 50; 50 snowballs
5. 0 10 20 30 40 50 60 70 80 90 100; 10 buckets
   1 2 3 4 5 6 7 8 9 10

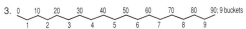

6. 0 5 10 15 20 25 30 35 40 45 50 55 60 65 70 75 80 85 90 95 100; 20 minutes
   1 2 3 4 5 6 7 8 9 10 11 12 13 14 15 16 17 18 19 20

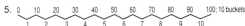

Bonus: 35 30 25 20 15 10 5 0; 7 days
       1 2 3 4 5 6 7

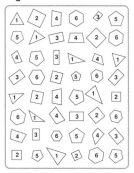

**Page 129**
Sections shaded will vary.

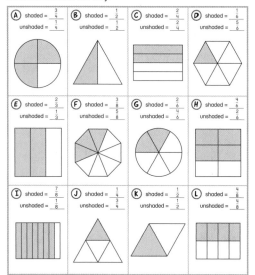

Bonus: Possible answers include the following:

**Page 131**
1. 24 ÷ ? = 3, 3 x 8 = 24 or 8 x 3 = 24, 8, Oclet
2. 32 ÷ ? = 8, 8 x 4 = 32 or 4 x 8 = 32, 4, Wapag
3. 18 ÷ ? = 9, 9 x 2 = 18 or 2 x 9 = 18, 2, Zorax
4. 30 ÷ ? = 5, 5 x 6 = 30 or 6 x 5 = 30, 6, Beezle
5. 12 ÷ ? = 4, 4 x 3 = 12 or 3 x 4 =12, 3, Tricaden

Bonus: 5; Answers will vary.

**Page 132**
Drawings will vary.

| | | True | False |
|---|---|---|---|
| 1. $\frac{1}{4}$ is less than $\frac{1}{2}$. | | H | P |
| 2. $\frac{4}{8}$ is less than $\frac{7}{8}$. | | B | G |
| 3. $\frac{4}{6}$ is greater than $\frac{2}{6}$. | | N | R |
| 4. $\frac{2}{3}$ is less than $\frac{1}{3}$. | | O | U |
| 5. $\frac{1}{2}$ is the same as $\frac{1}{3}$. | | S | C |
| 6. $\frac{2}{8}$ is greater than $\frac{6}{8}$. | | E | O |
| 7. $\frac{3}{6}$ is less than $\frac{1}{6}$. | | R | D |
| 8. $\frac{1}{4}$ is not the same as $\frac{3}{4}$. | | T | L |
| 9. $\frac{5}{8}$ is greater than $\frac{1}{8}$. | | M | E |
| 10. $\frac{2}{3}$ is not the same as $\frac{1}{3}$. | | F | G |

An "EGGS-PLORER"

Bonus: Possible answers include the following: 4. $\frac{2}{3}$ is greater than $\frac{1}{3}$. 5. $\frac{1}{2}$ is not the same as $\frac{1}{3}$, or $\frac{1}{2}$ is greater than $\frac{1}{3}$. 6. $\frac{2}{8}$ is less than $\frac{6}{8}$. 7. $\frac{3}{6}$ is greater than $\frac{1}{6}$.

**Page 133**
A. 4 + 4 = 8 or 2 + 2 + 2 + 2 = 8
B. 4 + 4 + 4 = 12 or 3 + 3 + 3 + 3 = 12
C. 4 + 4 + 4 + 4 + 4 = 20 or 5 + 5 + 5 + 5 = 20
D. 1 + 1 + 1 + 1 + 1 = 5
E. 5 + 5 + 5 + 5 + 5 = 25
F. 3 + 3 + 3 = 9
G. 5 + 5 + 5 + 5 = 20 or 4 + 4 + 4 + 4 + 4 = 20
H. 2 + 2 + 2 + 2 = 8 or 4 + 4 = 8
I. 1 + 1 + 1 + 1 = 4
J. 5 + 5 = 10 or 2 + 2 + 2 + 2 + 2 = 10
K. 3 + 3 = 6 or 2 + 2 + 2 = 6
L. 5 + 5 + 5 = 15 or 3 + 3 + 3 + 3 + 3 = 15

Bonus: Answers should be the other equation from A–C above.

**Page 134**

1. 25 inches
2. 14 inches
3. 36 inches
4. 78 inches
5. 16 inches
6. 33 inches

"CELLAR-Y"

Bonus: Answers will vary.

**Page 145**
Circled details will vary.
1. Pumpkins go through stages as they grow.
2. A pumpkin is a healthy food choice.
3. Not all pumpkins look the same.
4. Pumpkins need bees to grow.

Bonus: The details in paragraphs 2 and 4 tell why. The details in paragraphs 1 and 3 tell how.

**Page 147**
1. in a tree, enjoying an acorn
2. The plant provides food and shelter for the squirrel.
3. The squirrel helps the plant spread its seeds when it buries them in the fall.
4. They rely on each other to survive.

Bonus: Answers will vary.

**Page 148**
1. A drought is a period of time when the amount of rainfall is much less than normal.
2. Crops can die. Forest and grass fires are more likely to pop up. Streams and lakes can dry out, and the soil below can be blown away.
3. *Conserve* means to save.
4. Possible answers include the following: turn off the water when you brush your teeth; turn off the faucet as you lather your hands; choose one cup as your cup for the day; put leftover ice cubes in a houseplant's pot; take a shower instead of a bath; keep your shower under five minutes; and drop used tissues in the trash instead of the toilet.

Bonus: Answers will vary.

**Page 149**
"The Ruler Trick"
The book was easier to lift with a long lever because the fulcrum was farther from the load.

"Want to Race?"
1. It takes more force to lift the car straight up, so the rubber band stretched farther.
2. an inclined plane

**Page 150**
"Winding Down"
1. a screw
2. Possible answers include the base of a lightbulb, a spiral staircase, and a corkscrew.

"Give Me a Lift"
1. Pulling the rope exerted force on the brooms, making them hard to keep apart.
2. a pulley

**Page 156**
1. George Washington, James Madison, and Benjamin Franklin
2. May 1787
3. The newly formed United States needed one government.
4. The men shared ideas. They talked about what a strong government should look like. They wanted laws that would help people in every state.
5. It is a written plan for the government.

Bonus: four months; There were many disagreements among the men.


**Page 158**

| | | |
|---|---|---|
| Veterans Day is a holiday in the United States. It is on November 11. | On Veterans Day, people thank the men and women who served in the armed forces. | The armed forces include the Army, Navy, Air Force, Marine Corps, and Coast Guard. ☆ |
| In the United States, parades are held and speeches are given on Veterans Day. | In 2011, there were more than 21 million veterans in the United States. | Other countries have holidays like Veterans Day. |
| People in Canada, Australia, and New Zealand observe Remembrance Day on November 11. They honor those who died in war. | Remembrance Sunday is held in the United Kingdom. It is held on the second Sunday in November. | Memorial Day also honors men and women who served in the armed forces, but it remembers those who died while serving. It is observed by Americans in May. |

Bonus: Paragraphs will vary.


**Page 159**
1. one big rock split into two boulders; at the entrance
2. a statue with Dr. King's image carved into it
3. Tidal Basin
4. It faces the place where Dr. King gave his "I Have a Dream" speech.
5. near the intersection of Independence Avenue and West Basin Drive

Bonus: Civil rights are the freedoms and rights that a person may have as a member of a community. They include freedom of speech, of the press, and of religion; the right to own property and to receive fair and equal treatment from government, other persons, and private groups.


**Page 162**
1. D4
2. A3
3. E2
4. D1
5. B1
6. C5
7. E5
8. C2
9. A4
10. A5

Bonus: Answers will vary.


**Page 188**
Card 1
A. sock
B. steps
C. watch
D. stand
E. water

Sentences will vary.

Card 2
A. loyalty
B. courage
C. friendship
D. weakness
E. beauty

Abstract nouns will vary.

Card 3
A. *impossible*, not possible
B. *preload*, to load in advance
C. *mislabel*, to label incorrectly
D. *dislike*, the opposite of *like*
E. *uncork*, to remove a cork

Words will vary.

Card 4
Answers will vary.


**Page 193**
"A Gigantic Home"
The bold word is an important word for the reader to know; Answers will vary.

"Good Times Ahead"
Order will vary.
My friend is coming over. Is my friend coming over?
Expanded sentences will vary.

"Word Chains"
Short vowels
```
n e t
    u
  b i g
      a
    s l i p
        l
        u
      g a l
          i
          p
          s
```
Long vowels
```
s e e m
      o
      a
    n i g h t s
          l
          e
          e
        p a i l
            a
            i
            d r e a m
                  i
                  n
                  e
```

**Page 194**
"My Family"
1. S
2. W
3. W
4. W
5. S
6. S
7. W
8. S

"Busy Words"
1. combination: the act or process of combining
2. expiration: the act or process of expiring
3. exploration: the act or process of exploring
4. imagination: the act or process of imagining

"Set to Sail"
Page numbers will vary. The misspelled words are *anchor*, *biscuits*, and *parrot*.


**Page 195**
"Book It!"
A glossary and a dictionary both give meanings for words. A glossary is found in the back of an informational text. A dictionary is its own book or website.

"Make New Words"
Order will vary.
isn't, wasn't, he's, he'll, she's, she'll, they're, they'll, we're, we'll, don't, can't

"Break New Ground"

| | | |
|---|---|---|
| afraid | unafraid | not afraid |
| checked | unchecked | not checked |
| chewed | unchewed | not chewed |
| sent | unsent | not sent |
| | | |
| check | recheck | check again |
| freeze | refreeze | freeze again |
| paint | repaint | paint again |
| read | reread | read again |


**Page 196**
"Use Your Noggin!"
central nervous system; It takes the reader to another screen and gives more information on that specific topic.

"On the Lookout"
agree*able*, break*able*, collect*ible*, distract*ible*, prevent*able*, resist*ible*, sens*ible*, wash*able*

"A Little Mystery"
    Sherlock Bones was very quiet. He looked closely at the evidence, snapped pictures, and took notes.
    "I will need just a little more time to gather these clues," Sherlock Bones said.
    "Is there anything I can do to help?" the park ranger asked.

Stories will vary.


**Page 197**
"Grouped Together"
Drawings and additional words will vary. The words shown are collective nouns. Each noun names one unit made of many parts.

"Explain the Rule"
The apostrophes signal to the reader that the nouns own or have something else.

"The Old Switcheroo"
1. Gary and Harry play tricks on their friends whenever they get the chance!
2. These twins will pretend to be the other and exchange shirts.
3. Will Harry and Gary fool their friends again? Gary and Harry will fool their friends again. Harry and Gary will fool their friends again.


**Page 198**
"Get to the Meaning"
*agreement*, the act of agreeing; *employment*, the act of employing; *equipment*, the act of equipping someone or something; *movement*, the act or process of moving (people, things, or body parts); *payment*, the act of paying

"Senses Aside"
Abstract nouns: kindness, goodness, luck, growth, anger
Sentences will vary.

"Rock On!"
1. she, Rita Rock Star
2. They, The fans
3. it, the show
4. he, My brother

**Page 199**

"They're Worth How Much?"
A. 15
B. yes
C. 150
D. 1 hundred flat, 5 ten rods

"Just for Giants"
A. ninety-nine
B. one hundred seven
C. one hundred thirty
D. one hundred sixty-five
E. one hundred eighty-two

**Page 200**

"Seating Chart"
Answers will vary but should indicate four rows of five, five rows of four, two rows of ten, or ten rows of two.

"A Ballpark Estimate"
Brody; Explanations will vary.

"Fair and Square"
Drawings will vary.

| thirds | fourths | sixths | eighths |
|---|---|---|---|
| 1/3 | 1/4 | 1/6 | 1/8 |

**Page 201**

"Super Solver"
A. He added the numbers in the ones column and wrote the sum. Then he added the numbers in the tens column and wrote it under the first sum. He wrote the sum of each column to show the final answer.
B. He broke apart each number. Then he subtracted the tens and the ones. He found the sum of those values to show the final answer.
Answers will vary.

"A Shape Parade"
A. 3    B. 4    C. 0    D. 5    E. 6
Drawings will vary.

**Page 202**

"Student Work Space"
32; Word problems will vary.

"Busy Bakers"
They each have 42 cookies. The commutative property states that the same factors result in the same product.

"Proclaim the Same"
A, B, and are D are equivalent, C and E are equivalent; explanations will vary.

**Page 203**

"Put in Parts"
Possible answers include 6 rows of 3, 2 rows of 9, 9 rows of 2, 1 row of 18, and 18 rows of 1.

"Growing Up"
Pictures and equations will vary.
A. 14 centimeters    B. 17 centimeters

**Page 204**

"Involve the Inverse"
A. 8, 8 × 7 = 56
B. 7, 7 × 9 = 63
C. 9, 9 × 5 = 45
D. 9, 9 × 4 = 36
E. 5, 5 × 8 = 40

"What Makes a Dozen?"
Order will vary.
12 = 6 × 2 = 4 × 3 = 3 × 4 = 2 × 6

"Too Much or Too Little?"
more than a liter: bathtub, paint
less than a liter: cup, glass

"It All Adds Up"
He found the area of the two tall rectangles. Then he found the area of the square. He added each amount together to find the total area of the shape.

**Page 213**

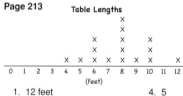

Table Lengths

```
                      x
                      x
          x           x
          x   x       x
      x x x x x x x       x
    0 1 2 3 4 5 6 7 8 9 10 11 12
            (feet)
```

1. 12 feet
2. 4 feet
3. 8 feet
4. 5
5. 6
6. 1 foot, 2 feet, 3 feet, 11 feet

Bonus: Answers will vary.

**Page 220**

A. 109    B. 119    C. 88    D. 186
E. 100    F. 80    G. 110
H. 89    I. 112    J. 118

Bonus: Answers will vary.

**Page 231**

Explanations will vary.
A. 36    B. 57    C. 16    D. 19    E. 28

Bonus: Addition and subtraction are related operations.

**Page 232**

 George Washington ate few desserts.

 Andrew Johnson was a tailor before he became president.

 Ronald Reagan was once an actor.

 Abraham Lincoln knew how to swing an ax.

William Henry Harrison died of pneumonia.

One of George Washington's favorite foods was ice cream.

William Henry Harrison was president for only 31 days.

Abraham Lincoln had a job chopping wood for fences before he took office.

Andrew Johnson knew how to sew.

Ronald Reagan was in many movies.

GW    George Washington ate few desserts, but one of his favorite foods was ice cream.

WHH    William Henry Harrison was president for only 31 days, for he died of pneumonia.

AL    Abraham Lincoln knew how to swing an ax, for he had a job chopping wood for fences before he took office. Abraham Lincoln had a job chopping wood for fences before he took office, so he knew how to swing an ax.

AJ    Andrew Johnson was a tailor before he became president, so he knew how to sew.

RR    Ronald Reagan was once an actor and was in many movies.

Bonus: Answers will vary.

**Page 233**

A. 7:40 AM
B. 35 minutes
C. 8:05 AM
D. 45 minutes
E. 7:35 AM
F. 1 hour 10 minutes, or 70 minutes
G. 8:25 AM
H. 8:40 AM

Bonus: Number lines will vary; 6:05 PM.

**Page 237**

1961 When Mae was five years old, she knew she wanted to be an astronaut.

1973 Mae worked hard. When she was 16 years old, she finished high school and went to Stanford University.

1983 Mae wanted to help people. After she became a doctor, she joined the Peace Corps and cared for sick people in Africa for two years.

1985 When Mae was 29, she applied to the space program.

1992 When Mae was 35, she went into space.

Bonus: Answers will vary.

**Page 241**

1. a lettuce nto pepper cucumber sala celery espinach afooledyou
2. reptile, B; insect, D; amphibian, C; bird, A
3. Answers will vary.
4. paper money, yes; real giraffes, no; tea, yes; eyes, yes; tomatoes, yes; fingernails, yes
5. green-eyed monster, B; green behind the gills, C; green thumb, A; green, E; green light, D

**Page 245**

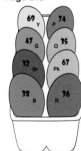

A. 35, addition or subtraction
B. 69, addition
C. 38, addition or subtraction
D. 47, addition or subtraction
E. 67, addition
F. 36, addition or subtraction
G. 32, addition or subtraction
H. 74, addition

Bonus: Answers will vary.

**Page 254**

1. terribly (blue)
2. local (green)
3. beautiful (green)
4. eager (green)
5. quickly (blue)
6. carefully (blue)
7. loudly (blue)
8. brave (green)
9. quickly (blue)
10. playful (green)

Bonus: adverbs—*nearby, today,* or *very*; adjectives—*hot, many,* or *cool*

**Page 255**

Circled clues will vary.
1. expands
2. thunderous
3. flukes
4. krill
5. throat pleats
6. blowhole
7. lunges
8. baleen

Bonus: expands; Answers will vary.

# INDEX